IMAGES
of America

SULLIVAN COUNTY

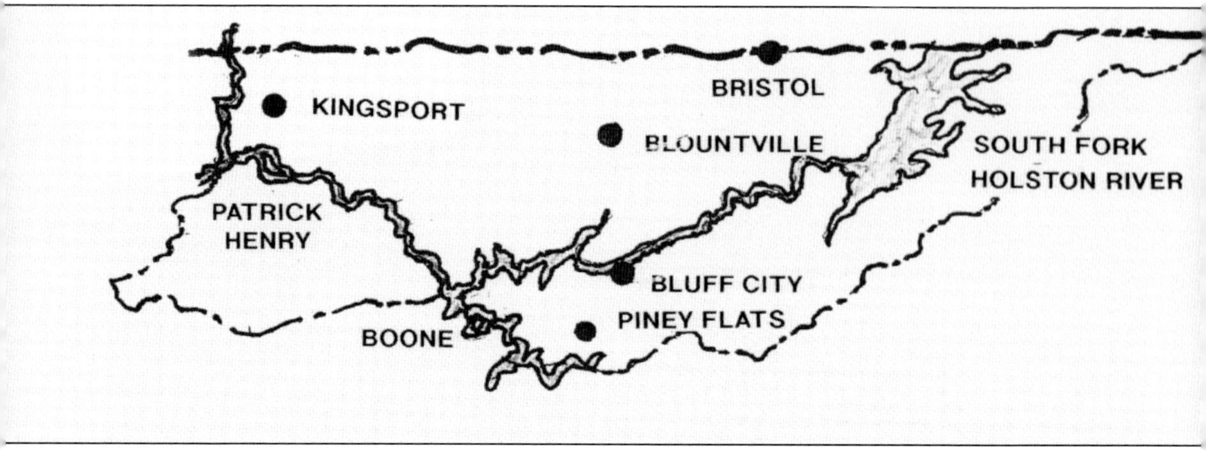

COUNTY MAP. Shaped like Tennessee, present-day Sullivan County borders Johnson, Carter, Washington, and Hawkins Counties in Tennessee and extends along the Virginia border, touching Washington and Scott Counties. This original map shows the major towns of Kingsport, Bluff City, Blountville, Piney Flats, and Bristol, plus the Tennessee Valley Authority's reservoirs at South Holston, Boone, and Fort Patrick Henry. (Courtesy of Shelby Edwards.)

ON THE COVER: Two young boys go fishing, *c.* 1946, at the "Old Mill Dam" beside a railroad trestle on the South fork of the Holston River in Bluff City. Photographer Bill Inscho shot this scene for a postcard. The mill dam was torn down about five years later for the completion of Boone Lake in the early 1950s. Locals still remember this site as a great fishing hole. (Courtesy of the Bluff City Public Library.)

IMAGES
of America

SULLIVAN COUNTY

Joe Tennis

ARCADIA
PUBLISHING

ISBN 978-0-7385-5409-9

Published by Arcadia Publishing
Charleston, South Carolina

Printed in the United States of America

Library of Congress Catalog Card Number: 2008921155

For all general information contact Arcadia Publishing at:
Telephone 843-853-2070
Fax 843-853-0044
E-mail sales@arcadiapublishing.com
For customer service and orders:
Toll-Free 1-888-313-2665

Visit us on the Internet at www.arcadiapublishing.com

*For my parents, Richard and Jeanette Tennis;
and for my wife's parents, Walter Wolfe and the late Louisa Wolfe—your stories of South Holston Lake, Bristol, Kingsport, Sullivan County, and Tennessee have been a great inspiration*

CONTENTS

ACKNOWLEDGMENTS

Foremost thanks goes to Shelby Edwards, who generously shared postcards, pictures, and knowledge of Sullivan County; Bill McKee, who offered invaluable assistance; V. N. "Bud" Phillips, who provided consistent encouragement; and David McGee, who initially suggested this idea to me. I also sincerely thank Shelia Steele Hunt, who inspired me with images from her vast collection of historic photographs, and Kathryn Nichols, the Bluff City librarian, who became an early cheerleader for this project.

George Stone, a local author, shared his collection of photographs and postcards, as did Tim Buchanan, Tony Marion, John and Julie Slagle, Billy and Irene Wells, and Earl Neikirk.

Many others contributed information and images along the way, including Dr. Nancy Hamblen Acuff, William Lawrence Inscho, Jim Thomas, Krisna Goodwin, Bob Carpenter, Betty Thomas, David Vance, Gary Rose, Ruth King, Carolyn Williams, Rita Forrester, Bill Hartley, Suzanne Brewster, Freddie Boyd, Tim White, Harry Scanlan, Merle Dickert, Darlene Cole, Suzanne Lawson, Brenda Otis, John Beach, David Patton, Ben Brown, Brianne Johnson, Helen Whitaker, Frank Brumit, Charlie Aesque, George DeVault, Ken Childress, Suzanne Burow, T. J. DeWitt, Gary Walrath, Jo McDavid, Ethel Ketron, Peggy Sutherland, Mary Olinger, Azel Olinger, Charlotte Wilson, the Bloomingdale Ruritan Club, Larry Proffitt, Carol Gouge, Betty Lou Nelson, Mary Lou Fleenor, James Thomas, Mike Pierry Jr., Peter Koserski, Pat Dannhardt, Gil Francis, Betsy Carrier, Betty Carrier, June Presley, and Arlene Royer.

I must also thank many friends and colleagues who provided advice and patience, including Carol Jackson, Tim Cable, Carl Esposito, Cara Ellen Modisett, Jan Patrick, Steve and Kim Rhodes, John Molley, Rex and Lisa McCarty, Todd Foster, Peggy Hensley, Ken Heath, Kim Byrd, Bill Kovarik, Ben Jennings, Robin Bagnall, Patsy Phillips, Sherry Austin, Kim Moore, and Daniel Rodgers.

This book would also not have been possible without the patience, help, and encouragement of my editors, Maggie Tiller Bullwinkel, Anne Tate, and Lori Gildersleeve.

Additional thanks goes to family members: Maggie Caudill; Sam Caudill; Melissa Caudill; Jo Boswell; Cheryl Karant; Rob Tennis; John Wolfe; Homer Wolfe; my daughter, Abigail; my son, John Patrick; and my wife, Mary, a Sullivan County native.

INTRODUCTION

Tennessee's Sullivan County lays claim to being the center of the Tennessee Tri-Cities—Kingsport, Bristol, and Johnson City. It is among the oldest counties in the Volunteer State. It is also an area that has grown increasingly urban, as its historic farms are sliced into subdivisions and its old post office stops meld into newer neighborhoods. Yet Sullivan County is also simply diverse—a place where the steep mountains surrounding Denton Valley bear little resemblance to the industrialization of Kingsport and much of Bristol.

In many ways, the story of Sullivan County follows the course of the Holston River, a waterway draining the rocky mountains of Southwest Virginia and the tumbling creeks of Johnson County, Tennessee. This river lends its name to landmarks and communities—Holston Valley, Holston Mountain, and simply "Holston." It has provided the power for gristmills and the water to cool locomotives. Large logs have floated its surface and so have flatboats, once taking off in regular runs from Kingsport.

How this river took its name comes from legend. A man named Stephen Holstein carted a canoe to the river near its headwaters in Virginia and sailed away in what must have seemed like an endless journey in the 1740s. Legend says he made it as far as the Mississippi River. But, in truth, there is no telling how far he went. Some early settlers later called the river "Holston," spelling it how they would pronounce Holstein's name.

About 200 years later, the Tennessee Valley Authority (TVA) came to Sullivan County and made the communities of Bluff City and Blountville a land between the lakes. By the mid-1950s, TVA's South Holston Reservoir would provide a scenic shoreline for Sullivan County on the east, while Boone Lake to the south formed a border that could be boated from the Watauga River at Piney Flats to what is now a sandy beach near the Tri-Cities Regional Airport.

This place is truly Tennessee, a place where the "Vols" are celebrated with Big Orange flags on the front porches of Kingsport, and the strains of old-time Appalachian performers and traditional country music remain popular in Bristol, a unique two-state town straddling the Tennessee-Virginia border.

Before Sullivan County was created, much of the area was considered part of Virginia. Every place north of the Holston River, in fact, was assumed to be inside the Old Dominion, reaching west to the North fork of the Holston River's confluence, with the South fork in what is now Kingsport.

Just below the Virginia line, and not far from present-day North Carolina, Sullivan County formed in 1779—a time when there was no Tennessee. Originally, this was Sullivan County, North Carolina, and the county name originated from John Sullivan, a Revolutionary War officer and member of the Continental Congress. The first court met at the fort of Moses Looney in 1780.

The affiliation with the Tar Heel State did not last. In a time of great financial constraints, North Carolina ceded lands west of the mountains to the United States, including what is now Sullivan County, to help pay its share of debts incurred by the Revolutionary War.

Soon after, some early settlers gathered in 1784 to form a new state—one called Franklin—in hopes that the country's senior statesman, Benjamin Franklin, might be so flattered that he would rally strongly for statehood. But Franklin did not lend his support. In a short time, the State of

Franklin turned into a state of turmoil as its leaders fought the officials of North Carolina in a turf war across present-day Northeast Tennessee.

As it turned out, North Carolina had opted not to give away this land after all, leaving the State of Franklin simply no space to exist.

Franklin faded by the spring of 1788. But, again, the North Carolina connection was broken. In 1790, what is now Sullivan County became part of the Territory of the United States South of the River Ohio. The capitol was established at Rocky Mount in what is now Piney Flats, a Sullivan County community on the northern edge of Johnson City.

In 1796, finally, Sullivan County's long, legislative, roller coaster ended as it became part of the newly formed State of Tennessee.

Centuries later, the Holston River continues to connect the crossroads of this county. Free flowing in some stretches and dammed in others, this river laps the banks of islands named Boy's, Long, and Osceola. It drains branches called Beaver and Weaver. Like a funnel, too, it catches all of that water streaming down from Virginia, culled from creeks as far north as Tannersville, Tumbez, and Teas.

Sullivan County's charms are many—from the towering spine of Holston Mountain in the Cherokee National Forest to the cool escapes of its caverns. From Rock Springs to Cold Spring, State Street to Church Circle, it is a land with many stories to tell.

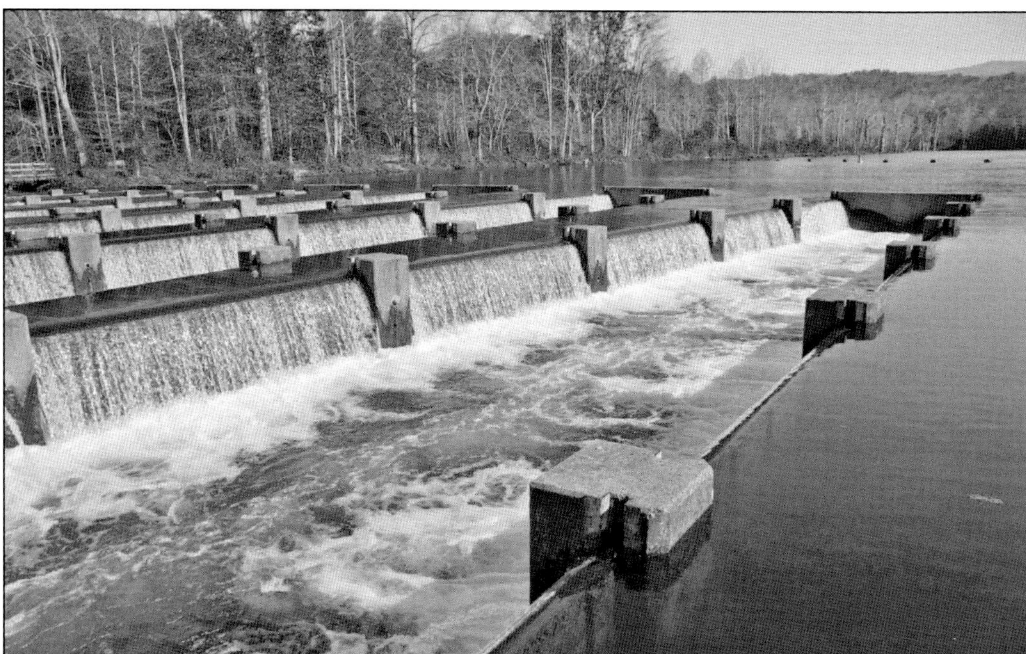

WEIR DAM. The Weir Dam breaks up the flow of the South fork of the Holston River just below South Holston Dam in the Emmett community. Installed in the early 1990s, the weir provides oxygen in the water, which, in turn, provides a great habitat for trout. At the center of the South fork lies Osceola Island, a nature sanctuary accessible by a footbridge. (Photograph by Earl Neikirk.)

One

Blountville

Founded in 1792, the courthouse town of Blountville shares its name with Tennessee's Blount County and took its name from William Blount, governor of the Territory of the United States South of the River Ohio.

For a while in the 19th century, Blountville was incorporated as its own town along the Great Stage Road, and many early businesses depended on the trade of overnight travelers. But, after a few years, Blountville would later give up its incorporation in a dispute over whether liquor could be served in town.

The Sullivan County Courthouse stands at the center of Blountville. Built in 1853, this stately structure faced the wrath of an approaching Union army on September 22, 1863, in a skirmish that became known as the Battle of Blountville.

For several hours, Confederate forces commanded by Col. James E. Carter fought a Union brigade led by Col. John W. Foster. The Union forces launched an artillery barrage from the Blountville Cemetery, then commonly called the "City of the Dead," and many places burned, including the courthouse, several businesses, hotels, and private homes.

Near the county courthouse, the Deery Inn has stood on Blountville's Main Street since the late 1700s, attracting visits by such presidents as James K. Polk, Andrew Johnson, and Andrew Jackson. In more recent times, politicians, including Richard Nixon and Bob Dole, have also visited Blountville, stopping at the Tri-Cities Regional Airport.

One of the Blountville's most famous political visits came in 1980 when Pres. Jimmy Carter attracted thousands to the airport and several thousand more pedestrians to Blountville's sidewalks. Carter also stopped to see the Deery Inn's genteel owner, Virginia Caldwell. The president kissed the 79-year-old woman five times and signed the back of a Deery Inn door.

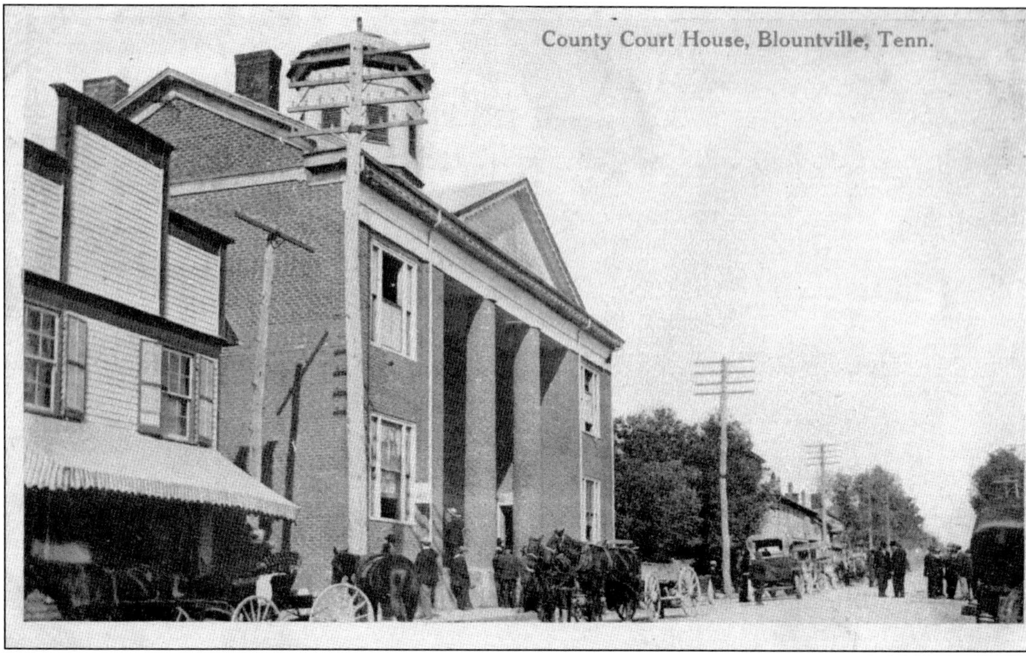

SULLIVAN COUNTY COURTHOUSE. Standing on Blountville's Main Street, the Sullivan County Courthouse was built in 1853. It sustained damage in 1863 when cannon fire struck the structure during the Civil War's Battle of Blountville. In turn, many records were lost. The courthouse was rebuilt by 1866 and was remodeled in 1920. (Courtesy of George Stone.)

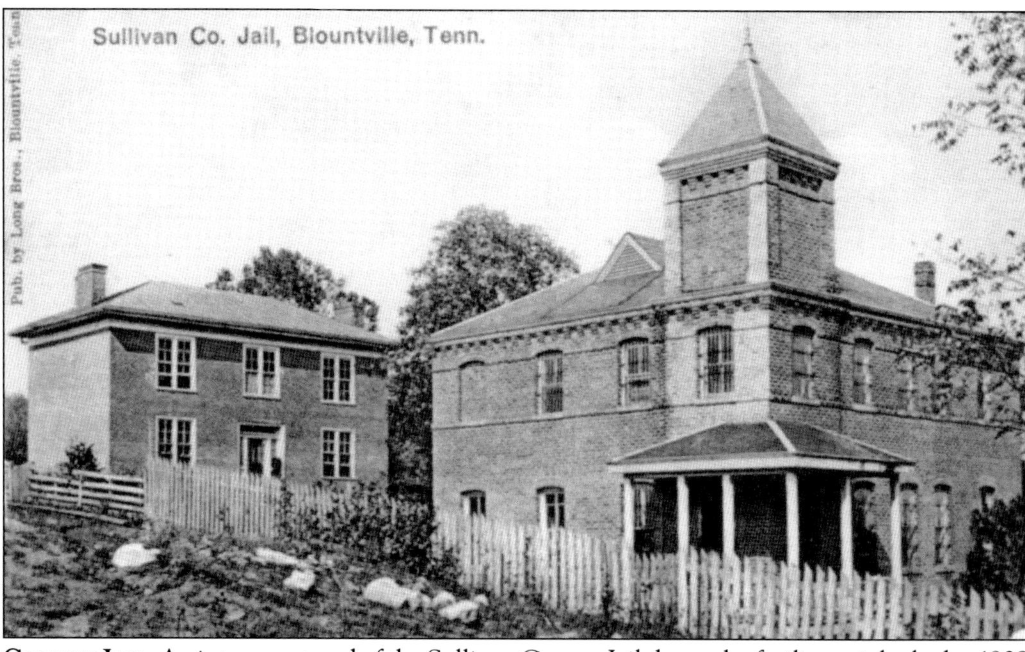

COUNTY JAIL. A vintage postcard of the Sullivan County Jail shows the facility as it looked *c.* 1908. Located behind the county courthouse in downtown Blountville, the jailhouse, at left, was built in 1870. The larger building, at right, no longer stands. (Courtesy of Shelia Steele Hunt.)

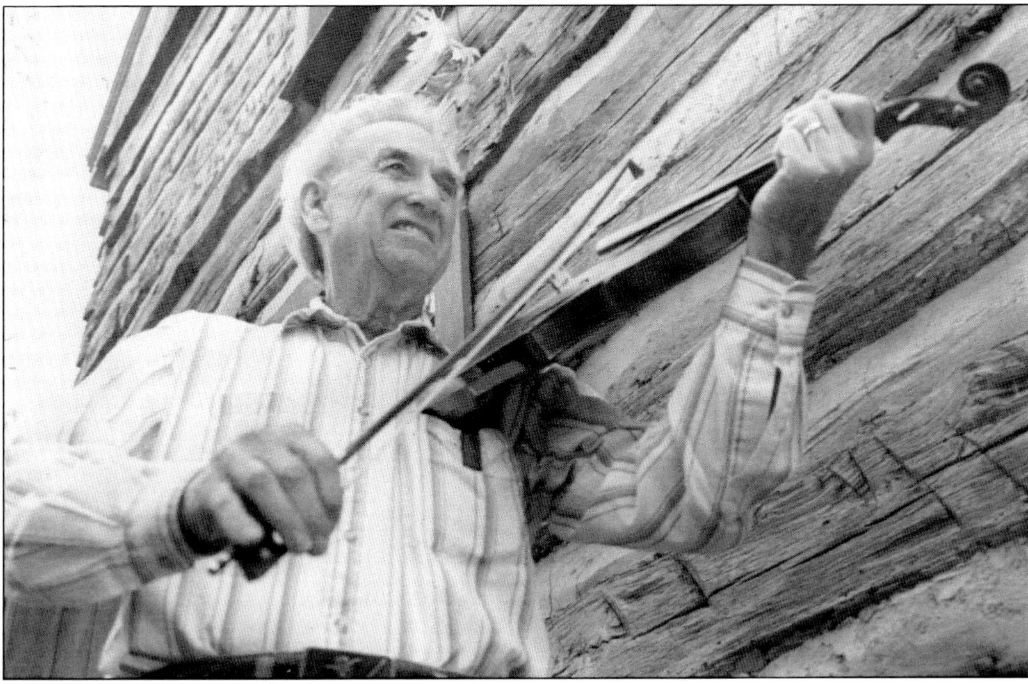

One Z, Please. Fiddler Ralph Blizard became a Blountville institution as both a musician and an advocate for protecting the town's history. Blizard (1918–2004) played on local radio stations WOPI, WKPT, and WJHL with a band of high school classmates. He also played with the New Southern Ramblers. Along the way, the World War II veteran gently suffered his surname often being misspelled with two Z's. (Photograph by David McGee.)

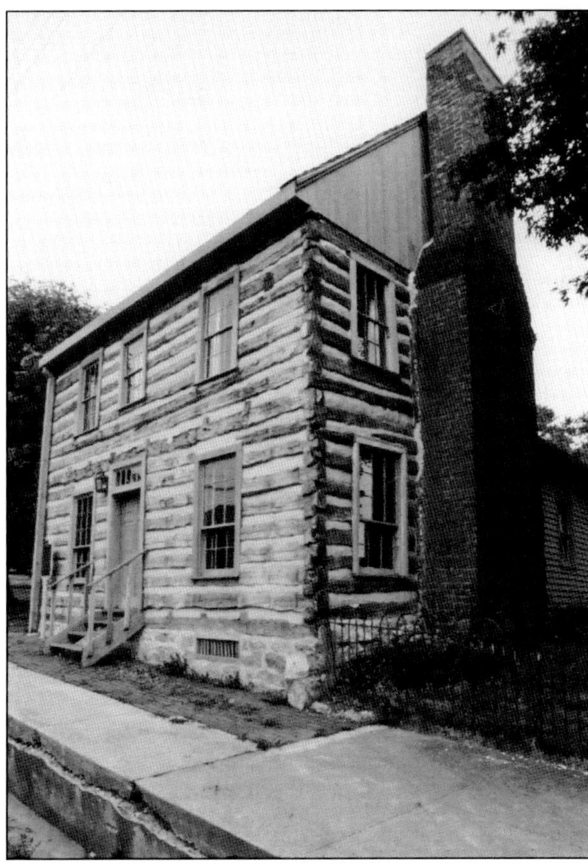

Anderson Townhouse. Col. John Anderson built the Anderson Townhouse with hand-hewn logs near the center of Blountville, *c.* 1792–1795, and early county leaders used the home as a gathering place. Anderson also built a townhouse—or fort—in nearby Scott County, Virginia, along the Wilderness Road near Big Moccasin Gap. The logs of the Anderson Townhouse, photographed in 1983, remain original to the structure. (Courtesy of the *Bristol Herald Courier.*)

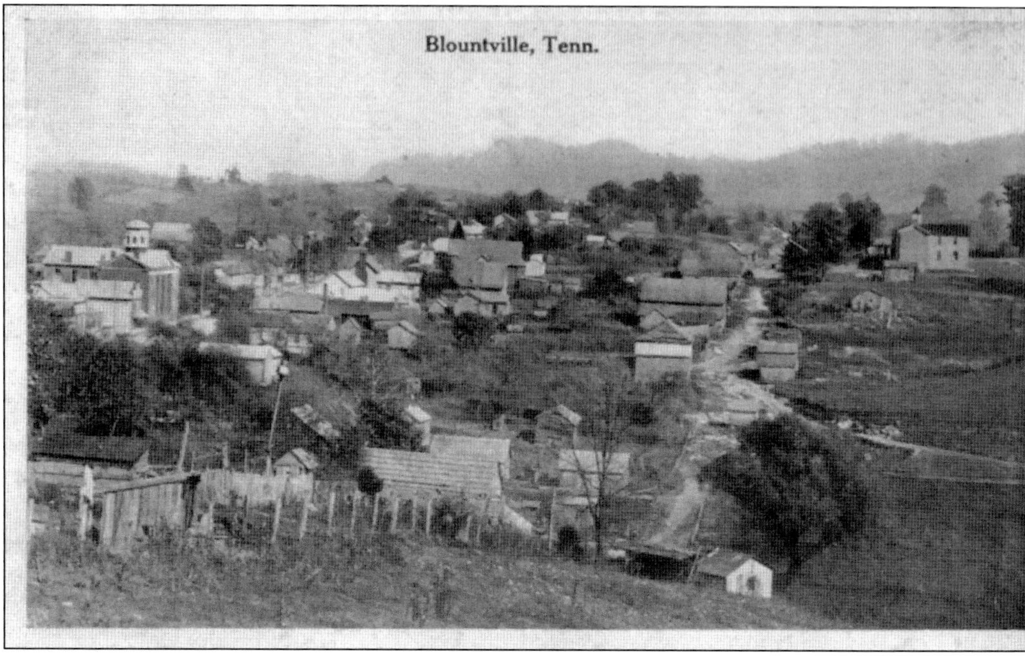

OLD TOWN. An early 1900s view of Blountville in this postcard reveals dirt paths for streets and rows of wooden buildings. Many of the historic district's most charming structures also stood at this time, including the county courthouse, seen in the lower left corner. (Courtesy of Tony Marion.)

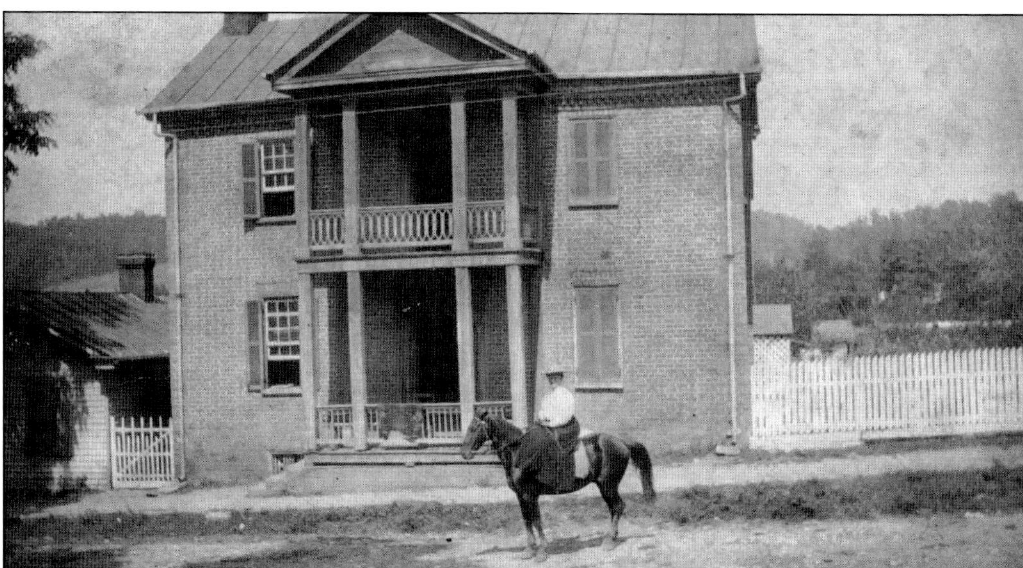

ANDERSON HALL. Dr. Elkanah Dulaney built Anderson Hall with hand-fired bricks sometime after 1800. The structure took its present name from William S. Anderson, who bought the house in 1891. The dirt road fronting the house is Blountville's Main Street. This *c.* 1900 photograph shows Anderson Hall in the days before cars, when horses were a common way to travel around town. (Courtesy of Bud Phillips.)

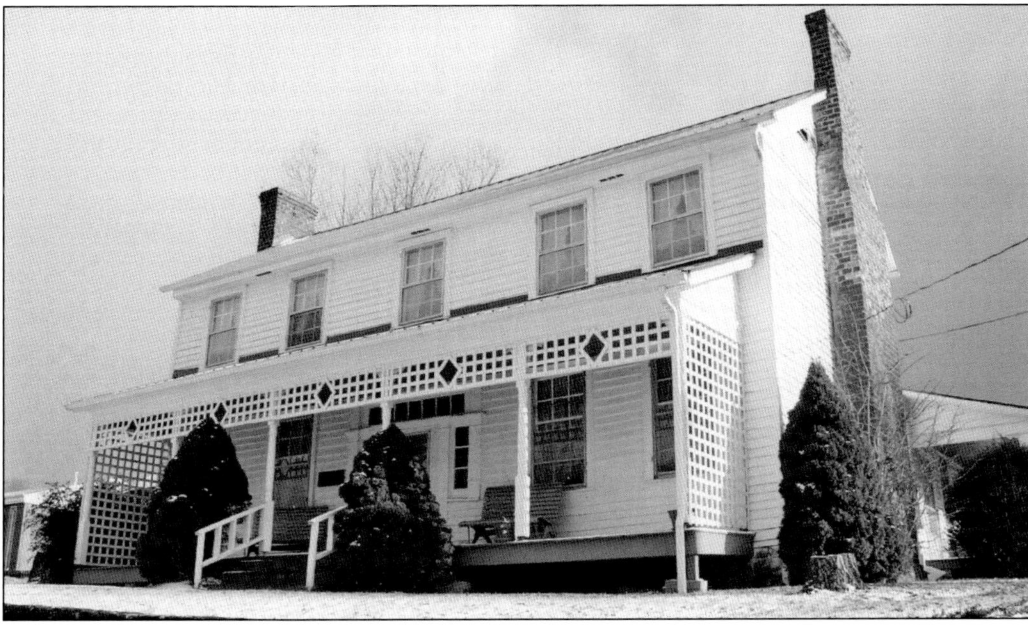

CANNONBALL HOUSE. Built in 1848, Matthew Taylor Haynes's two-story home on Main Street acquired its nickname, "The Cannonball House," when Union army cannonballs struck the house on September 22, 1863, during the Battle of Blountville. Union troops had targeted Haynes, a Confederate official, because he kept records of seized Union property. (Photograph by Joe Tennis.)

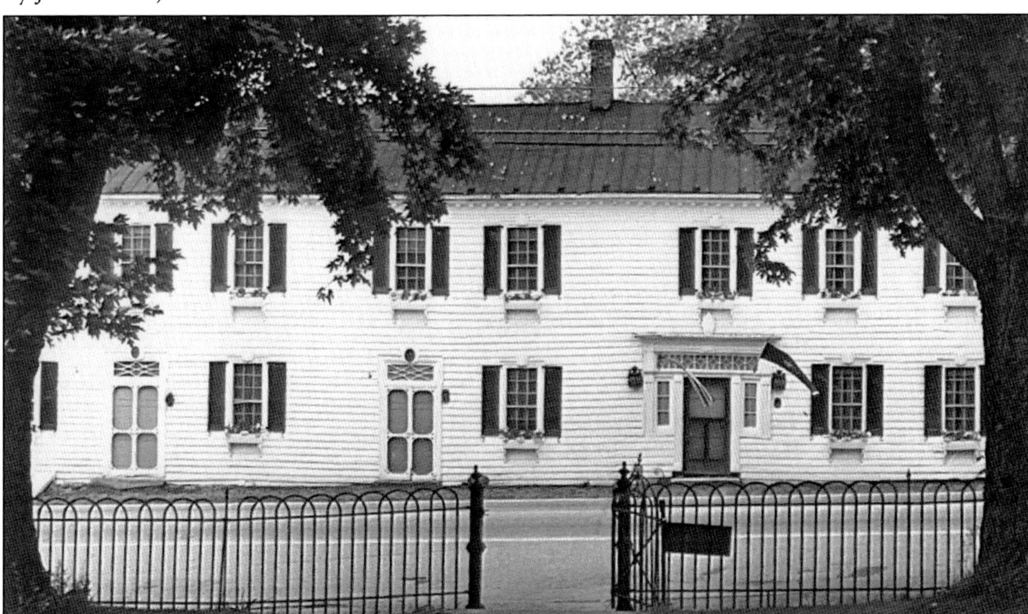

DEERY INN. Once a restaurant and stop for travelers along the Great Stage Road, the Deery Inn was built sometime after 1785. The three-story clapboard structure took its name from its second owner, William Deery (1768–1845), an Irish trader who owned stores in Blountville and Pulaski, Virginia. Briefly, in the 1880s, the Deery Inn was known as "Cates Hotel" for owners Gideon and Mary Cates. (Courtesy of Shelia Steele Hunt.)

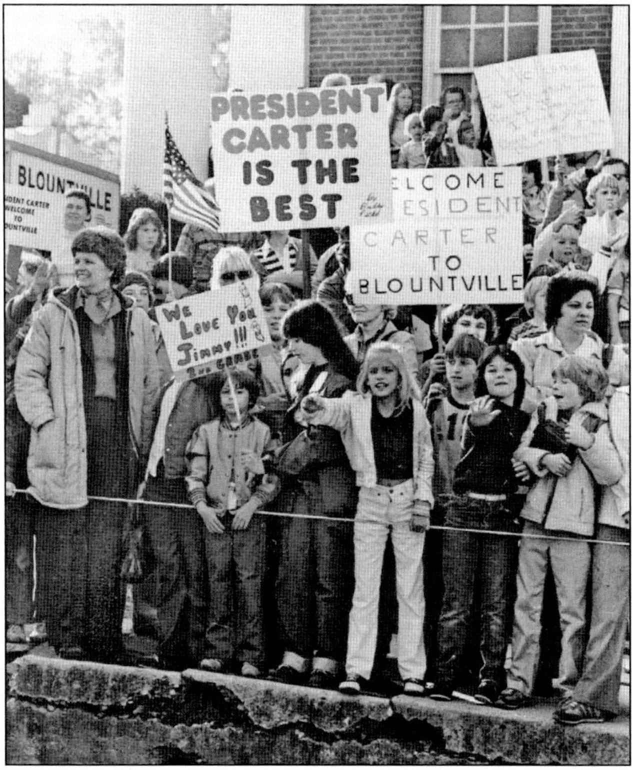

Welcome to Blountville. Local schoolchildren and teachers lined the steps of the Blountville United Methodist Church when Pres. Jimmy Carter stopped on October 9, 1980—a Thursday—to campaign for re-election. The sign in the upper right corner says: "Welcome to Blountville, Tenn.—President Jimmy Carter—I Love You—David Weaver—3rd Grade—Blountville Elementary." (Courtesy of the *Bristol Herald Courier*; photograph by Wayne Sharrett.)

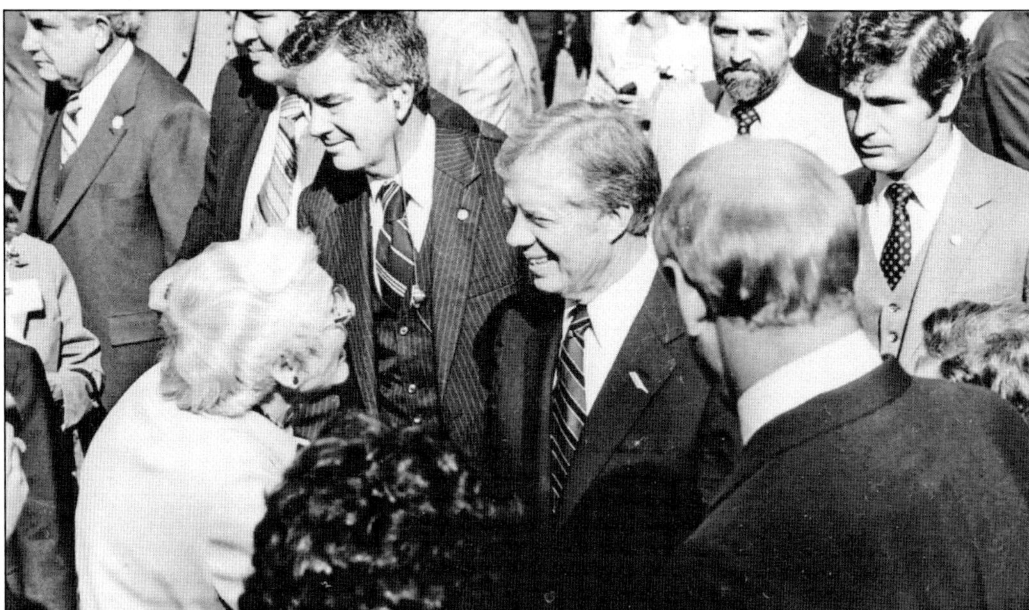

Mr. Carter. Pres. Jimmy Carter greeted a crowd of 10,000 well-wishers at the Tri-City Regional Airport on October 9, 1980. President Carter, center, also made a stop at the Deery Inn in Blountville, answering a request made by the home's owner, Virginia Caldwell. Carter campaigned that year to win another four years in the White House but lost to Ronald Reagan. (Courtesy of the *Bristol Herald Courier*; photograph by Wayne Sharrett.)

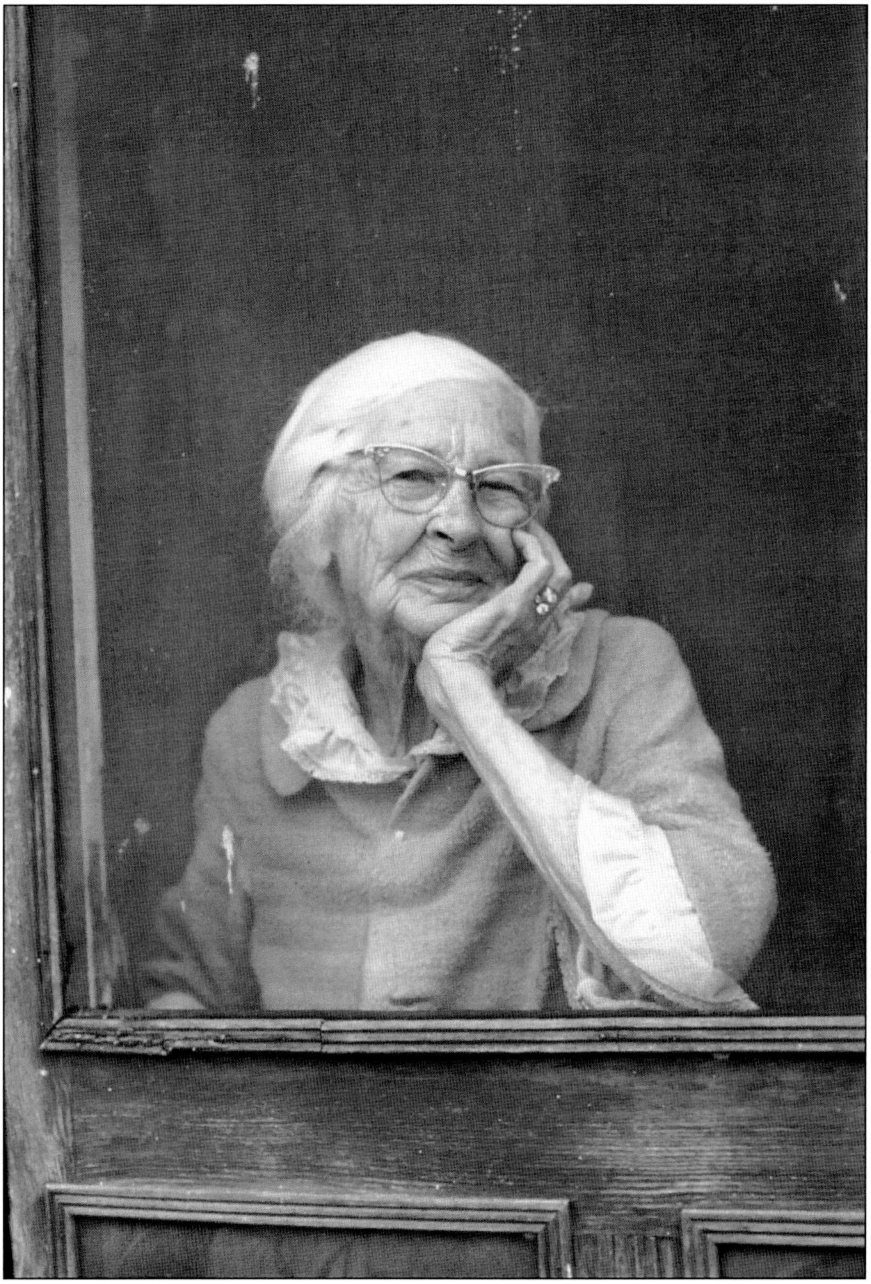

MISS VIRGINIA. Peering out the screen window of the Deery Inn on Blountville's Main Street often became the place to find Virginia Byars Caldwell. A Bristol native, "Miss Virginia" had lived in Norfolk, Virginia, as well as Hawaii, before she bought the Deery Inn in 1940. Over the next 50 years, Caldwell lovingly restored the historic structure as well as a collection of cabins. The wife of Joseph A. Caldwell, a county judge, Caldwell became known for her love of history, sense of humor, and servings of homemade English tea cake. "I belong to the covered-wagon era," Caldwell said in 1982, several years before she died at the age of 98. "I have no business being in this time. I'm not a computerized person. I'm not electronic in any way." (Courtesy of the *Bristol Herald Courier*; photograph by Bill McKee.)

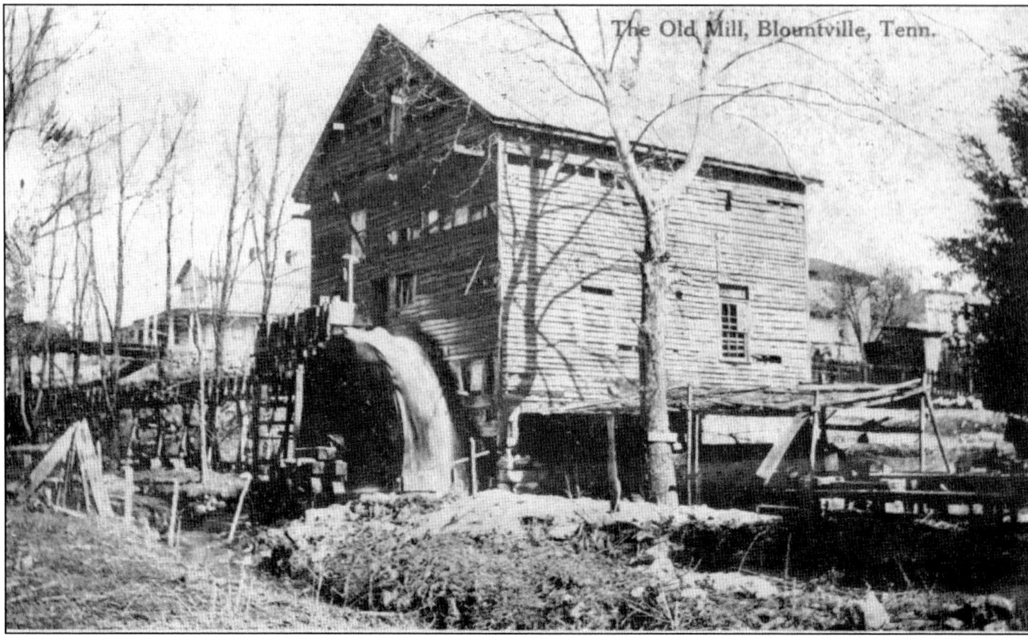

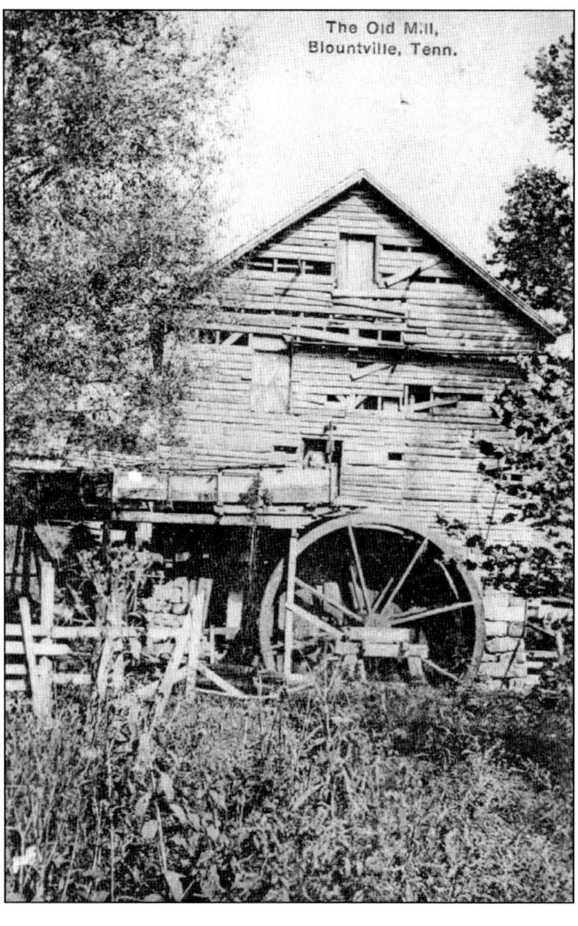

OLD MILL. The wooden gristmill on Muddy Creek in downtown Blountville inspired a pair of postcards, c. 1914, depicting its rustic charms. For many years, this landmark was known as the Bedwell-Millard Mill. In 2008, the building still stands on Main Street between the Sullivan County Courthouse and the Blountville Cemetery, but it can barely be recognized as a mill house. (Both, courtesy of Tony Marion.)

METHODIST CHURCH. An early 1900s postcard of the Blountville United Methodist Church on Main Street displays a brick church of the 19th century, a structure that has since been replaced with a more modern building. This Methodist congregation traces its roots in Blountville to 1806. (Courtesy of Tony Marion.)

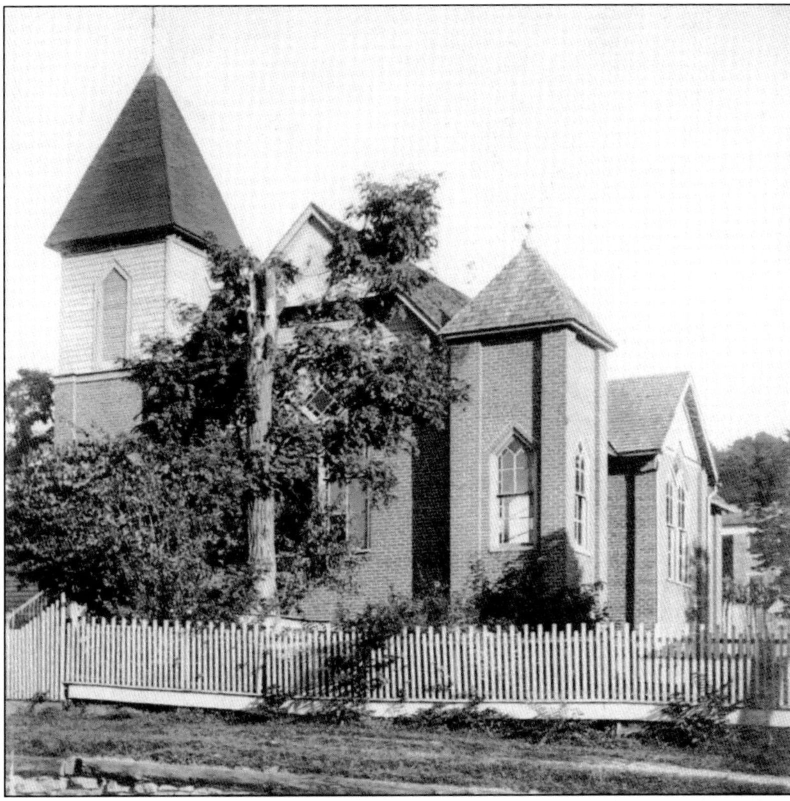

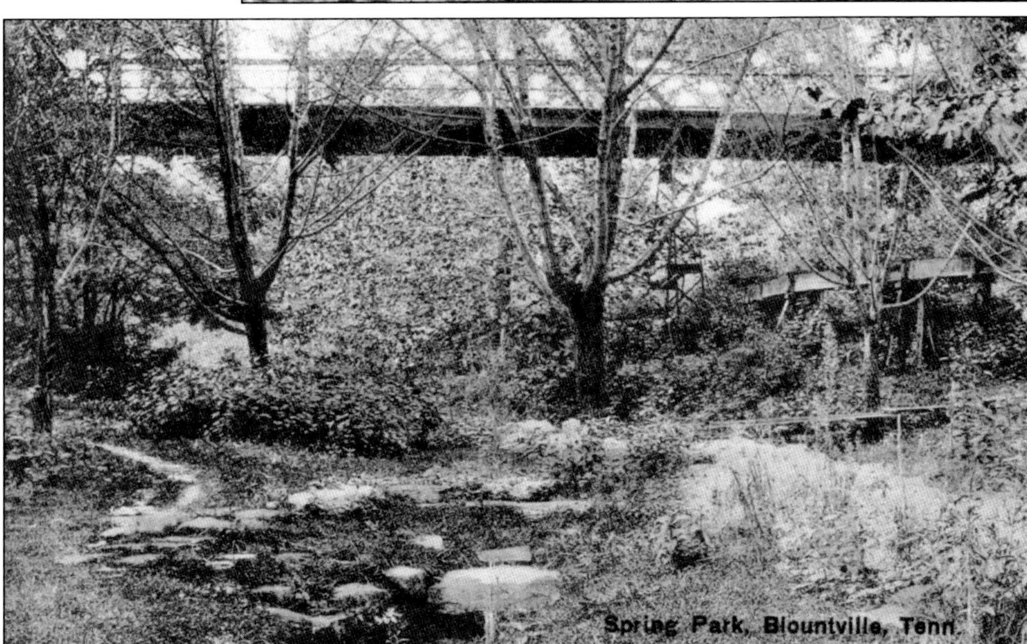

SPRING PARK. A vintage penny postcard shows Blountville's Spring Park, *c.* 1910, largely overgrown with vegetation. The park once provided residents a place for picnics near Blountville's Old Mill. (Courtesy of George Stone.)

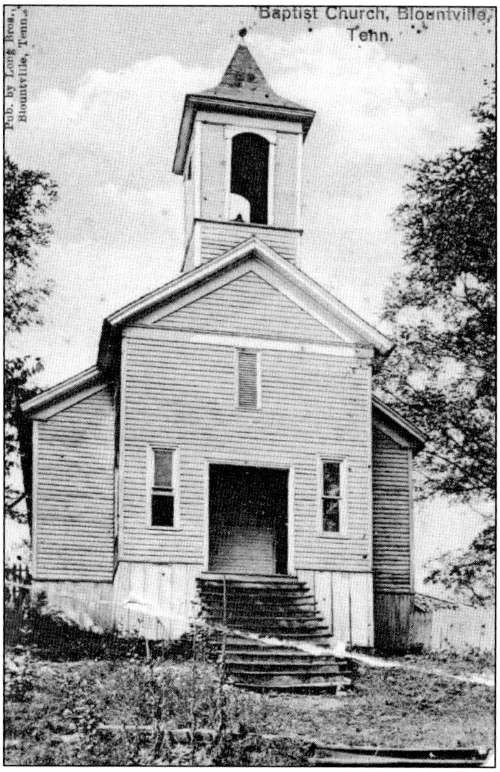

Baptist Church. A postcard of the old Baptist Church of downtown Blountville, c. 1912, displays simple wooden steps used to access the otherwise stately structure on Main Street. This building has been replaced by a newer structure. (Courtesy of George Stone.)

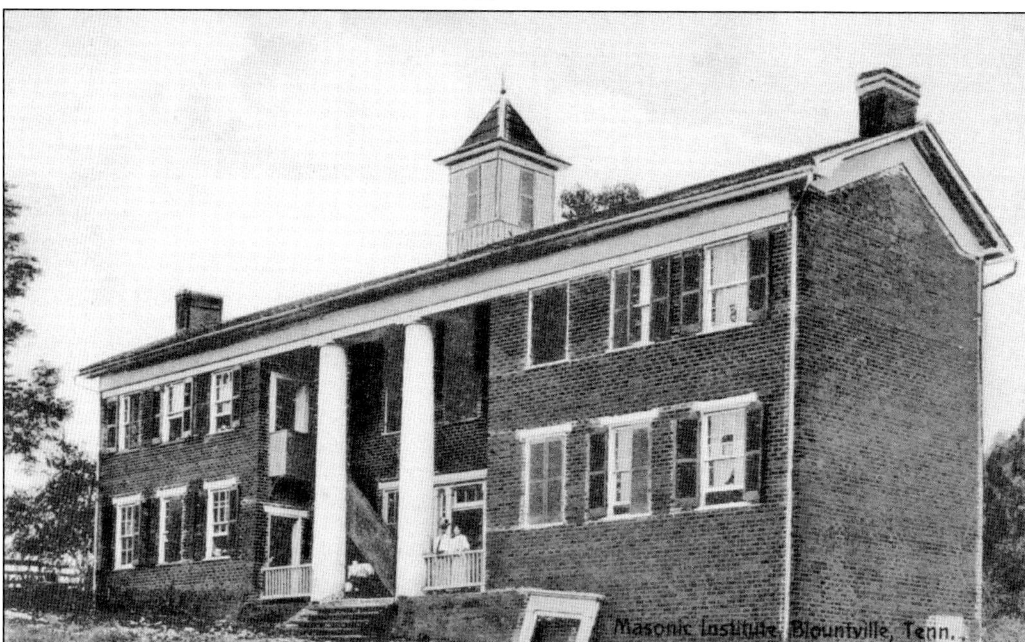

Masonic Institute. In the early 1900s, students could receive their entire education, from elementary grades to high school courses, at the Blountville Masonic Institute. The brick structure, once known as the "Female Institute," stood on Back Street until it was demolished about 1919. (Courtesy of George Stone.)

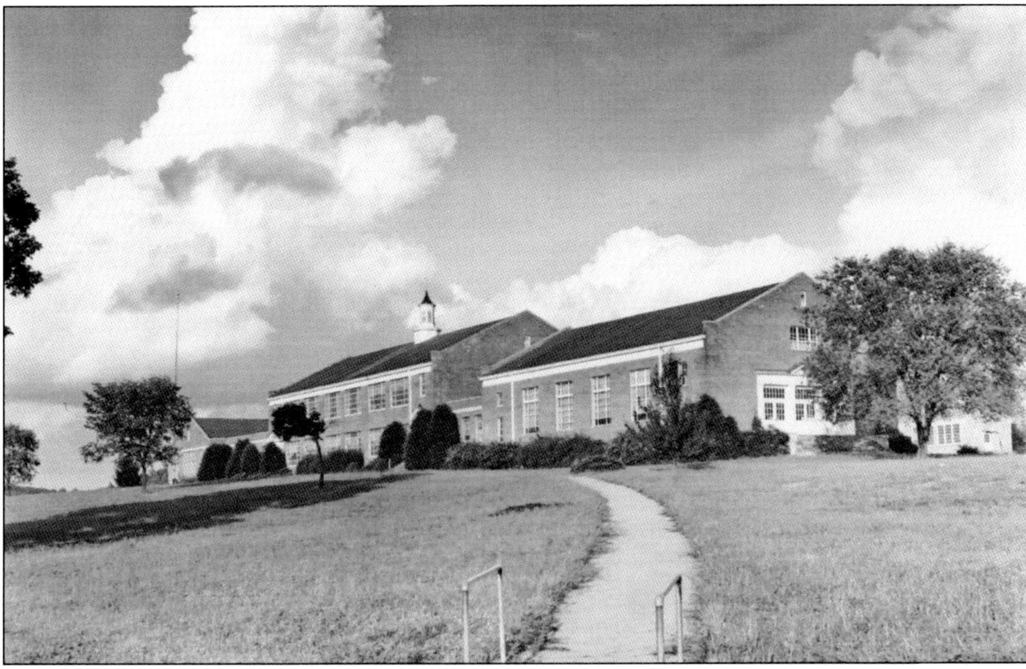

BLOUNTVILLE HIGH SCHOOL. This photograph of the old Blountville High School shows how the building looked soon after its construction in 1932. The upper-class students were transferred in 1968 to the new Central High School, located just off Interstate 81, in the Gunnings community. (Courtesy of the Bluff City Public Library.)

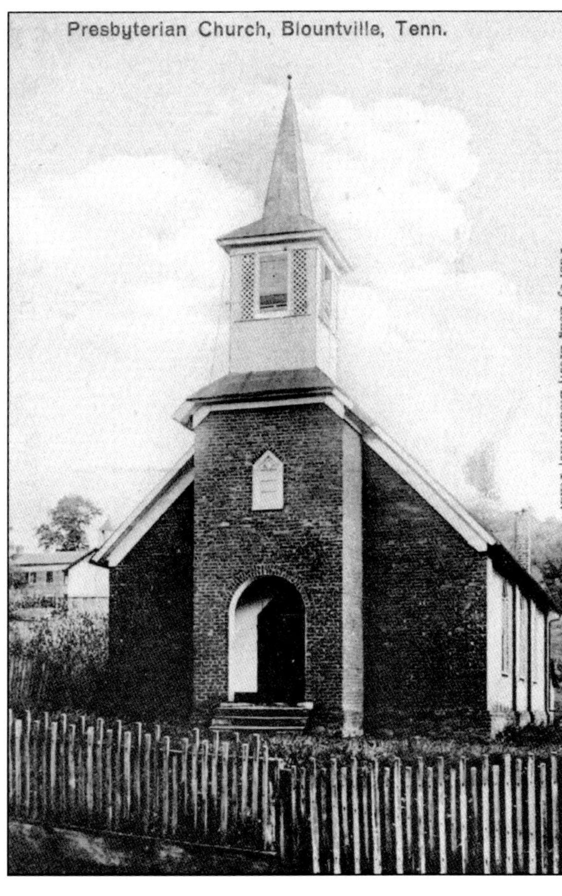

PRESBYTERIAN CHURCH. A vintage postcard, c. 1915, shows the brick structure of the Blountville Presbyterian Church prior to the construction of the present church in 1935 on Main Street near the Anderson Townhouse. This congregation was organized at Blountville in 1820 at the home of Samuel Rhea. (Courtesy of George Stone.)

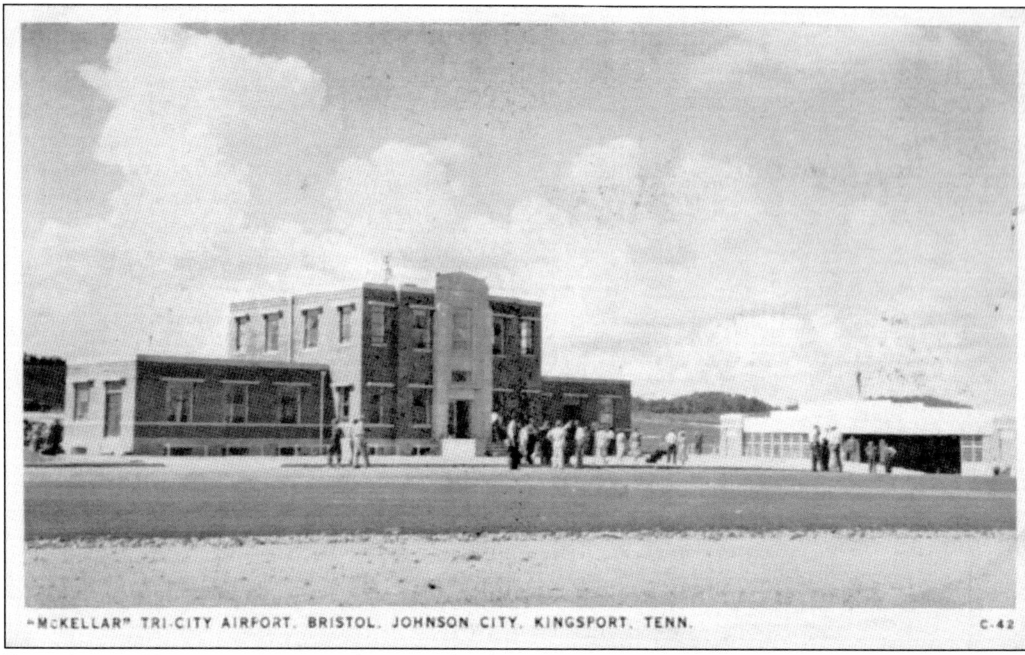

JUST AFTER TAKEOFF. A regional airport for the Tri-Cities had been planned in the 1930s at Gray Station, Tennessee, but officials ultimately chose to build runways on farm fields slightly south of Blountville in 1937. The McKellar Tri-City Airport took its name from Sen. Kenneth McKellar, who was instrumental in helping get the airport off the ground. (Courtesy of George Stone.)

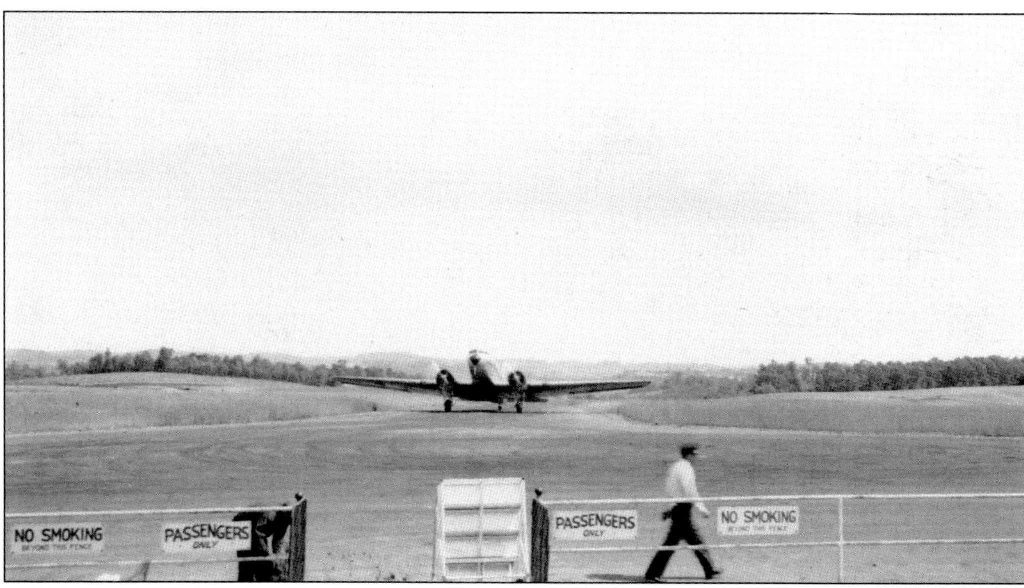

EARLY BIRD. Officials had to warn passengers that there would be "No Smoking Beyond The Fence" at the Tri-City Airport in the late 1930s. Notice the plane coming in for a landing in this photograph, made years before the nearby South fork of the Holston River became Boone Lake, just beyond the airport's boundaries. (Courtesy of Bristol Historical Association.)

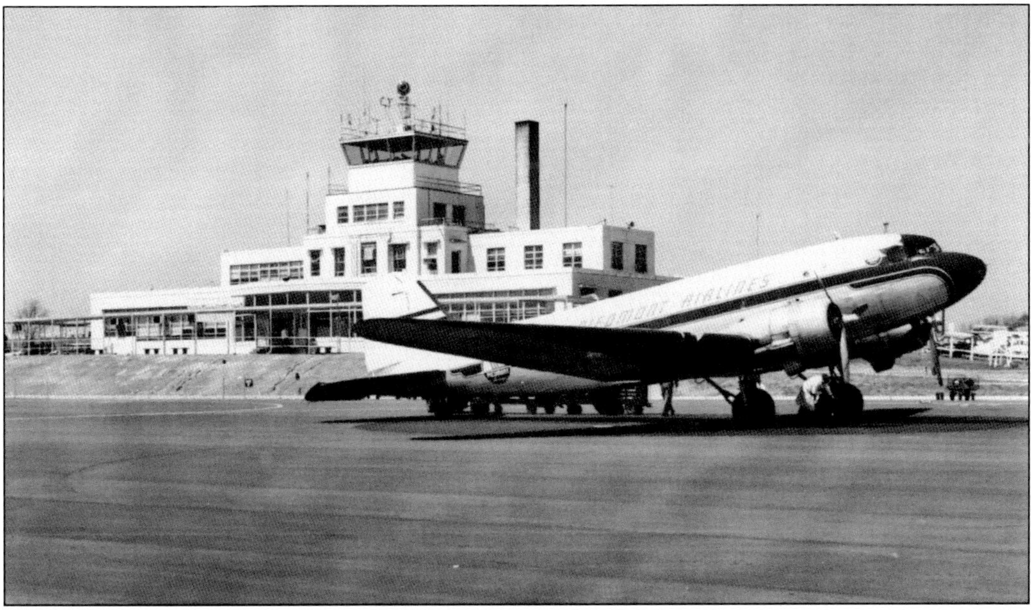

BIG BIRD. By the 1950s, Piedmont Airlines made regular flights at Tri-City Airport. In May 1959, Piedmont advertised a special "Fun Pak Vacation," flying from the Tri-City Airport to Virginia Beach, with rates as low as $79.80 for a round-trip ticket plus six nights "at a leading ocean-front hotel." (Courtesy of Bud Phillips.)

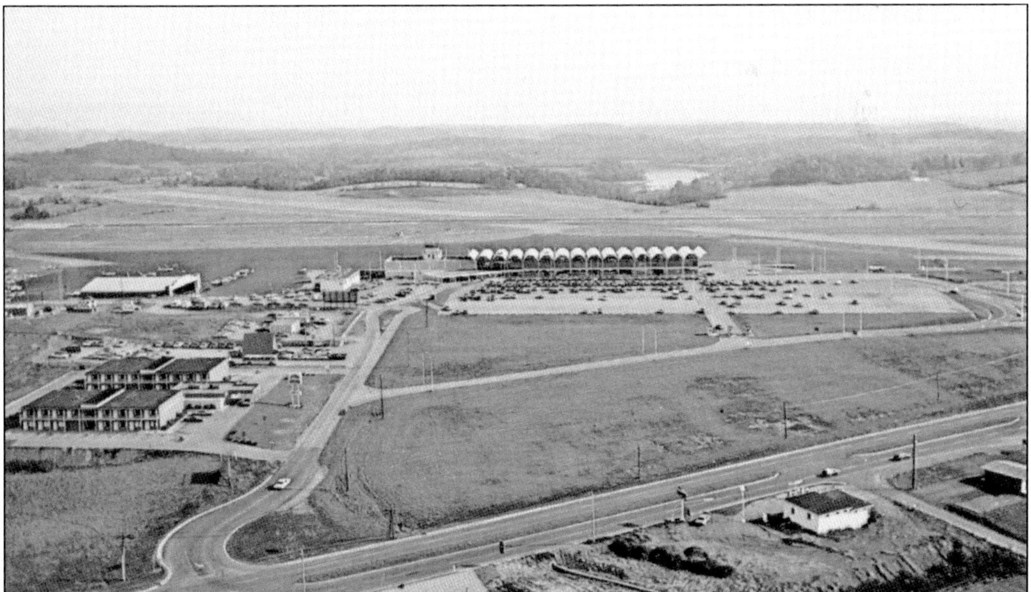

OVERLOOKING THE AIRPORT. A large terminal building (center) was added to the airport in the late 1960s. Just beyond, Boone Lake can be seen in the background, showing a *c.* 1970 aerial view of the Tri-City Regional Airport. The facility's name changed from Tri-City to Tri-Cities in the 1990s. (Courtesy of Shelby Edwards.)

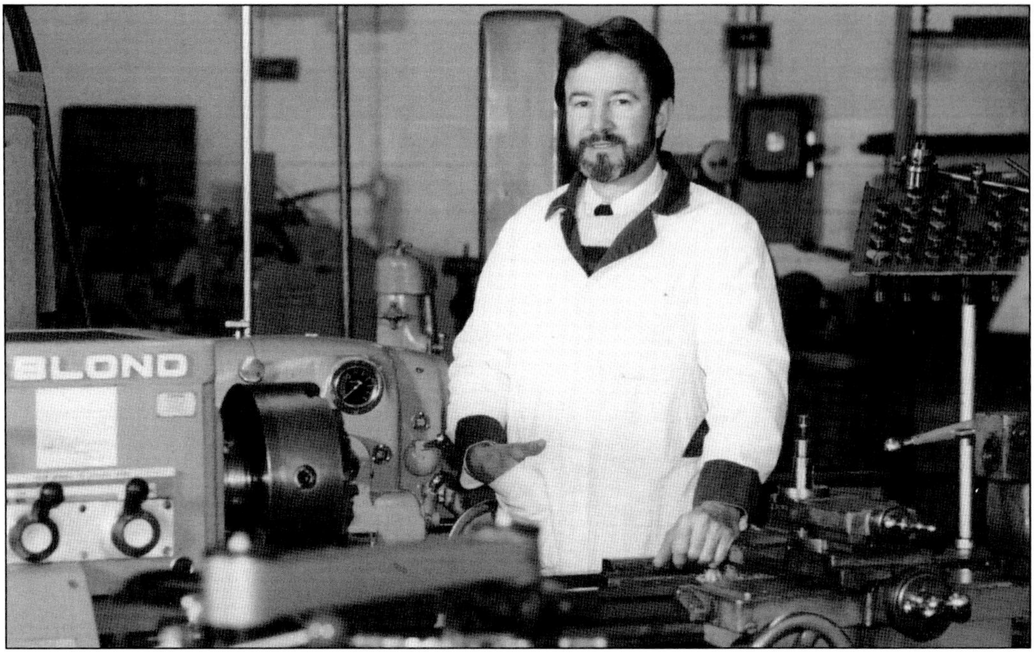

LAST MAN STANDING. Tom Jarrell of Bluff City was one of the first teachers when Tri-Cities Area Vocational-Technical School opened in 1966 with 35 students. By 1994, Jarrell was the last original member of this school's faculty. But, by then, the Blountville school had grown into the Northeast State Technical Community College, with an enrollment of more than 3,500 students. (Courtesy of the *Bristol Herald Courier*; photograph by Mike Jackson.)

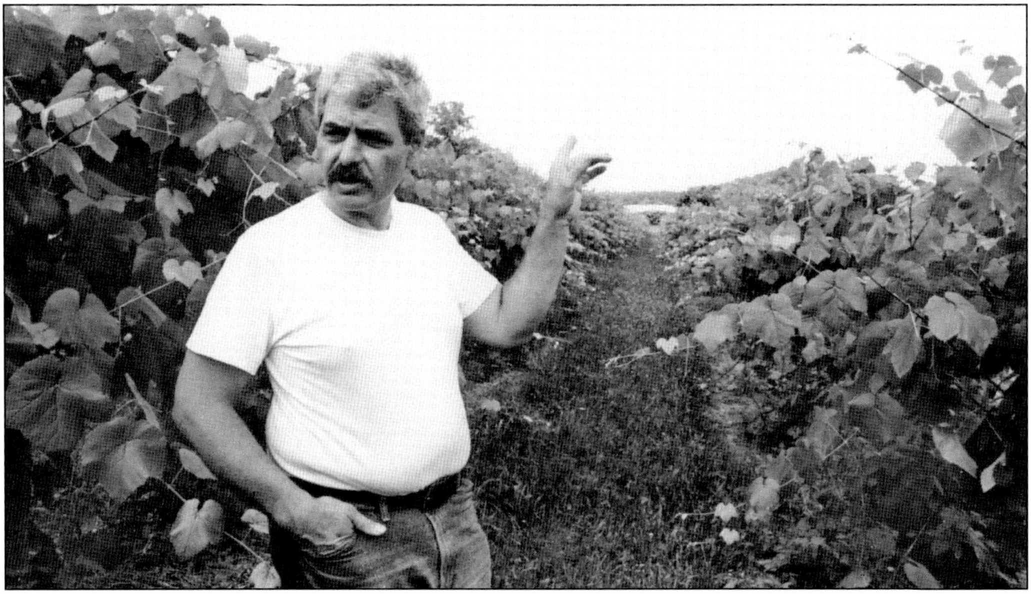

WINEMAKER. Jim Thomas led tours of the Countryside Vineyards and Winery on opening day in 1991, about four years after his family planted grapes and became a Sullivan County institution, near Interstate 81's Exit 66. The winery's most popular product, a red wine called Autumn Harvest, has been used for communion services at St. Dominic Catholic Church in Kingsport. (Courtesy of the *Bristol Herald Courier*; photograph by Bill McKee.)

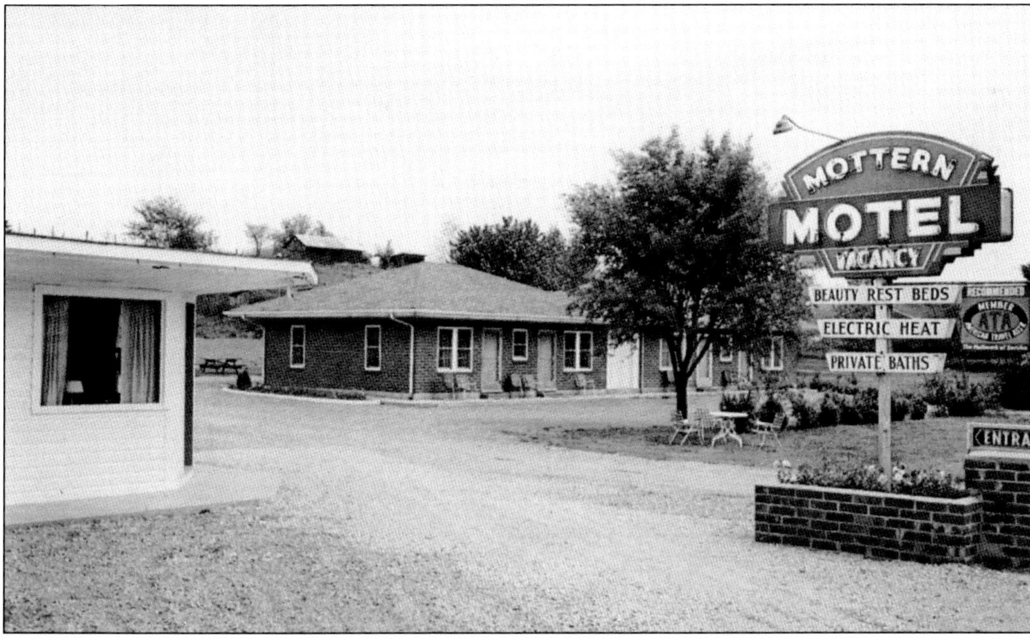

MOTTERN MOTEL. Boasting "Beauty Rest Beds," "Electric Heat," and "Private Baths," the Mottern Motel of Blountville once provided weary travelers a comfortable place to stay along the old U.S. Highway 11 West (now Blountville Highway). Mr. and Mrs. Clay Mottern operated the facility, promising visitors "Cross ventilation—Air cooled." (Courtesy of George Stone.)

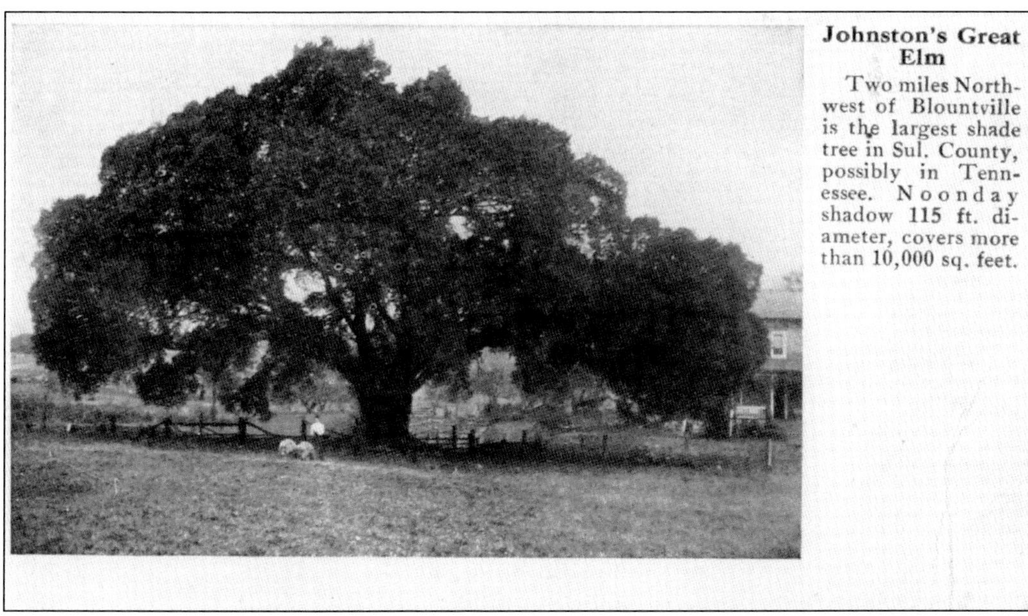

BIG TREE. The Johnston's Great Elm found fame on this penny postcard, made in the early 1900s. The tree was noted as being two miles northeast of Blountville and was the largest shade tree in Sullivan County. (Courtesy of George Stone.)

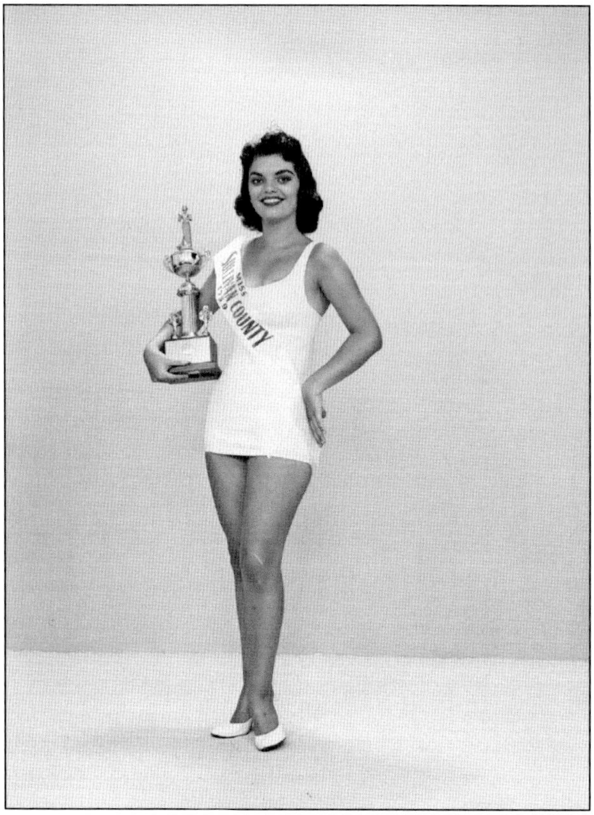

MISS SULLIVAN COUNTY. In the 1950s, the Miss Sullivan County pageant showcased the beauty and talents of young women across Upper East Tennessee, an area now more commonly called Northeast Tennessee. Sandra "Sandy" Nidiffer won the 1959 competition. (Courtesy of the Kingsport Archives; photograph by Carl Swann.)

ONE-STRING KING. Blountville resident "CanJoe" John L. VanArsdall makes instruments using only one string. He calls them "canjoes," and each handcrafted item is composed of a finger board with 10 frets, one tuner key, and one string pulled through a 12-ounce, aluminum beverage can, which is used as the resonator. CanJoe John has also performed on stages, including the Grand Ole Opry. (Courtesy of the *Bristol Herald Courier*; photograph by Joe Tennis.)

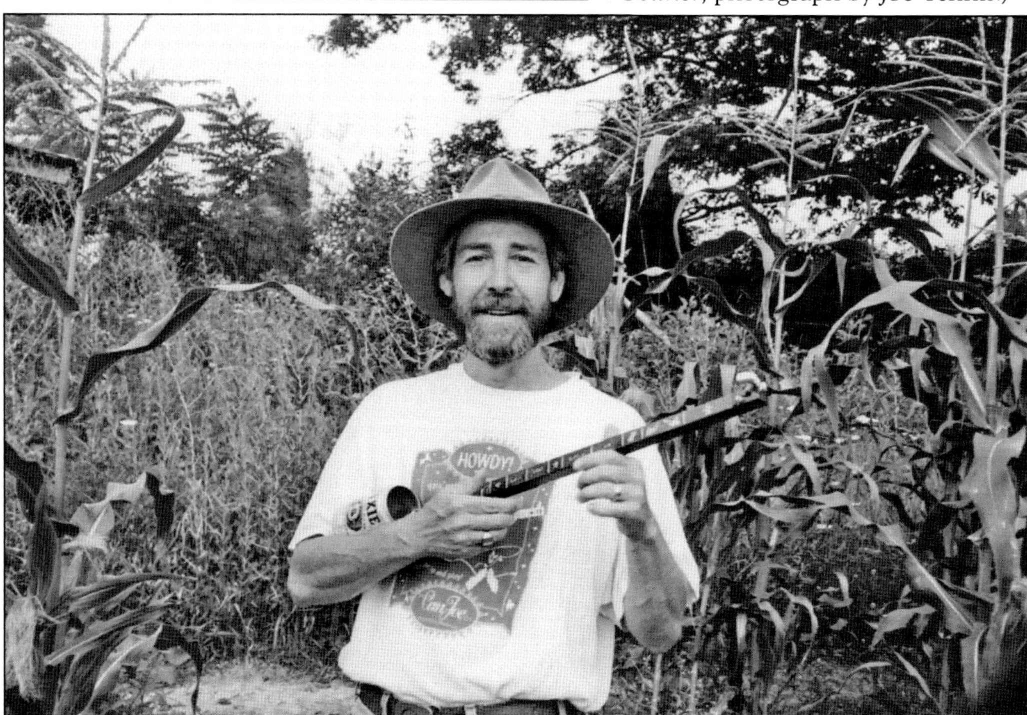

Two

Bluff City

It has been one name after another for Bluff City.

In 1777, the settlement was called "Shoate's Ford," or "Choate's Ford," for Edward Shoate, who settled near a crossing on the South fork of the Holston River. The ford was not far from Womack's Fort, an outpost established beside a spring a few years earlier and named for pioneer settler Jacob Womack.

A wagon road crossed Shoate's Ford about halfway between Abingdon, Virginia, and Jonesborough, Tennessee, and by 1805, this village naturally became known as "Middletown."

Then came the railroad in the late 1850s. Middletown was renamed Union Depot, a name soon shortened to simply "Union."

Not much later, the Civil War broke out, and locals feared a name like Union might be seen as sympathetic to the North. So the town's name changed yet again. In 1862, Union became "Zollicoffer" for Gen. Felix Zollicoffer, the man who controlled all Confederate military forces in East Tennessee.

During the war, Union raids passed through town and burned a railroad bridge at Bluff City.

After the war, the town reclaimed the name Union. Finally, in 1887, Bluff City adopted its present name, derived from the high bluffs overlooking the Holston River.

Incorporated in 1901, Bluff City claims fame for places like Stover Hall, a long-gone landmark. Destroyed in a 1906 fire, this mansion was once the home of Mary Johnson Stover, daughter of Pres. Andrew Johnson. Another historical footnote comes from L. V. Gerstle, a businessman who made a few drug products, including a liver regulator, at his shop on Main Street in the 1870s. Gerstle's operation later moved to Chattanooga and became the parent company behind the famous drug brand St. Joseph's.

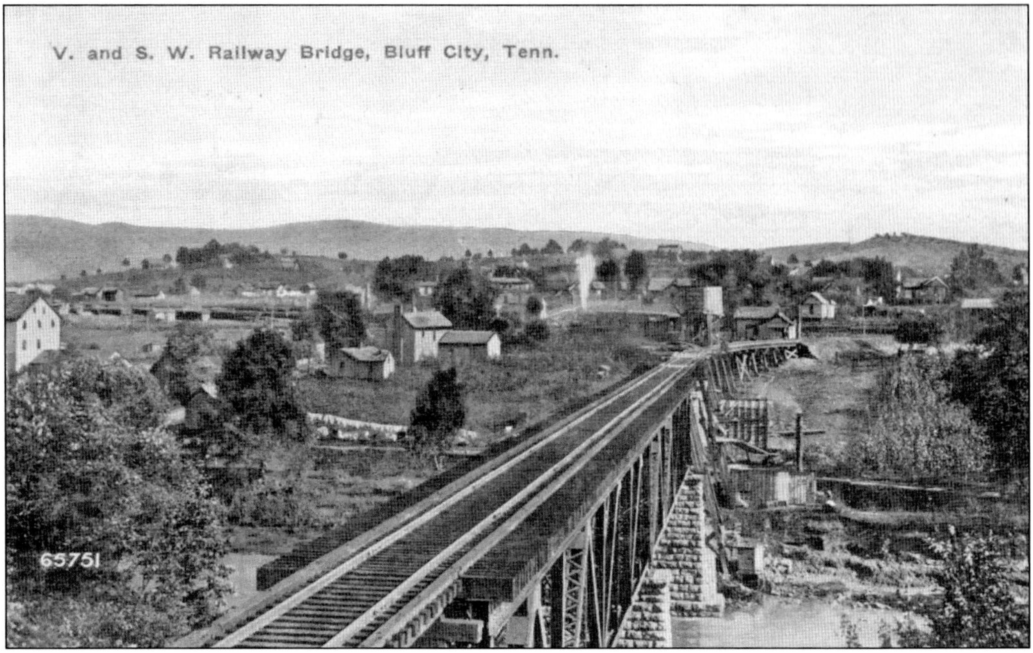

STEAMING INTO TOWN. It is easy to find beauty peering off the railroad tracks over the South fork of the Holston River in this postcard of the early 1900s. The wild river, at this spot, has since been tamed into the headwaters of Boone Lake. (Courtesy of George Stone.)

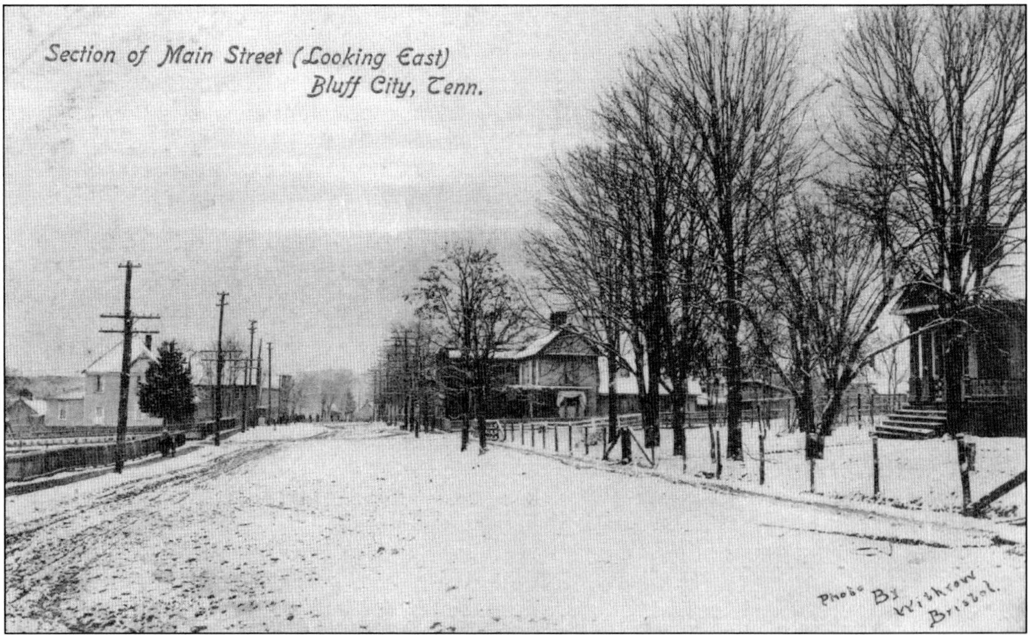

EARLY VIEW. A snowy scene from 1908 paints one of the earliest views of Bluff City's Main Street looking east. Much of the character of this corridor remains, with residential homes still situated among churches and small retailers. (Courtesy of George Stone.)

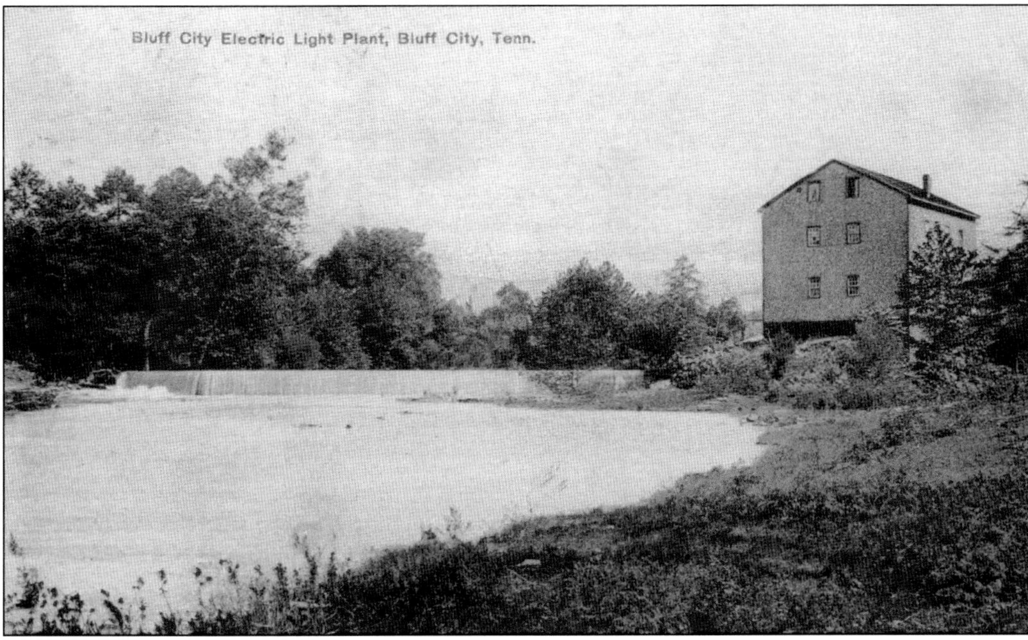

POWER OF THE RIVER. J. C. Henry operated the Bluff City Electric Plant, once standing on the banks of the South fork of the Holston River. In the early 1900s, the plant provided electricity by using the waterpower of a dam. (Courtesy of Billy and Irene Wells.)

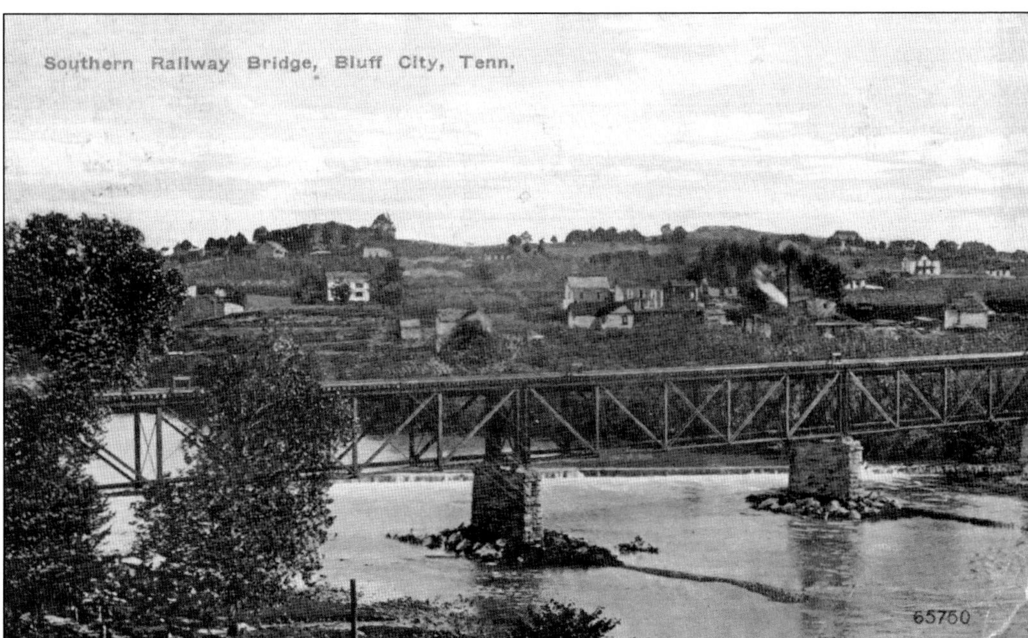

SOUTHERN RAILWAY BRIDGE. In the early 1900s, the Southern Railway Bridge became a popular point for making postcards of Bluff City, such as this one showing the crossing over the South fork of the Holston River. (Courtesy of George Stone.)

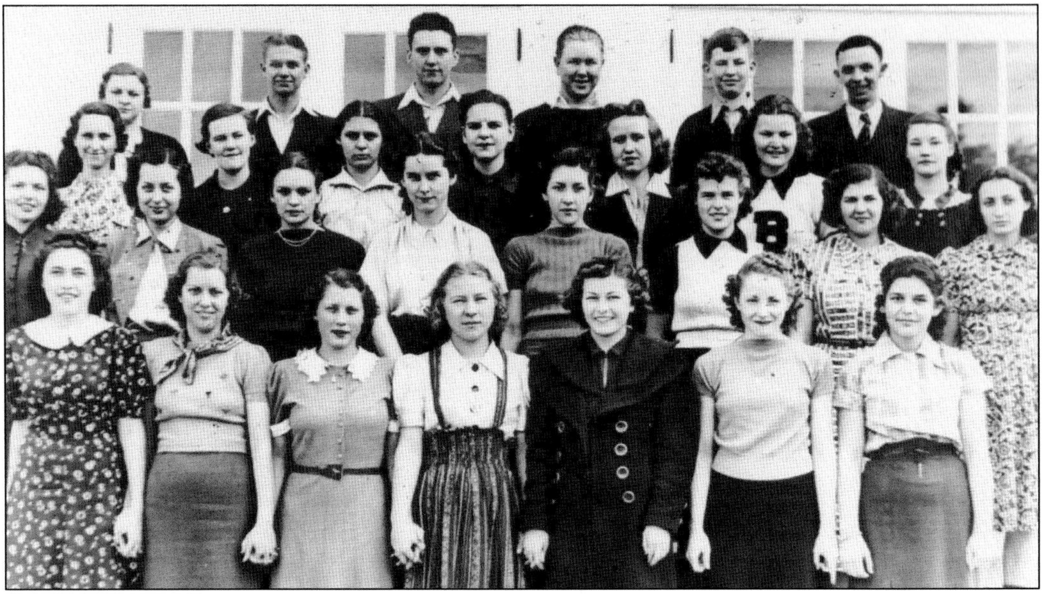

CLASS PORTRAIT. Members of the Bluff City High School class pose outside the school in 1939. From left to right, they are as follows: (first row) Nell Eads, Francis Allen, Ella Anderson, Luell Harkleroad, Dorothy Bryon, Helen Thomas, and Evelyn Webb; (second row) Swetta Morrell, Mary Allen, Maxie Massengill, Mary Virginia Miller, Ogle Smith, Elizabeth Morrell, Jessie Mae King, and Roberta Morton; (third row) Beulah Richards, Lenora Pierce, Janet Dempsey, Glenna Baumgardner, Helen Tinsley, Pearl Eads, and Pansy Mottern; (fourth row) teacher Ruth Boy, Earl O'Dell, Haskel Woods, Rollin Hicks, Warren Pierce, and teacher Herman O'Dell. (Courtesy of Shelia Steele Hunt.)

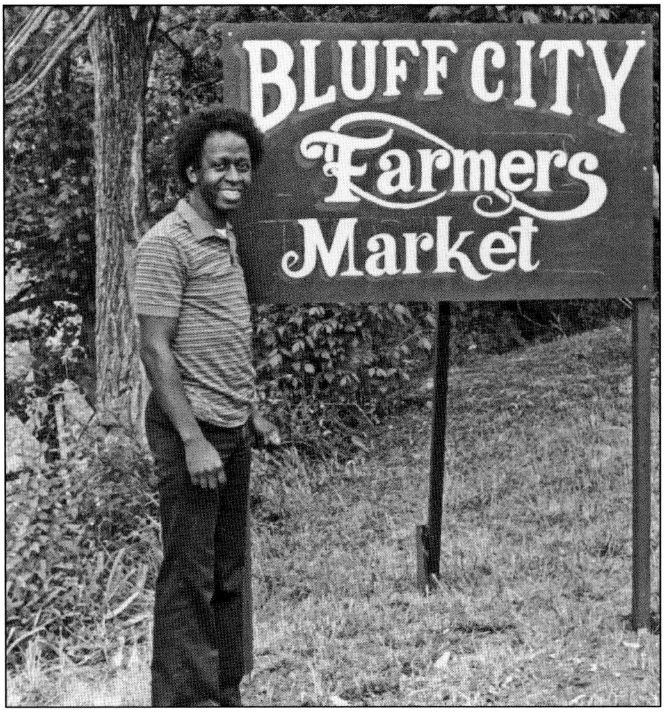

FAMOUS MAYOR. As Bluff City's mayor in the late 1980s, Billy Wells's achievements included building a boardwalk along Boone Lake and promoting the Bluff City Farmers Market. Wells also became famous as the first elected black mayor in Tennessee. (Courtesy of Irene Wells.)

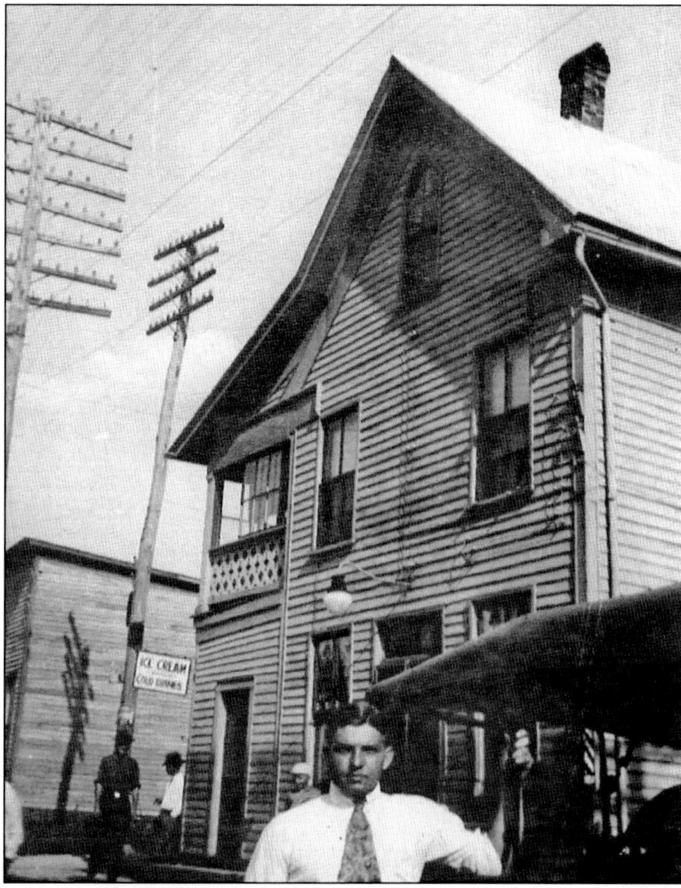

RYDEN'S STORE. Logue Ryden operated Ryden's Store in the 1940s, selling groceries, including ice cream and cold drinks, at Bluff City. This store building, at the corner of Main and Carter Streets, has since been torn down and made into a parking lot for Thomas Hardware. (Courtesy of Betty Thomas.)

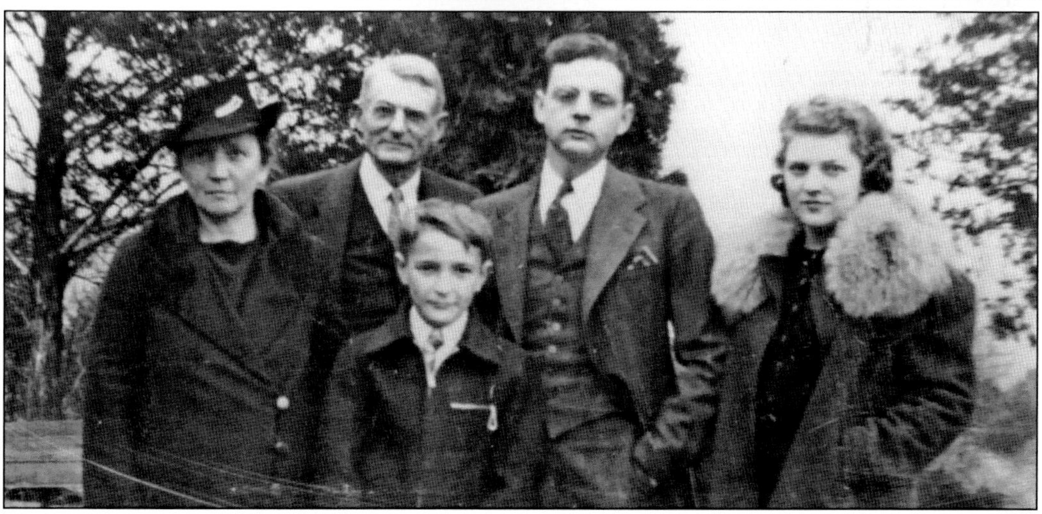

THOMAS FAMILY. Bluff City's prominent Thomas family posed for this photograph, c. 1940. From left to right are Margaret Thomas, Bert Thomas, Robert Thomas (in front), Forrest Thomas, and Willene Thomas. Forrest Thomas (1911–2001) began operating Thomas Hardware at the center of Bluff City in 1945. Robert Thomas, his brother, served for years on the town's board of mayor and alderman. (Courtesy of Betty Thomas.)

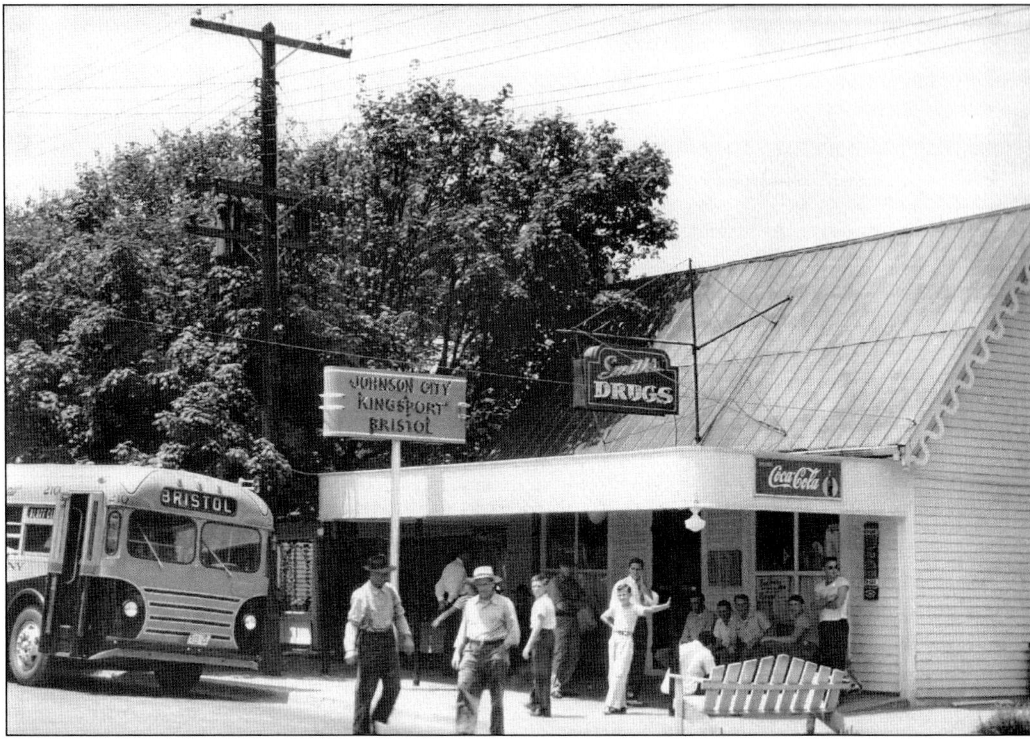

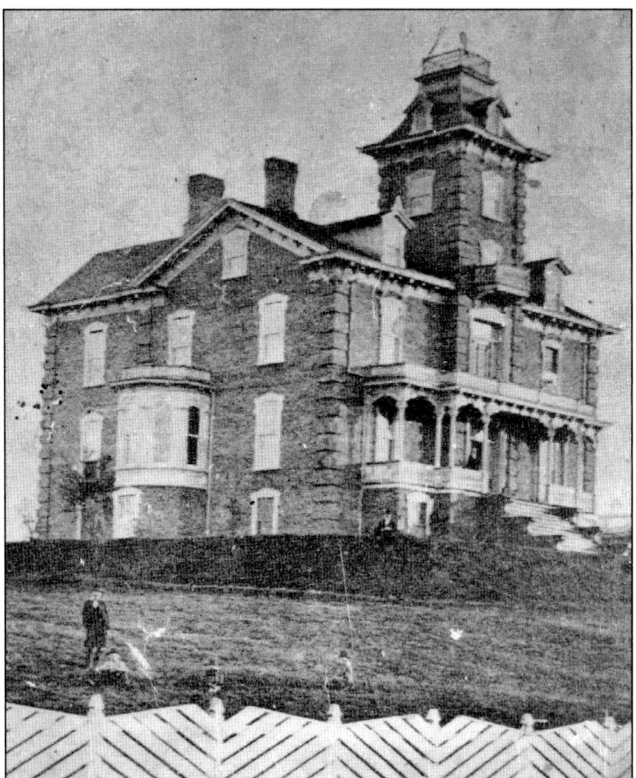

BUS STOP. Smith's Drugs on Main Street doubled as a bus stop, linking Bluff City to the Tri-Cities of Johnson City, Kingsport, and Bristol. This view captured the store in 1948 at the corner of Main and Carter Streets. The boy standing with his hand on the post is Kenneth Morrell. Behind him, near the door, is Charles Fleming. (Courtesy of Betty Thomas.)

STOVER HALL. Built in 1867, Stover Hall was once the home of Mary Johnson Stover, daughter of Pres. Andrew Johnson. Stover's family had a business interest in Bluff City's Holston Cotton Factory, and she came to live in town after her father died in 1875. Stover Hall was destroyed by fire in 1906. Long Shadows mansion was later built on its foundation. (Courtesy of the Bluff City Public Library.)

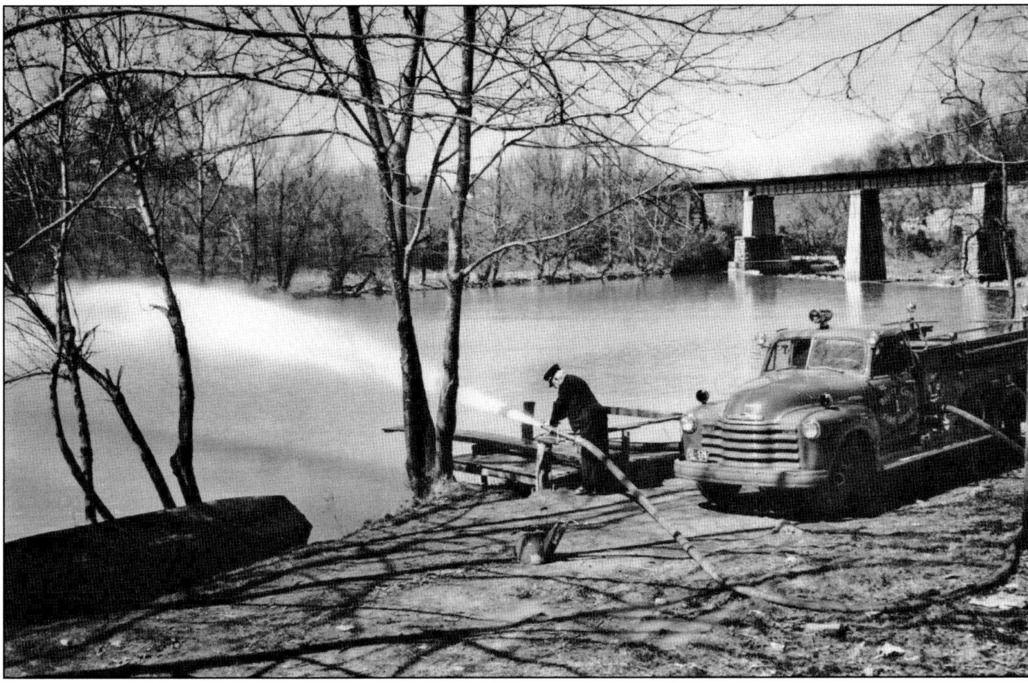

FIREMAN AND WATER. Harold Pratt, the owner of Pratt's Store, was a fireman for the Bluff City Fire Department. Here Pratt stops by the river and railroad tracks in Bluff City, *c.* 1952, in the vicinity of what was once known as "The Old Mill Dam." (Courtesy of the Bluff City Public Library.)

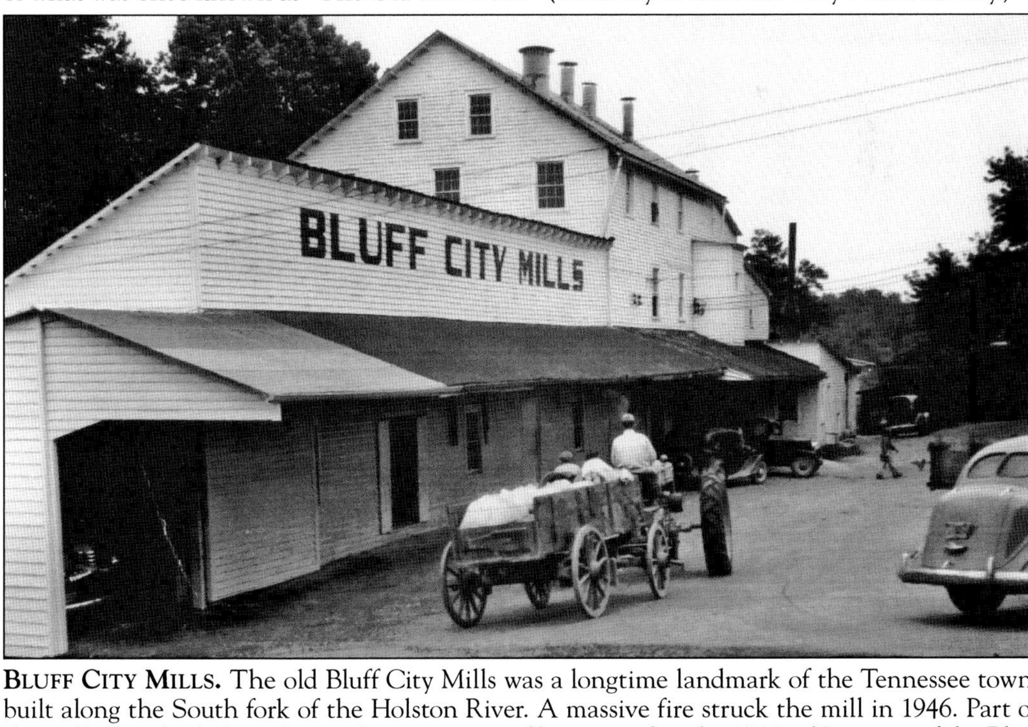

BLUFF CITY MILLS. The old Bluff City Mills was a longtime landmark of the Tennessee town, built along the South fork of the Holston River. A massive fire struck the mill in 1946. Part of the mill was rebuilt, but ultimately, it went out of business after the 1980s. (Courtesy of the Bluff City Public Library.)

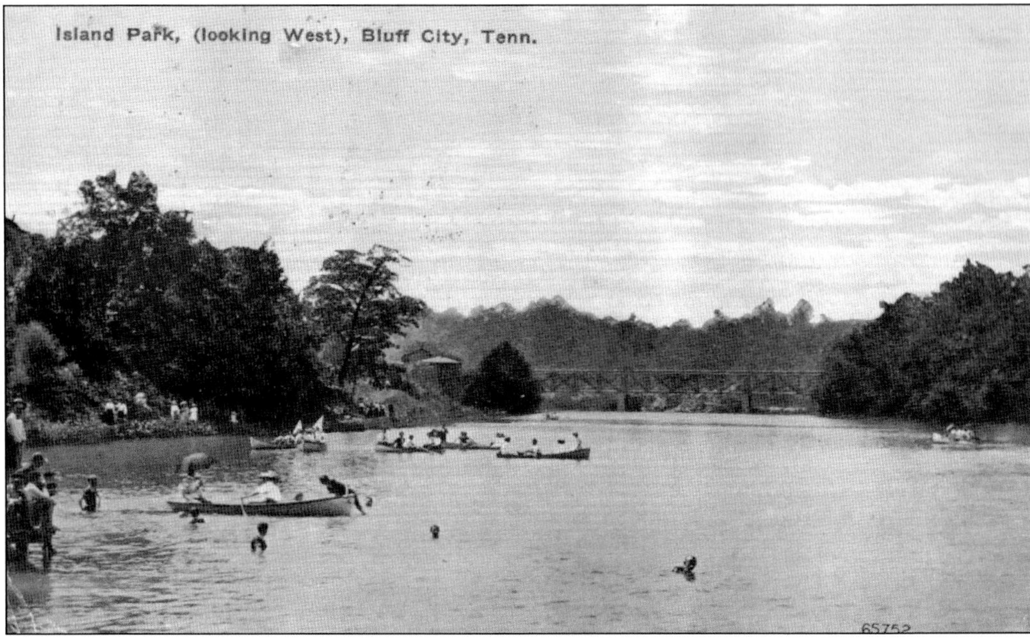

LOOKING WEST. Island Park provided a great place for recreation in the Bluff City area in the early 1900s. People flocked to the water with rowboats and canoes—and just to swim. The park also inspired many postcards, such as this one, looking west. Yet, unfortunately, Bluff City sometimes lost credit in the location. For example, this fun scene in 1914 is described on another edition of this same postcard as "near Bristol, Tenn.-Va." (Courtesy of Tim Buchanan.)

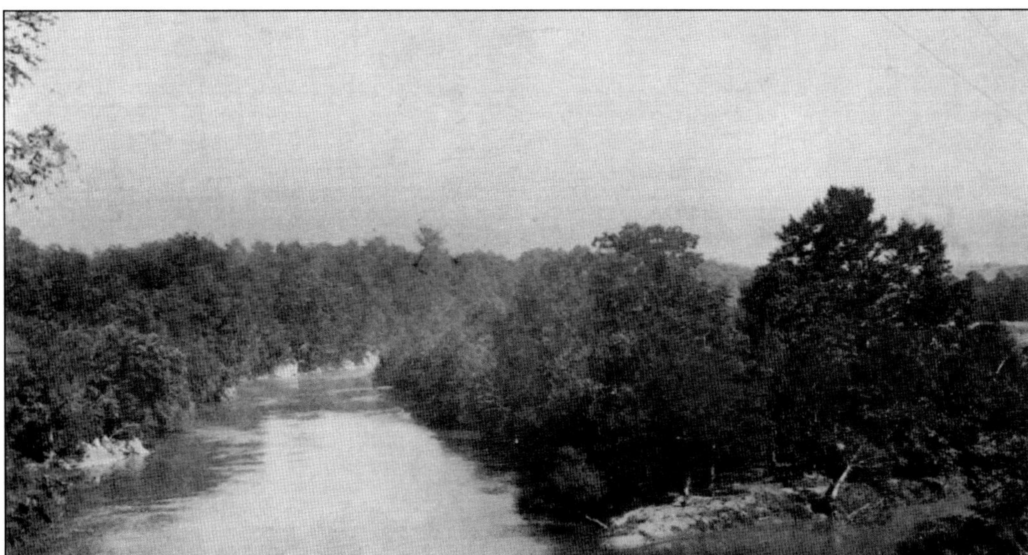

ISLAND PARK. The rugged scene of Island Park at Bluff City shows the natural island at the center of the South fork of the Holston River. This area is now part of the headwaters of Boone Lake. (Courtesy of George Stone.)

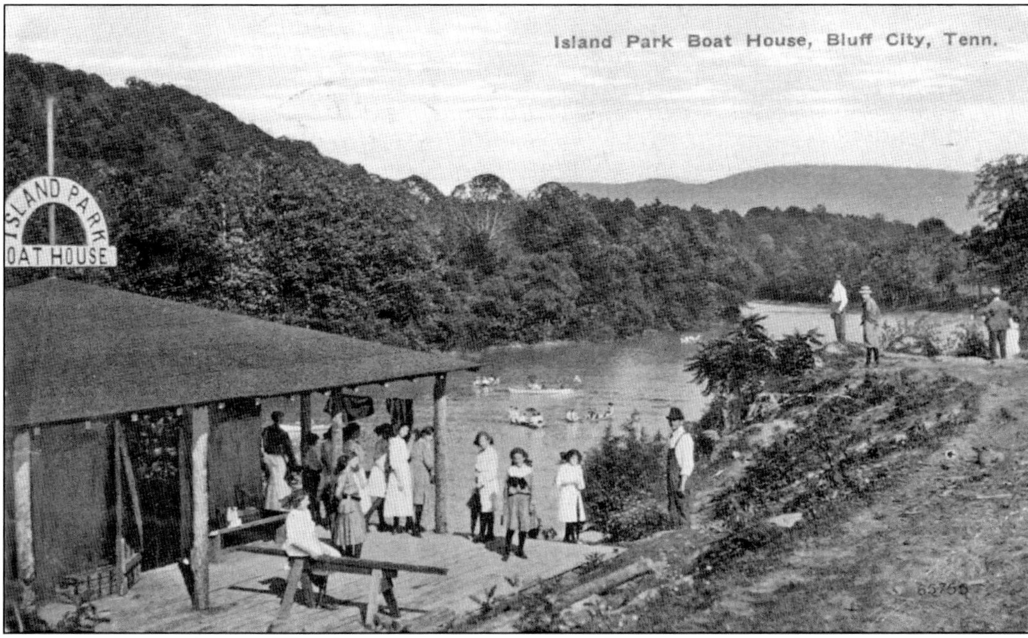

OAT HOUSE. No, "Oat House" is not a misspelling. But you actually need another "B" to fill in what should be the Island Park Boat House on the sign of this postcard, *c.* 1914. The boathouse provided a place to dock canoes and rowboats at Island Park. On the horizon, Holston Mountain can be seen on the eastern skyline in the upper right corner. (Courtesy of Billy and Irene Wells.)

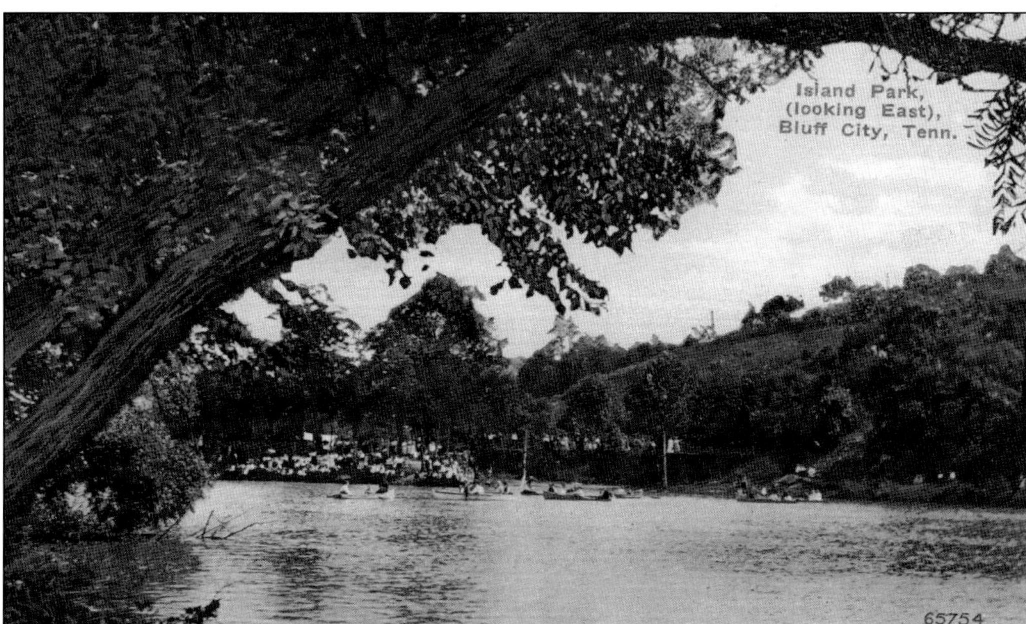

LOOKING EAST. A postcard of Island Park shows the view looking east from behind a tree. This area, like so much of Bluff City, now borders Boone Lake. (Courtesy of Tony Marion.)

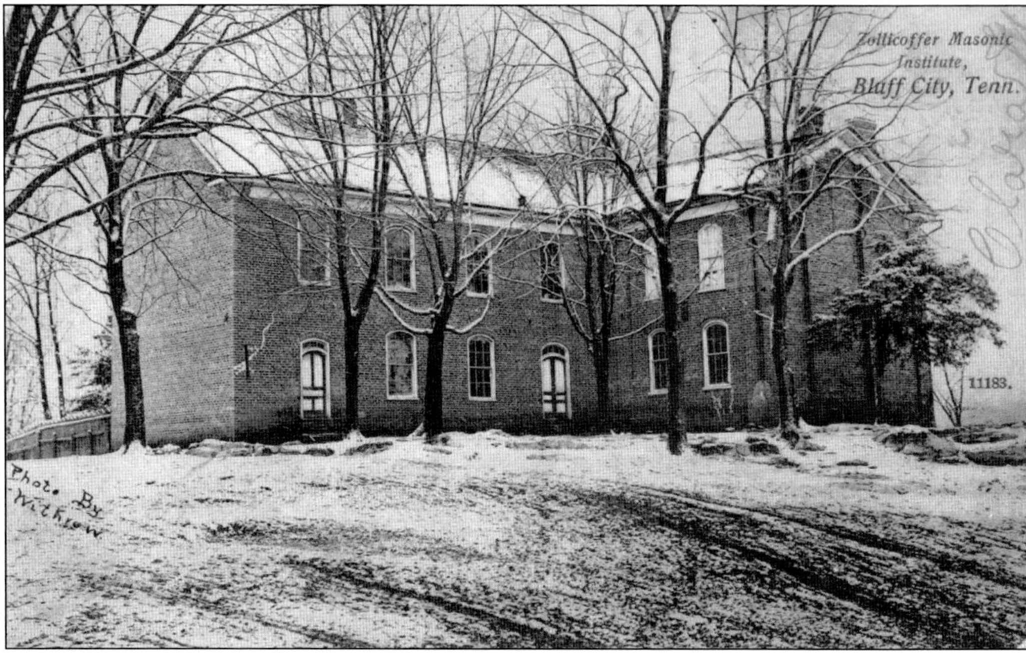

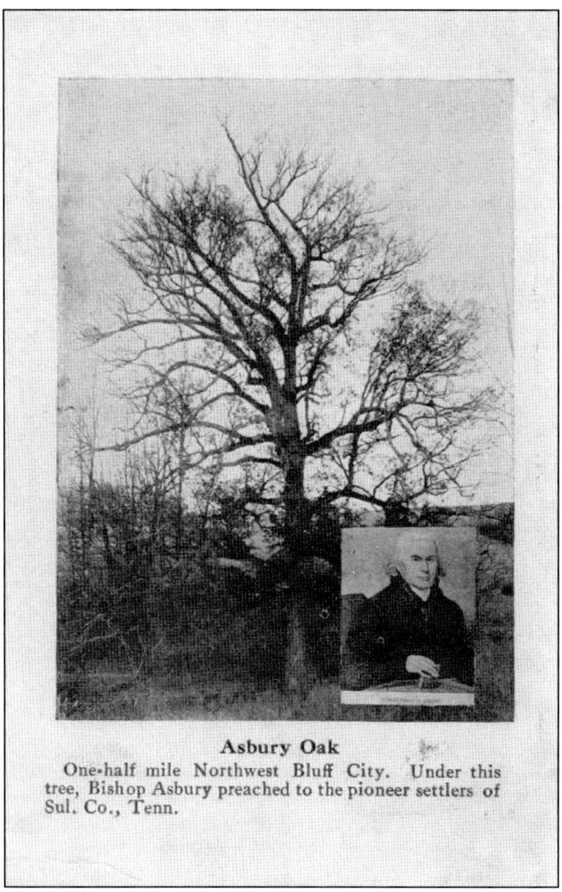

ZOLLICOFFER MASONIC INSTITUTE. A c. 1908 postcard showcases the Zollicoffer Masonic Institute, a brick structure built in 1889 and named for Bluff City's Civil War–era name, Zollicoffer. Here schoolboys were assigned to fetch water, but they would have to walk down the hill and cross the river to Mauk's springhouse. The institute was closed sometime after 1916. (Courtesy of George Stone.)

ASBURY OAK. Francis Asbury had a great influence on many settlers in what collectively became known as the Mountain Empire of Southwest Virginia and Northeast Tennessee. This postcard celebrates Asbury's life as a legendary Methodist bishop and a tree that became known as the Asbury Oak, noted to stand one-half mile northwest of Bluff City. (Courtesy of George Stone.)

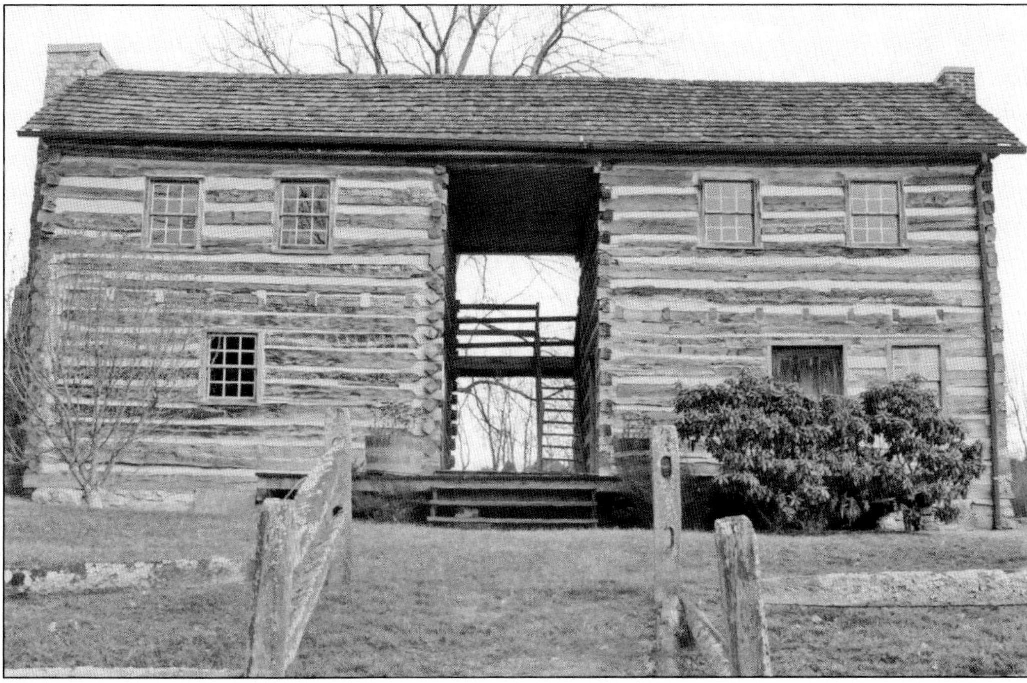

Cox House. Maryland native Edward Cox married his childhood sweetheart, Sallie Meredith, and had 10 children. Cox also built a double-hewn log house in the 1770s with a breezeway called a dogtrot. Methodist bishop Francis Asbury conducted Methodist services here, including what might have been the first Methodist conference in Tennessee. The Cox House stands slightly north of Bluff City, surrounded by modern homes. (Photograph by Joe Tennis.)

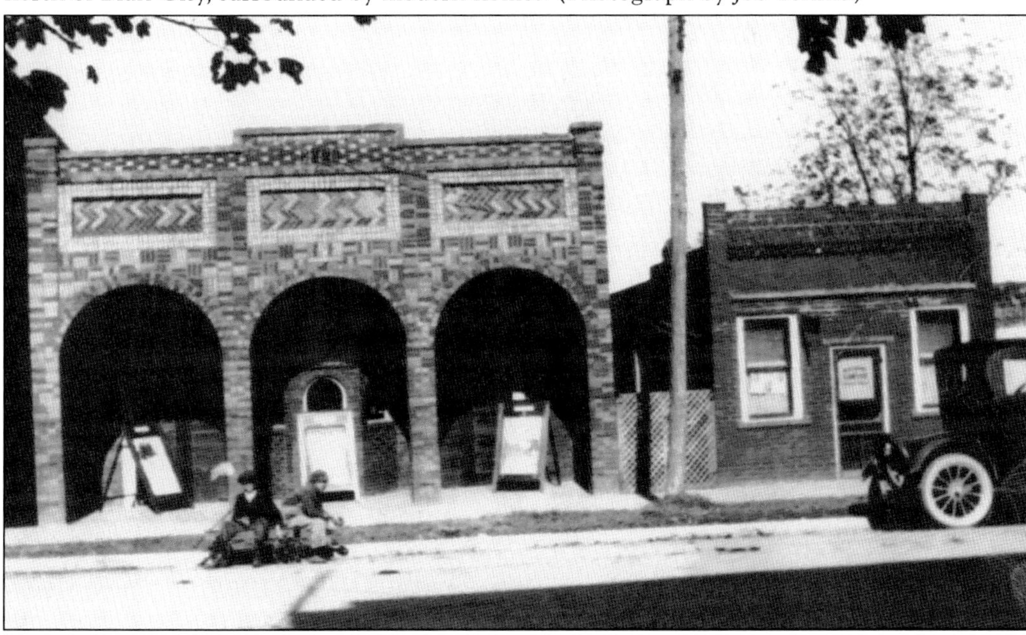

Early Business. A 1920s view of Bluff City's Main Street captures, at left, an early glimpse of the brick building that later became Hodge's Confectionery, affectionately dubbed "Banty's" by locals. (Courtesy of Betty Thomas.)

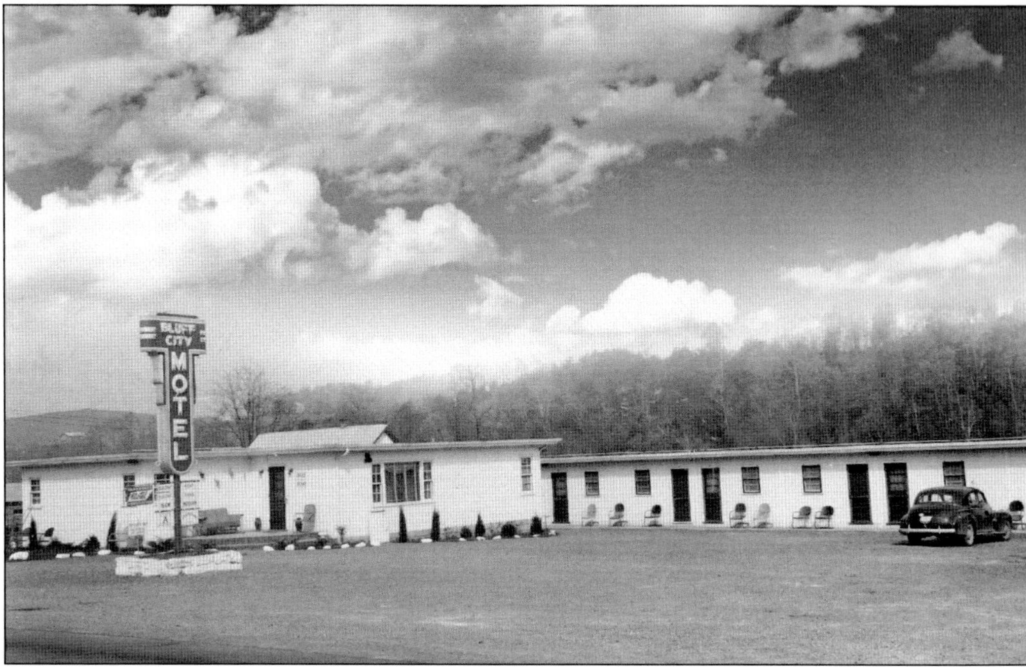

MOTOR LODGE. The Bluff City Motel boasted "Electric Heat" and "Electric Fans" in this *c.* 1940s photograph. The motel was located near what later became the Bluff City Fire Department. (Courtesy of the Bluff City Public Library.)

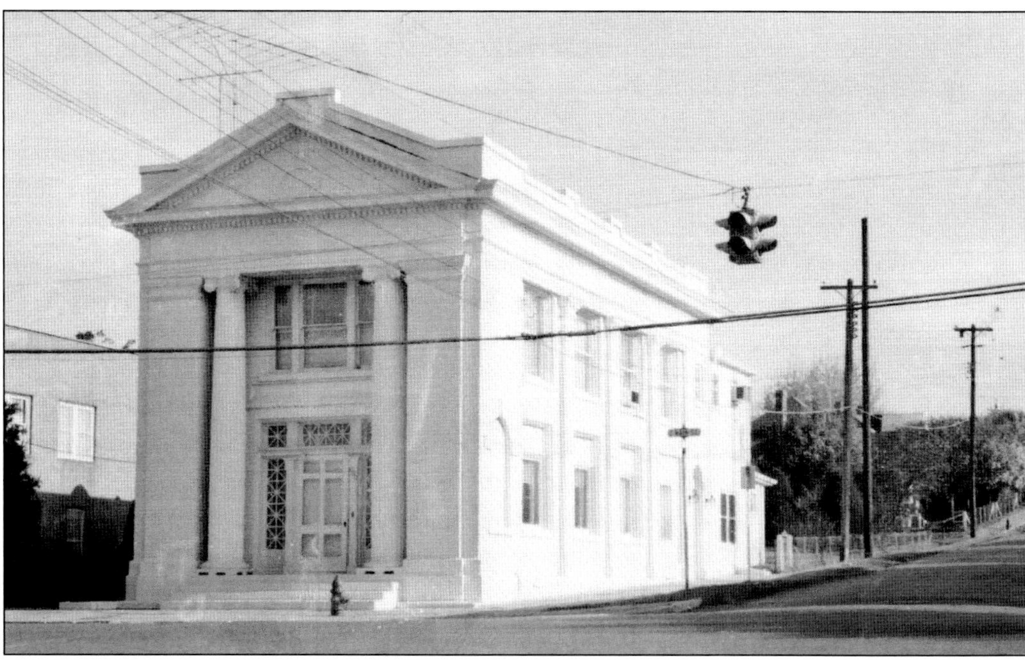

BLUFF CITY BANK. The old Bluff City Bank building on Main Street was built in 1912. From 1923 to 1945, part of the building served as Bluff City's town hall. The bank has since been used as a residence and apartment house. Hanging above the intersection of Main and Maple Streets, the traffic light seen in this *c.* 1958 photograph is no longer in place. (Courtesy of Betty Thomas.)

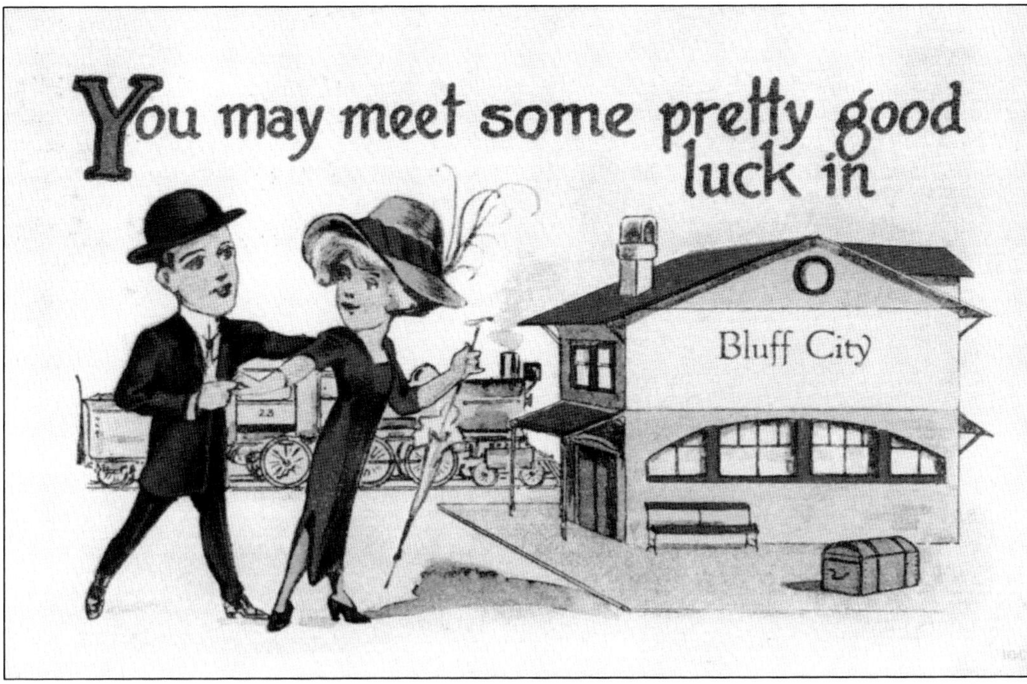

GOOD LUCK. Likely this funny relic of the early 1900s was a stock postcard with "Bluff City" simply printed in the blank space of the depot. In 1915, the sender wrote: "Hello; Don't guess you would think of hearing from me here. Am on my way to a ball-game near Piney Flats. There is also a game here this evening and no mistake this time." (Courtesy of Tony Marion.)

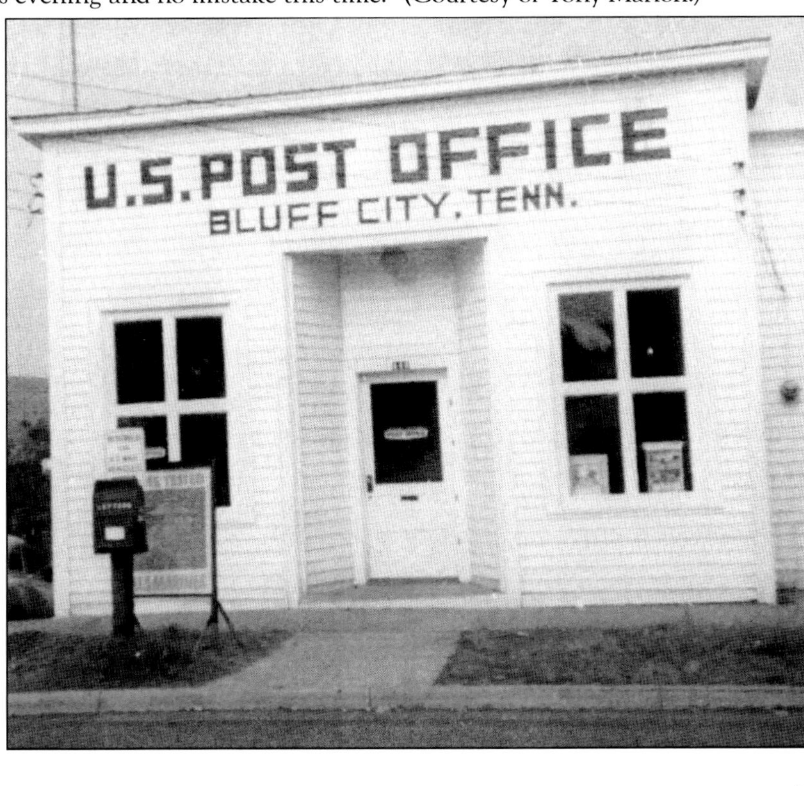

BLUFF CITY POST OFFICE. Pictured c. 1956, this little, white post office in Bluff City once stood on Main Street near Thomas Hardware. The postmistress was Inez Smith. Earlier post office names for Bluff City included Middletown, Union, and Zollicoffer. (Courtesy of Billy and Irene Wells.)

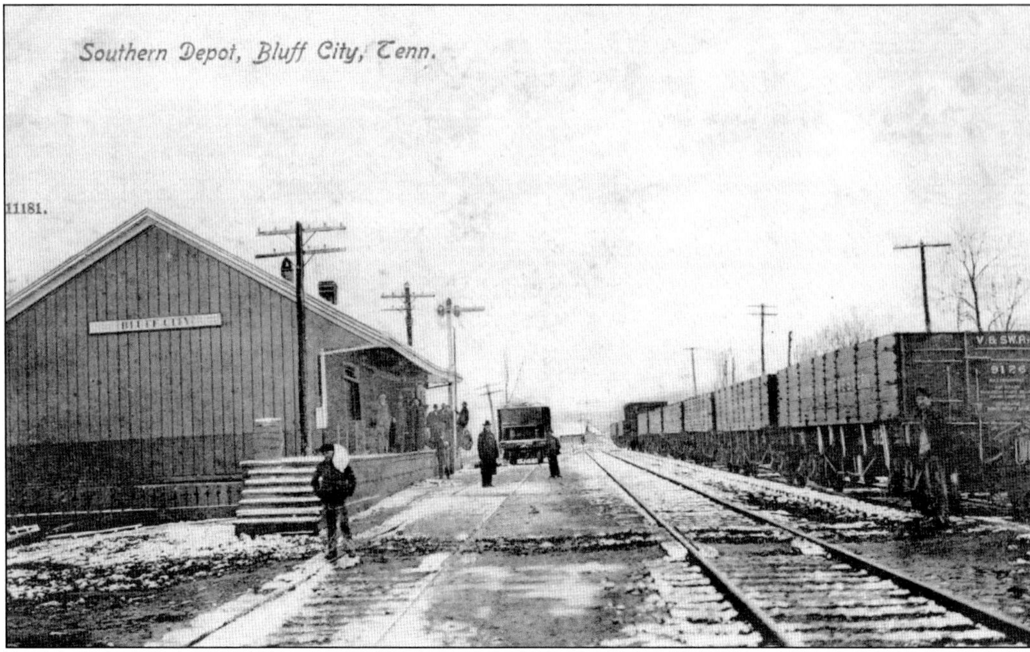

SNOW ON THE TRACKS. These postcards of Bluff City were likely made on the same day in 1908. The Bluff City Depot, above, is shown along the railroad tracks, when Bluff City was a major railroad stop south of Bristol. The Southern Railway Bridge, below, is shown crossing the South fork of the Holston River near a milldam. (Courtesy of George Stone.)

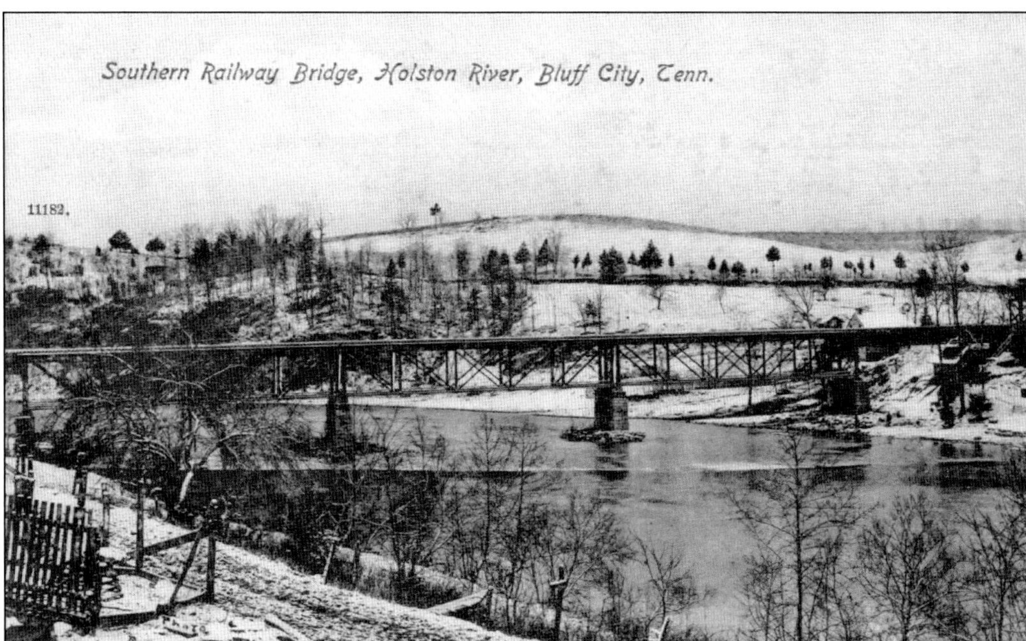

Three

Bristol

Call it the breezeway between Virginia and Tennessee.

Bristol spreads into both states—a Twin City that makes a resident of either town feel like their home state stretches from Memphis to Norfolk. Named for Bristol, England, the town was laid out by Joseph Anderson in 1852.

Actually, Bristol is two cities. There is a Bristol in Virginia and another in Tennessee. But they share the same post office, library, chamber of commerce, newspaper, and even stores built atop the state line.

At the center, the Twin City comes together on State Street. This is Bristol's main street, and it was called that until 1901, when it was renamed State Street to reflect where it ran—right atop the Tennessee-Virginia line. State Street also sounded soothing after years of bickering between Virginia and Tennessee over the location of the state border—in the middle of the road or smack against the buildings on the Virginia side of town.

The railroad came to town in 1856, and Bristol grew as an industrial base and shopping center for surrounding towns. For a while, some prospectors figured Bristol might become the "Pittsburgh of the South."

As it turned out, Bristol became most famous for its NASCAR track. The towering Bristol Motor Speedway, open since 1961, has been called the "World's Fastest Half-Mile Track." It is the site of major races each spring and summer.

Bristol, too, claims a rich musical heritage. This is the hometown of Tennessee Ernie Ford, known to millions as "The Ol' Pea Picker." It was also in Bristol in 1927, at a makeshift studio on State Street, that a talent scout discovered Jimmie Rodgers and the Carter Family—country music's first long-lasting stars—and gave Bristol the title of the "Birthplace of Country Music."

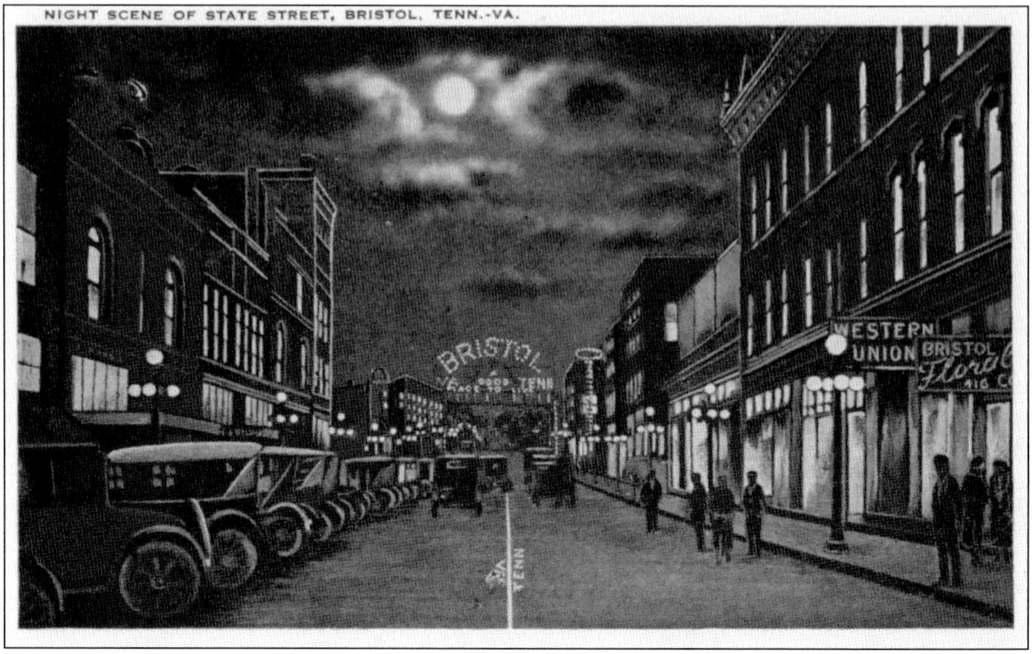

A Good Place to Live. The famous Bristol sign arches above the Virginia-Tennessee line in a "Night Scene of State Street," above, announcing the Twin City on the Sullivan County border as "A Good Place to Live." Published by the Knoxville Engraving Company, this 1920s-era postcard shows the Virginia side of town on the left and the Tennessee side on the right, with businesses including Western Union and Bristol Floral. Another night view of the famous road, below, depicts a similar view a few years later, when long-gone department stores like H. P. King, in Tennessee, competed with Virginia businesses like Raylass Department Store. (Courtesy of Tim Buchanan.)

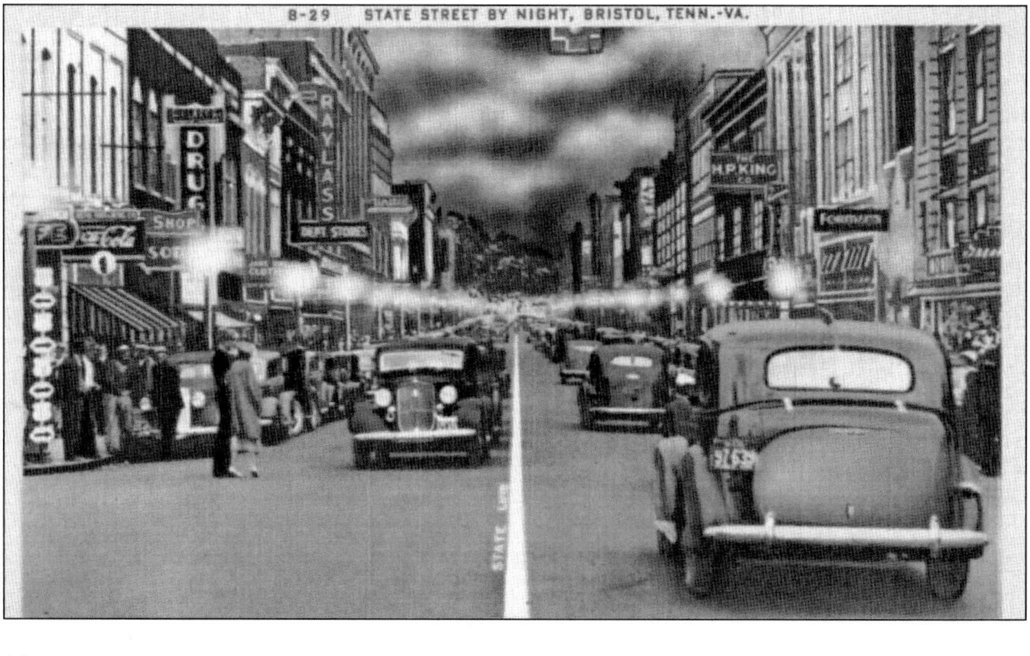

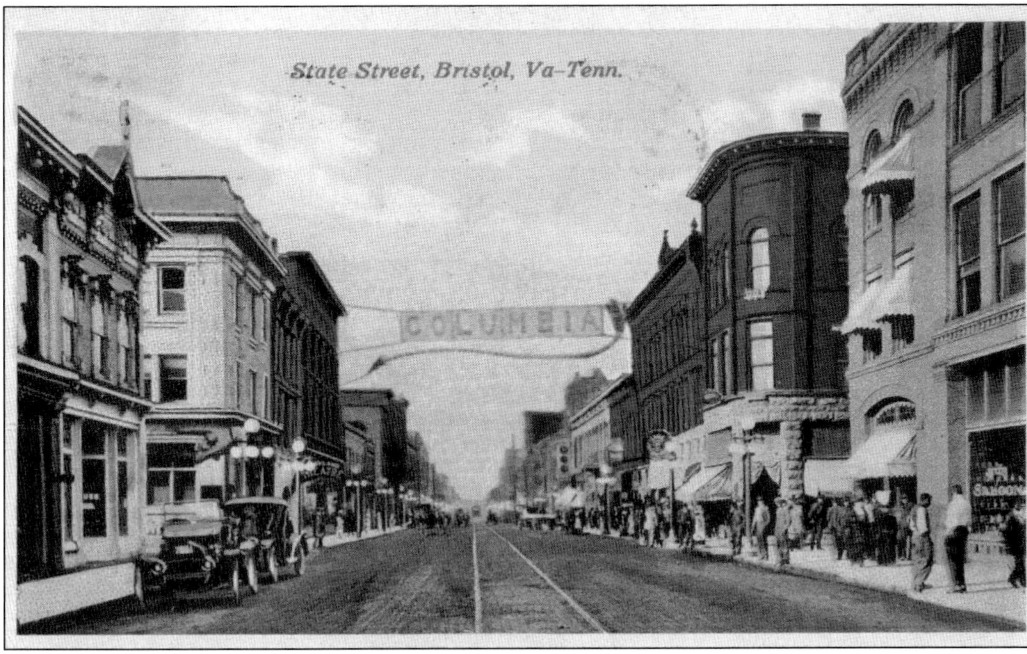

The Columbia. One of the many postcards made of State Street by S. H. Kress and Company in the early 1900s, this image announces the location of the Columbia Theater on the Tennessee side of State Street. The Columbia was built as a grand playhouse but, in time, became known as "The Rat House" for the rats heard running across the floor. (Courtesy of Tim Buchanan.)

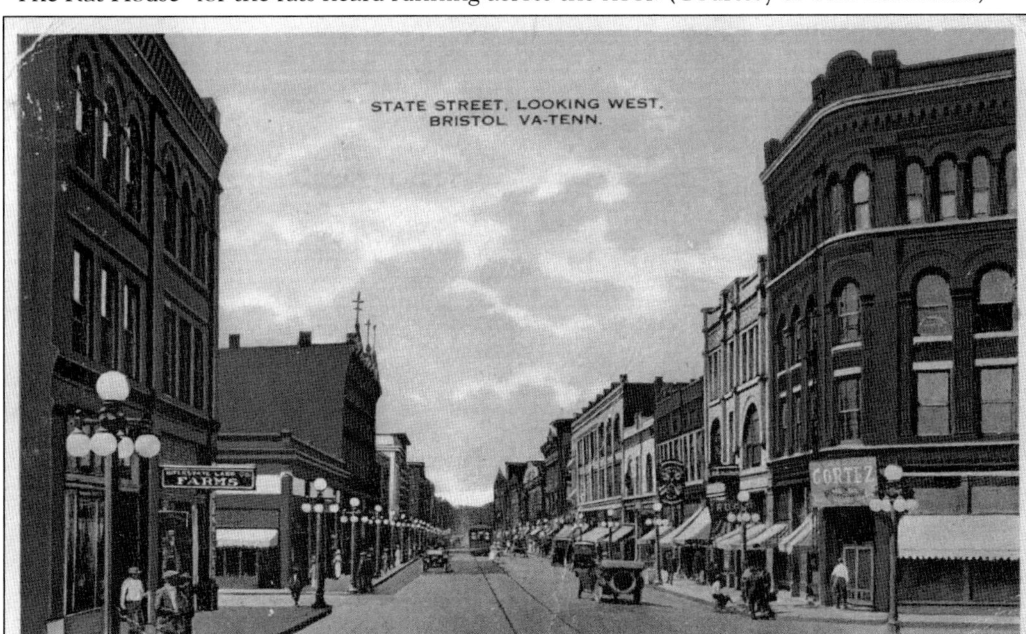

State Street Looking West. Early automobiles in Bristol had to navigate around the tracks of railcars, shown at the center of this postcard, produced about 1915. On the Tennessee side, at left, notice that the Interstate Land Company announces that "farms" are available. (Courtesy of Tim Buchanan.)

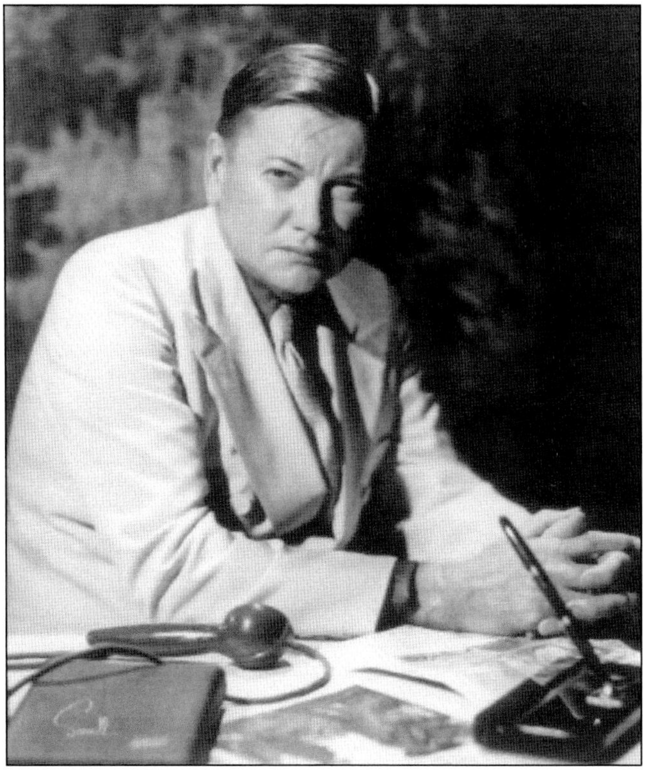

TALENT SCOUT. Think of Ralph Peer as the delivery doctor for Bristol's new identity—"The Birthplace of Country Music." In July–August 1927, this New York City talent scout operated microphones in Bristol for the Victor Talking Machine Company. What made these sessions historic were Peer's near-simultaneous discoveries of country music legends Jimmie Rodgers and the Carter Family. (Courtesy of the Birthplace of Country Music Alliance.)

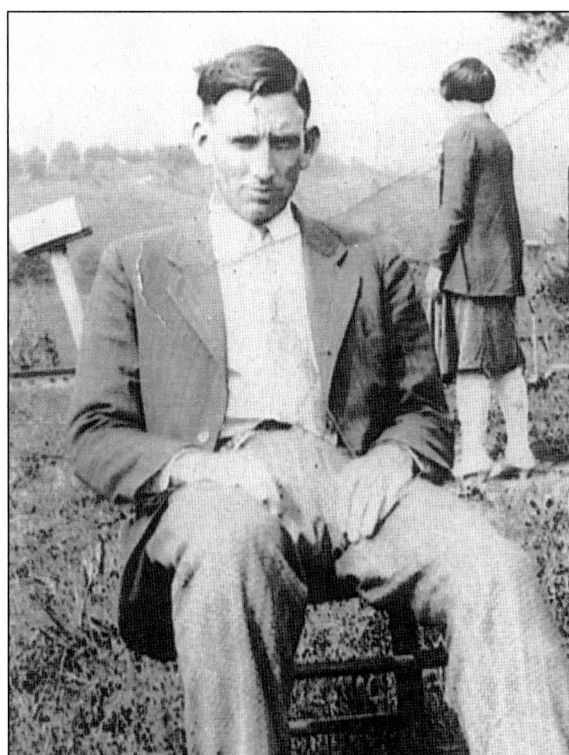

COUNTRY PIONEER. Alvin Pleasant Delaney "Doc" Carter (1891–1960) brought his family band, the Carter Family, from Maces Spring, Virginia, to record at Bristol in 1927. It was the first time the group had ever been recorded, and Carter's sister-in-law, Maybelle, was eight months pregnant at the time. Ultimately, the Carter Family built the cornerstones of country music, especially with Maybelle's widely imitated "chicken-scratch" guitar-picking style. (Courtesy of the Carter Fold.)

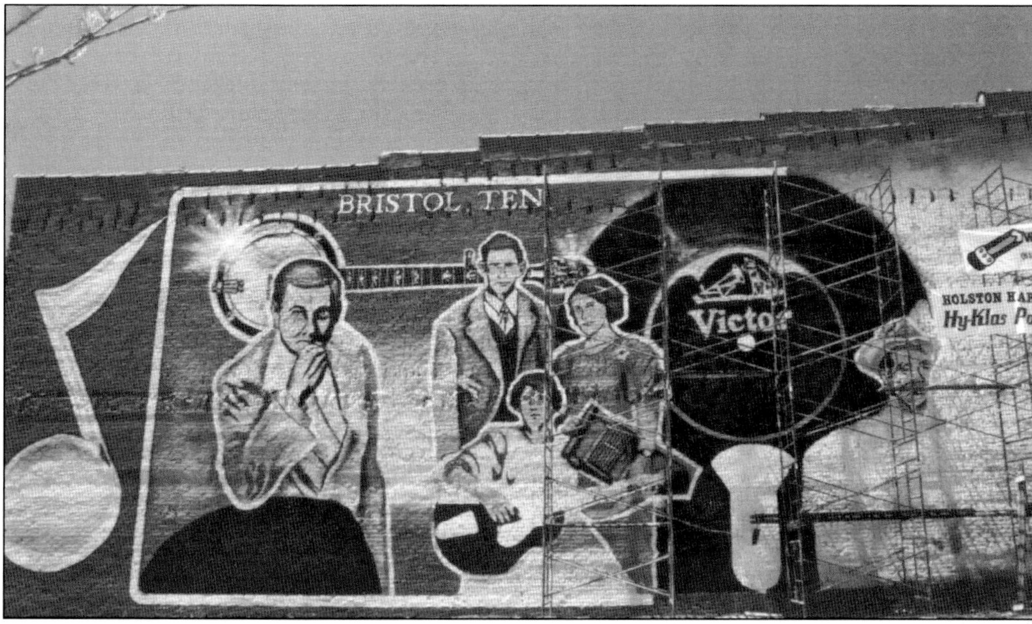

COUNTRY MUSIC MURAL. Tim White painted the *Birthplace of Country Music* mural on the 800 block of State Street in 1986. Here, at half-completion, the faces of talent scout Ralph Peer, left, can be seen, along with musicians A. P. Carter, Maybelle Carter (with guitar), and Sara Carter. At right is the half-drawn face of Ernest V. "Pop" Stoneman, named in 2008 to the Country Music Hall of Fame. (Courtesy of Shelby Edwards.)

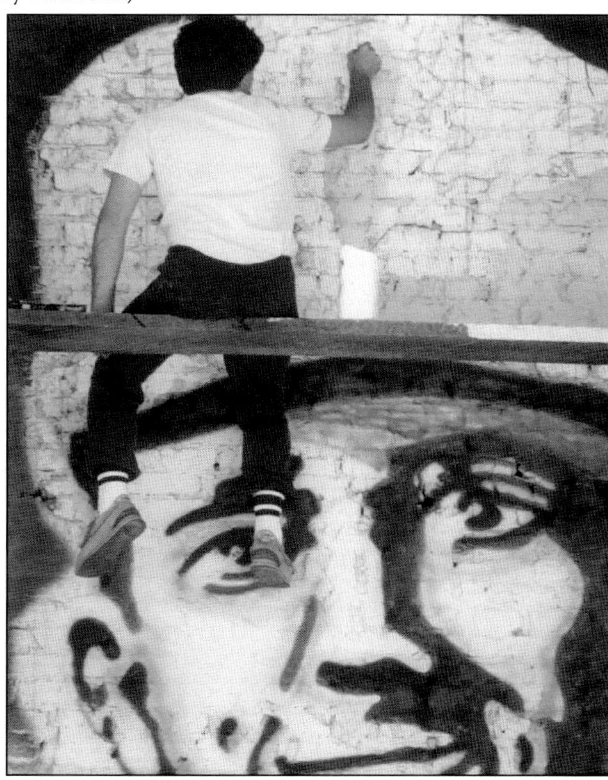

FATHER OF COUNTRY MUSIC. Jimmie Rodgers, of Meridian, Mississippi, became a yodeling sensation after being discovered in Bristol by talent scout Ralph Peer on August 4, 1927. Rodgers died in 1933, but his musical influence has continued for decades. In this 1986 photograph, Blountville artist Tim White sits on a scaffold while painting the face of Rodgers on Bristol's *Birthplace of Country Music* mural. (Courtesy of Tim White.)

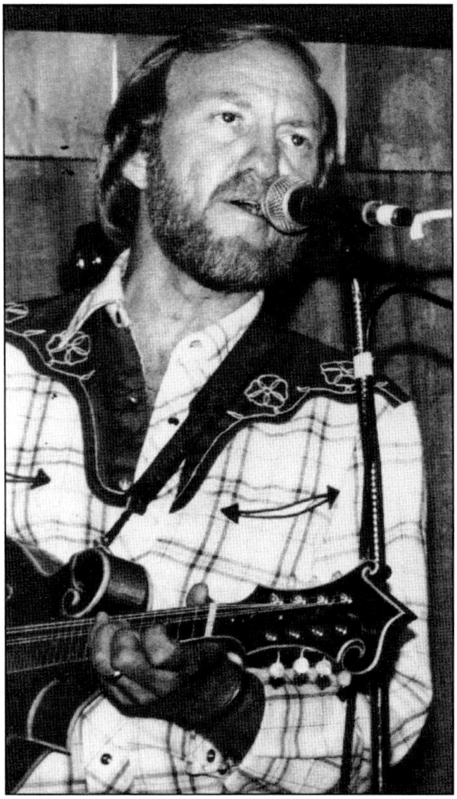

MANDOLIN MASTER. Bluegrass musician Doyle Lawson was born in 1944 at Fordtown, a Sullivan County community near Kingsport. He honed his craft in the 1960s as a member of J. D. Crowe and the Kentucky Mountain Boys. In the 1970s, he played with the Country Gentlemen. Lawson formed his own group, Quicksilver, in 1979 and moved to the outskirts of Bristol, Tennessee. (Courtesy of Suzanne Lawson.)

MAN IN BLACK. When country music superstar Johnny Cash married June Carter in 1968, he became the son-in-law of Maybelle Carter, a member of the Carter Family. Cash also became a regular around the Tri-Cities area, as he and June owned a Virginia home at nearby Maces Spring, June's hometown. Here, in 1987, Cash is shown performing in Bristol at the Viking Hall Civic Center. (Courtesy of Viking Hall Civic Center.)

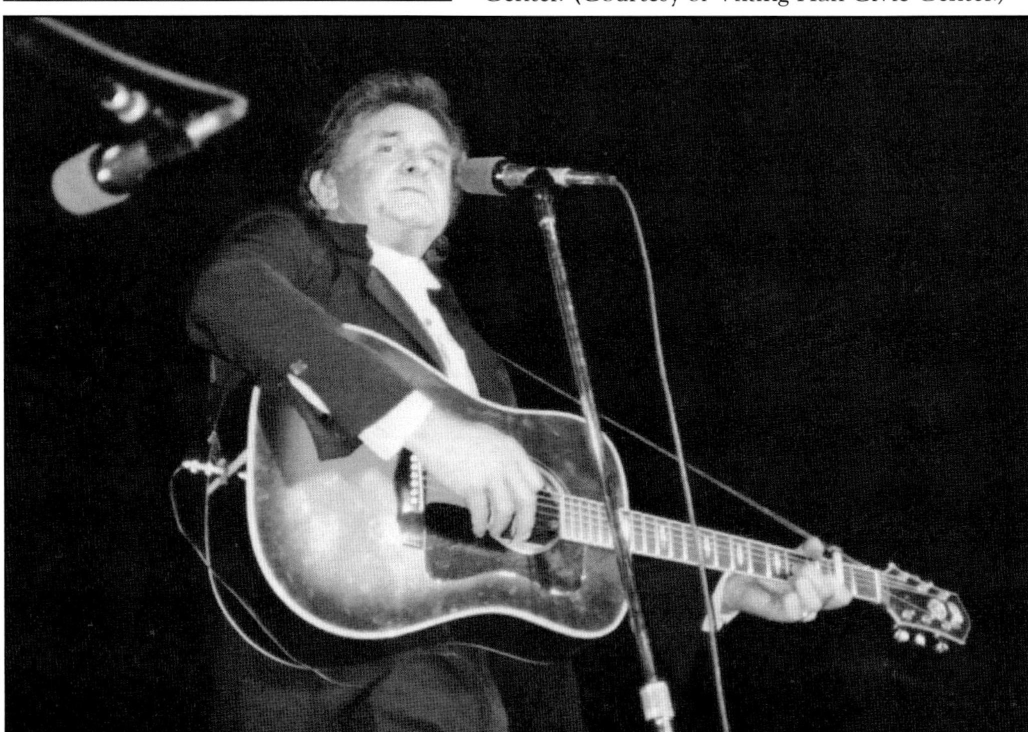

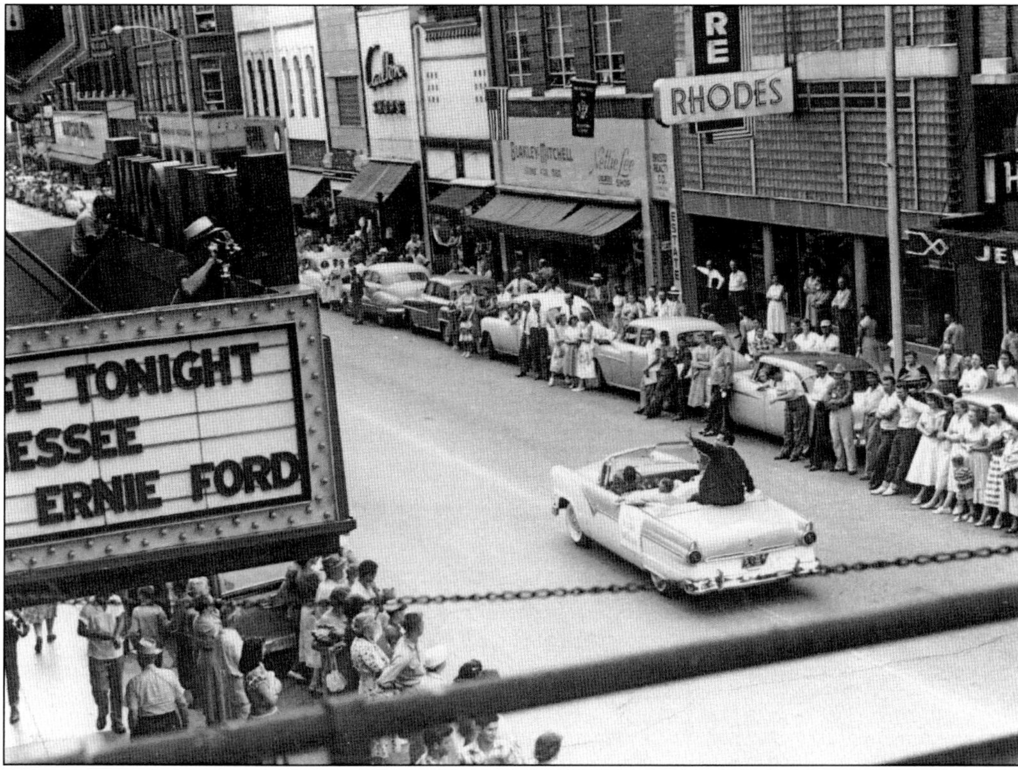

THE OL' PEA PICKER. Bristol native Ernest Jennings "Tennessee Ernie" Ford (1919–1991) was at the top of his career when he rode in a parade on Bristol's State Street in 1955. This year marked the release of his biggest hit, "Sixteen Tons." Millions also knew Ford as Cousin Ernie on television's *I Love Lucy.* As a child, Ford attended Bristol's Anderson Street Methodist Church. (Courtesy of Bristol Historical Association.)

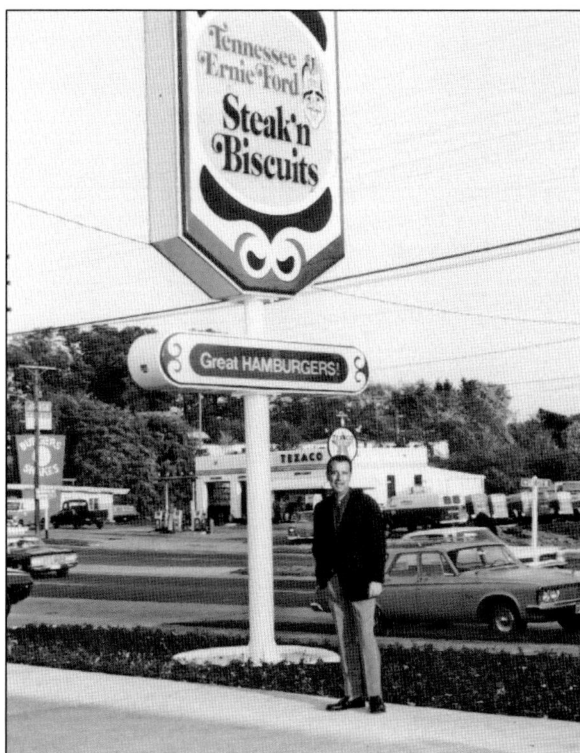

STEAK'N BISCUITS. Tennessee Ernie Ford came home to Bristol in 1969 to launch a quick-order restaurant at the three-way intersection of Blountville Highway, Euclid Avenue, and Gate City Highway. The menu included bean soup and black-eyed peas. A hamburger cost 20¢, and the signature "steak'n biscuits" was $1.19. Grand opening ceremonies included giveaway copies of Ford's albums to the first 1,000 customers. (Courtesy of Bristol Historical Association.)

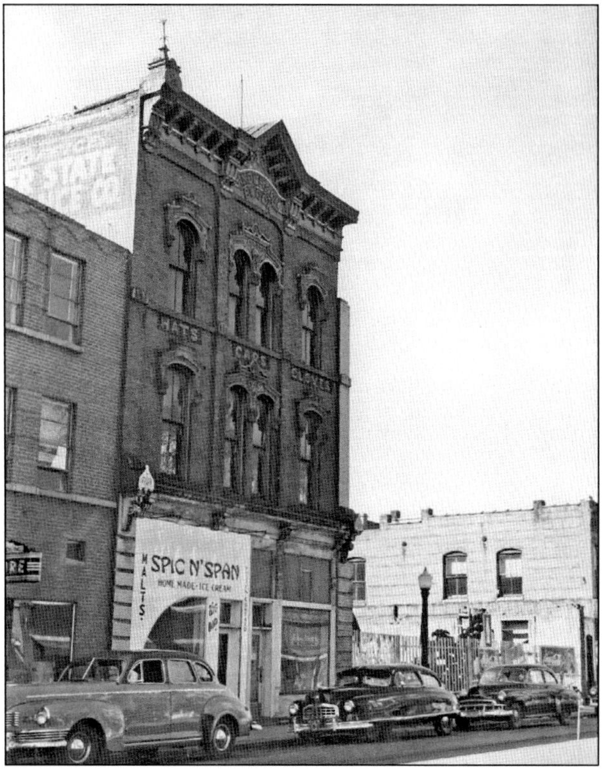

WHERE IT ALL BEGAN. This 1940s photograph shows the long-gone Taylor-Christian Hat Company building, located at 410 State Street, where the famous Bristol Sessions of 1927 took place, marking the first recordings of Jimmie Rodgers and the Carter Family. Notice the Spic N' Span at the street level of the building, offering malts, frozen custards, and the "big dip." (Courtesy of the Carter Fold.)

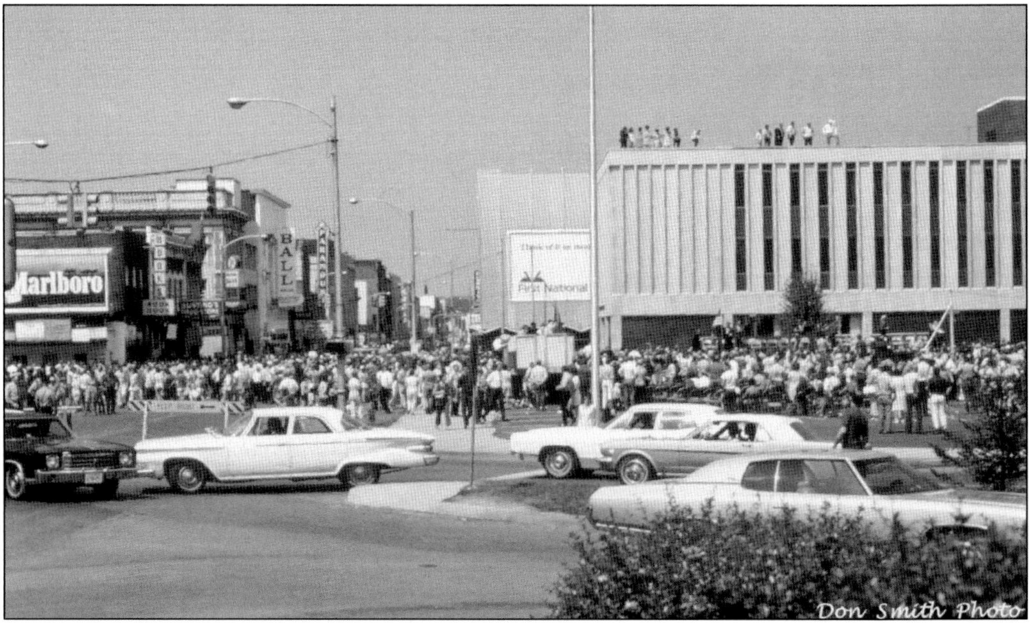

MARKING THE MONUMENT. Pedestrian traffic flooded both sides of State Street in August 1971 when Johnny Cash and June Carter helped dedicate Bristol's Country Music Monument. Originally placed in Virginia, the monument now stands in Tennessee near the site of the actual 1927 country music recordings. Notice signs, at left, for former State Street businesses like Book Nook and Bunting's Drug Store. (Courtesy of Don Smith.)

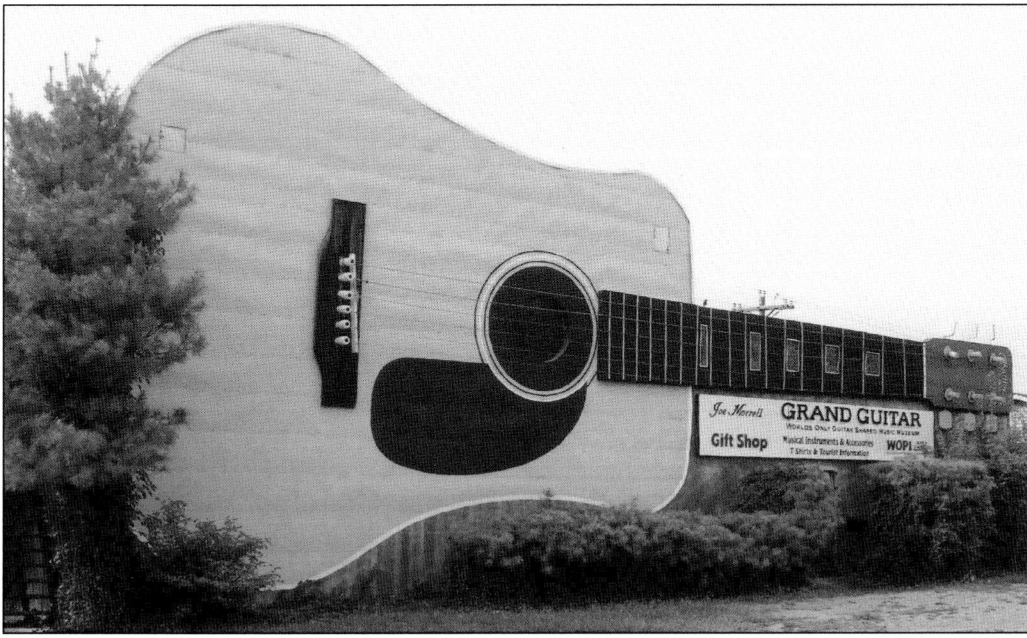

GRAND GUITAR. No one can miss the roadside oddity of the Grand Guitar, located near Interstate 81, just below the Tennessee-Virginia line. Standing 35 feet tall and stretching 70 feet long, this guitar-shaped building features two sets of six ropes—each a different size, just like real guitar strings. Joe Morrell built the "World's Only Guitar Shaped Music Museum" in 1983 with a cinder-block foundation. (Photograph by Joe Tennis.)

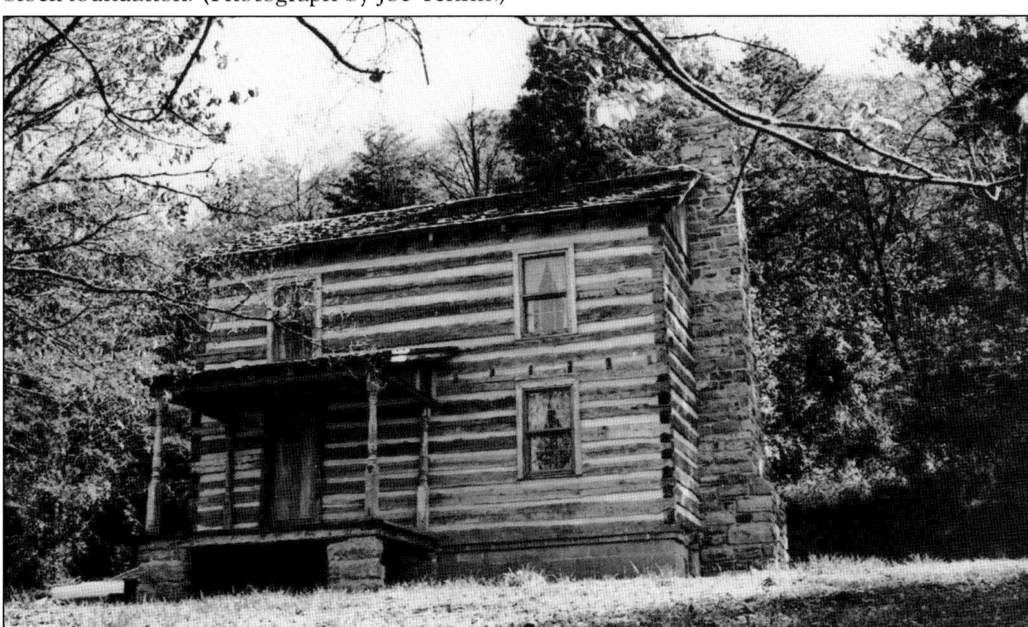

APPALACHIAN MUSIC MUSEUM. Bristol's short-lived Appalachian Music Museum of the 1980s showcased the stories of Jimmie Rodgers and the Carter Family inside a handsome log cabin at Steele Creek Park. Years later, in 1998, the U.S. Congress officially declared Bristol the "Birthplace of Country Music." (Courtesy of the *Bristol Herald Courier.*)

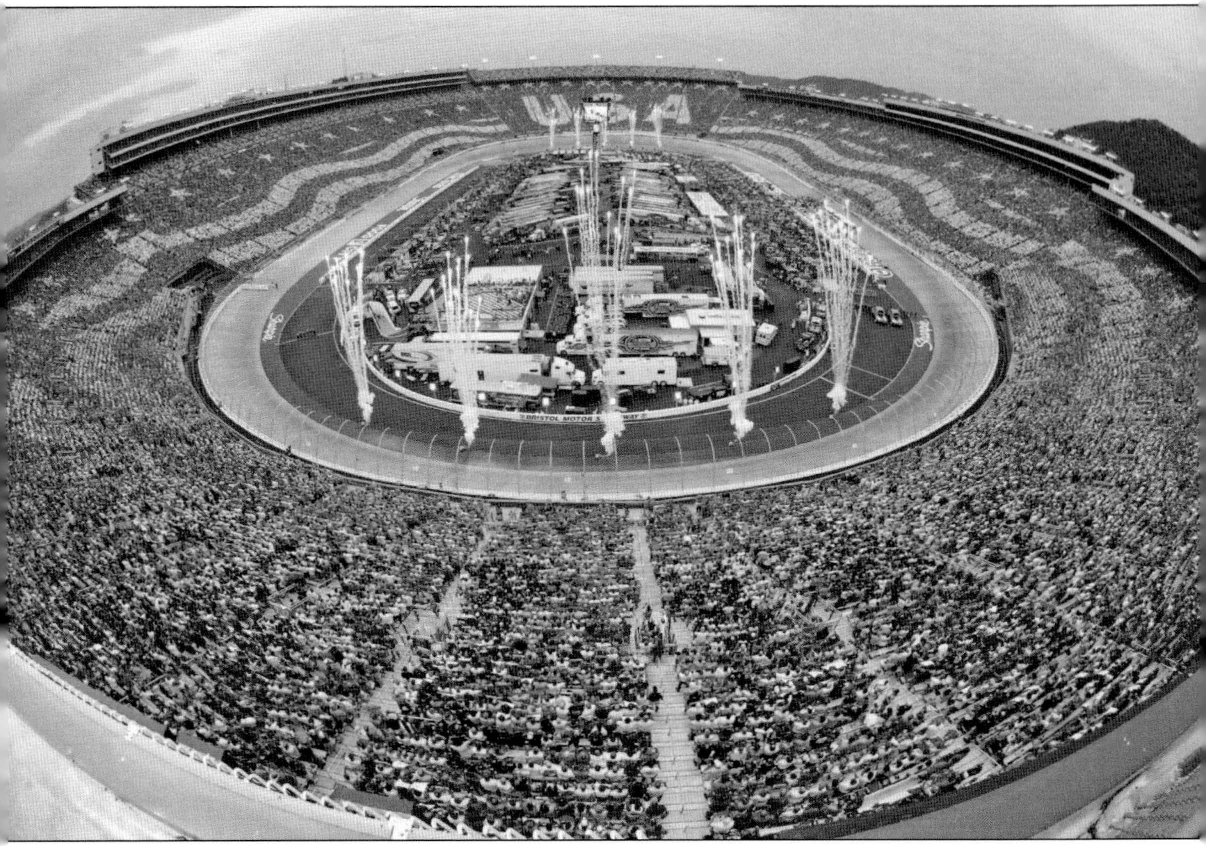

WORLD'S FASTEST HALF-MILE. Dating to the days of the John F. Kennedy White House, Bristol Motor Speedway was built in 1960–1961. The speedway attracts thousands of race fans to Sullivan County and has become famously known as the "World's Fastest Half-Mile Track." The track's popularity stems largely from its steep banks and reputation for bumper-banging competitions. Once called the "Bristol International Raceway," this 160,000-seat coliseum has hosted all the NASCAR heavyweights, from Junior Johnson and Cale Yarborough, to Darrell Waltrip, Dale Earnhardt, Rusty Wallace, Ricky Rudd, and Jeff Gordon. In this photograph, race fans made history in August 2007 by pulling off the world's largest card stunt, spelling out "U S A" with patriotic stars-and-stripes. (Courtesy of the *Bristol Herald Courier*; photograph by Earl Neikirk.)

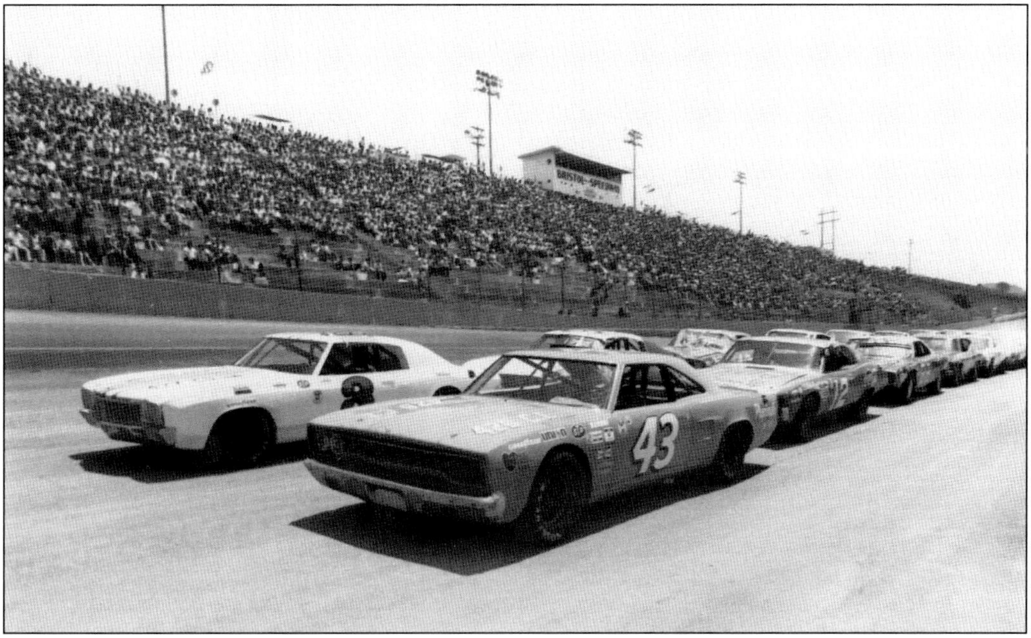

BRISTOL MOTOR SPEEDWAY. Racers gear up at the starting grid for the Volunteer 500 in 1971 at what is now the Bristol Motor Speedway. Richard Petty started on the pole, but the race win went to front-row starter "Chargin" Charlie Glotzbach, who averaged more than 101 miles per hour in the race. Petty finished third, six laps behind the winner. (Courtesy of David McGee; photograph by John Beach.)

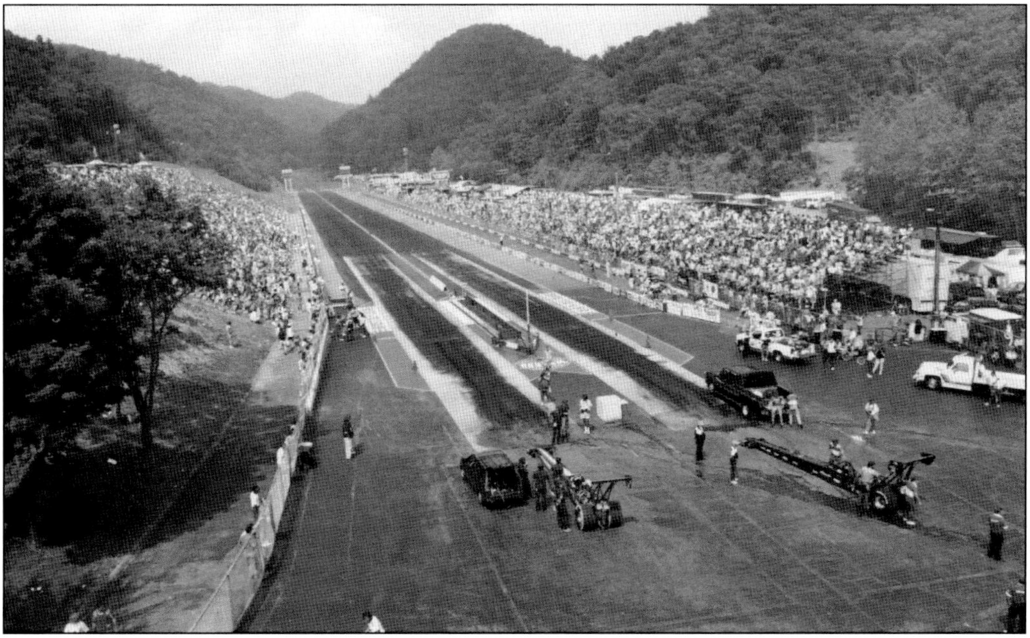

THUNDER VALLEY. Built in 1965 near the Bristol Motor Speedway, the Bristol Dragway served as the flagship track for the International Hot Rod Association for many years. It took its nickname, "Thunder Valley," from the roar of racing engines echoing against the dragway's location in a tiny valley. (Photograph by David McGee.)

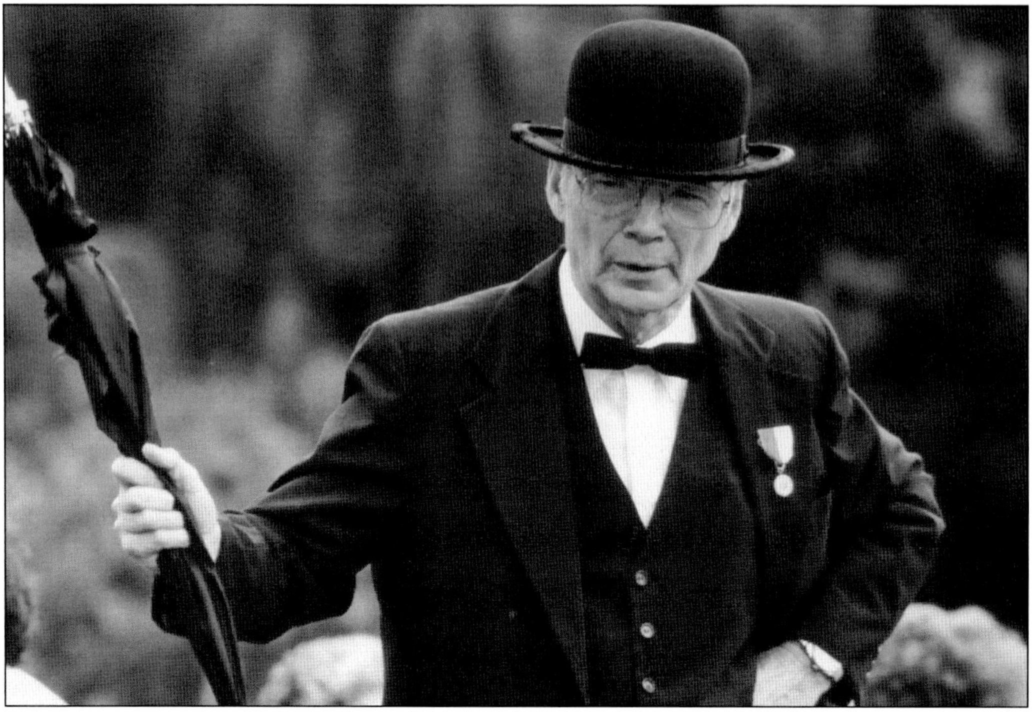

STORYTELLER. V. N. "Bud" Phillips adopted Bristol, Tennessee, as his home in 1953 and became the city's most recognized historian in 1992 after publishing his first book on Bristol history. A native of Arkansas, Phillips often dresses like he is a century behind the times as he conducts storytelling tours of East Hill Cemetery, a burial ground on the Tennessee-Virginia line. (Courtesy of the *Bristol Herald Courier*; photograph by Bill McKee.)

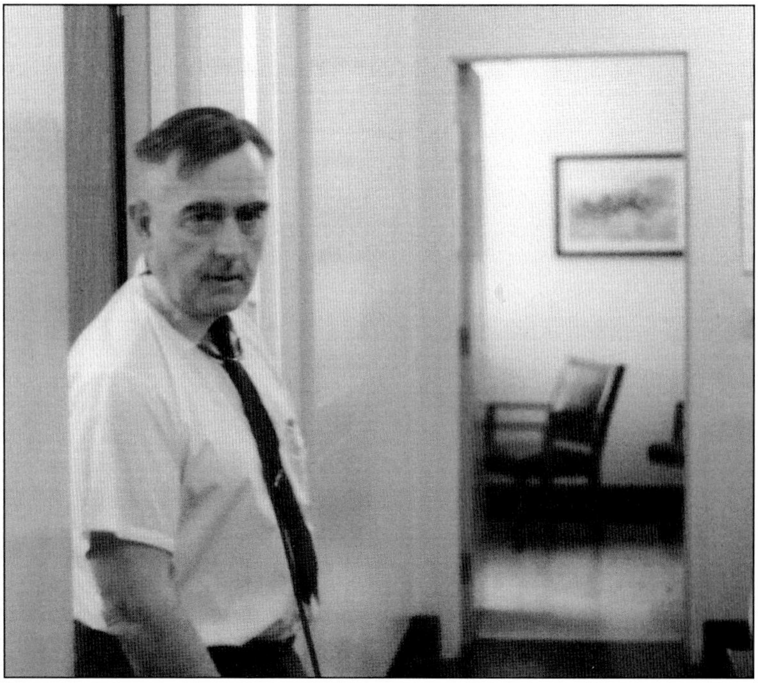

FRIENDLY PHYSICIAN. Bristolians remember Dr. Nathaniel John Chew (1911–1995) as an old-fashioned physician who was always willing to make house calls. The Maryland native came to Bristol in 1939 and, for years, lived on Holston Avenue. When not on call, he spent weekends at his cabin near Chinquapin Grove at the base of Holston Mountain. Dr. Chew retired in 1987 and is buried at Bristol's Glenwood Cemetery. (Courtesy of Betty Williams.)

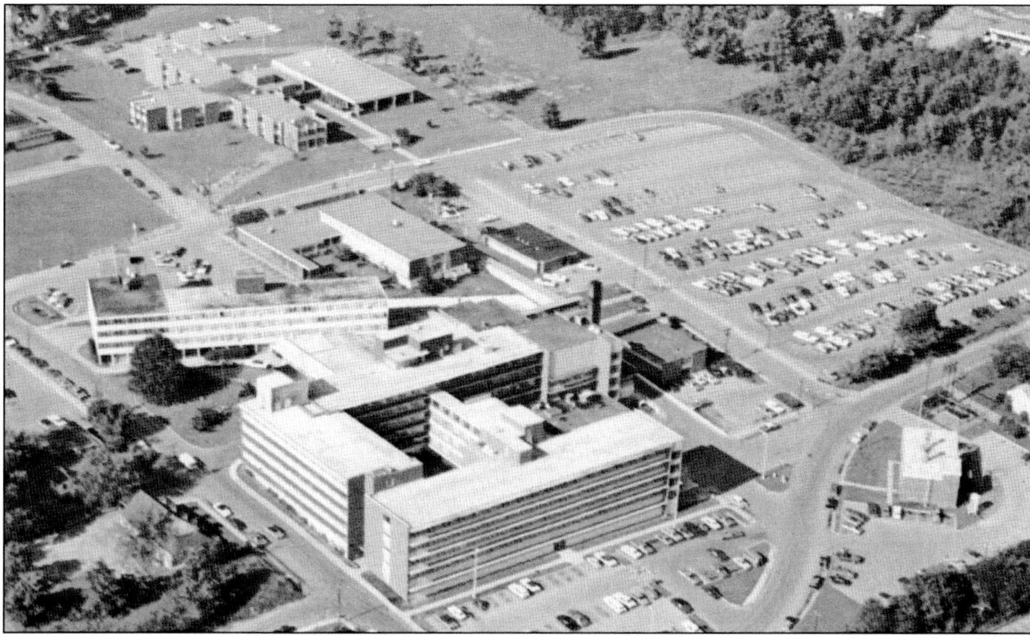

BRISTOL MEMORIAL HOSPITAL. This aerial view of the Bristol Memorial Hospital shows the structure, *c.* 1971. Built in the early 1950s, the hospital was named Memorial as a dedication to soldiers from all wars. It was razed in the mid-1990s after the new Bristol Regional Medical Center was dedicated in 1994. The area shown at the top right has since been made into a retail development. (Courtesy of Tim Buchanan.)

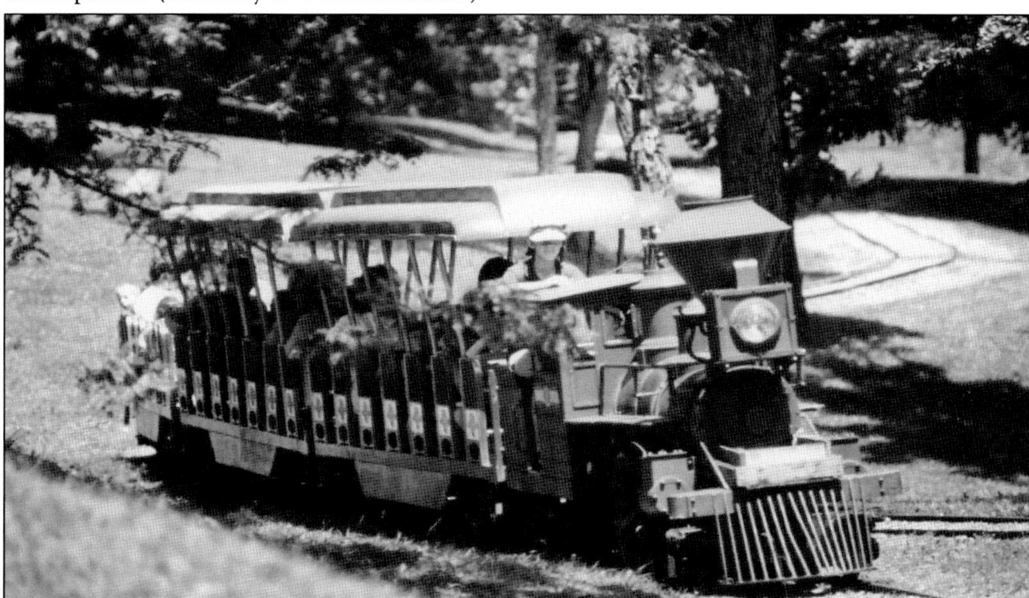

STEELE CREEK PARK. Starting in the 1960s, this popular train ran around the tracks at Bristol's Steele Creek Park for decades, shuttling visitors both young and old. Before this city park was built, plans proposed in the 1940s called this "Watauga State Park," when personnel from a nearby Civilian Conservation Corps began construction on the Steele Creek Lake project. (Courtesy of the *Bristol Herald Courier*; photograph by David Patton.)

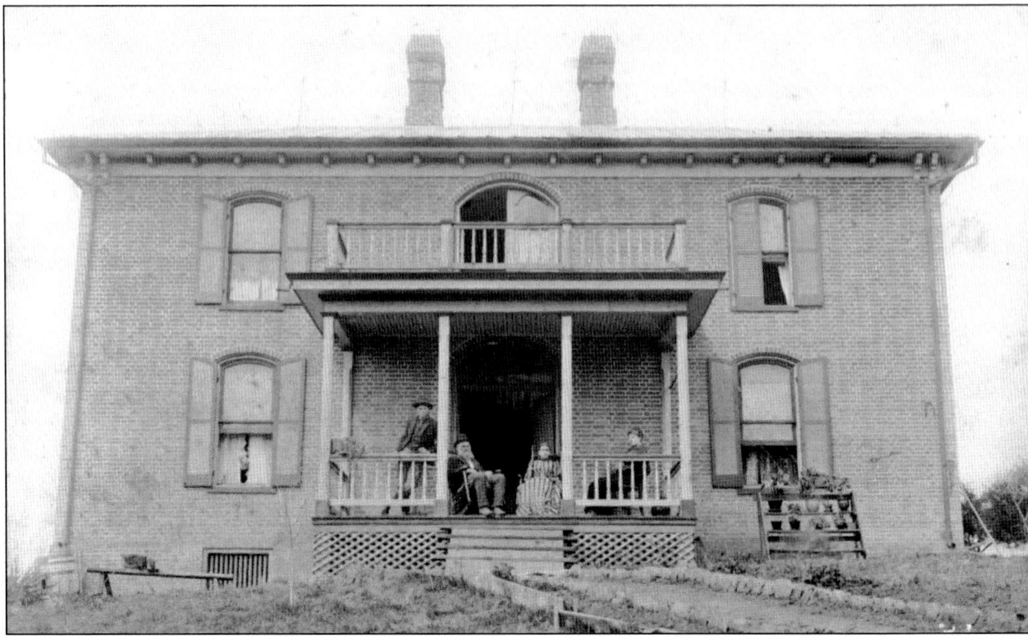

CARMACK HOME. Jacob Susong Carmack built a brick home near King College in 1884, and his 1,000-acre plantation later became part of the Middlebrook and Redstone housing subdivisions of Bristol, Tennessee. Shown here on the home's front porch around 1900 are, from left to right, Robert Carmack, Jacob Carmack, Jane Bushong Carmack, and Ellen "Ella" Carmack. (Courtesy of Bud Phillips.)

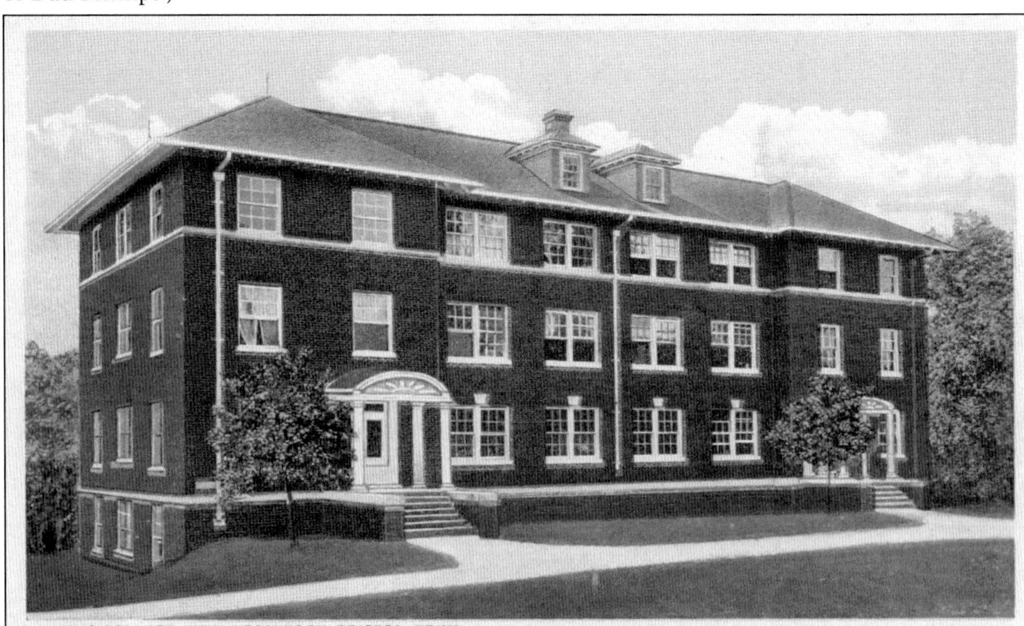

KING COLLEGE. Founded in 1867, King College was originally located on Fifth Street near downtown Bristol. The Presbyterian school moved to its present location, east of Bristol's State Street, in 1917. The college took its name from its founder, Presbyterian minister James King. (Courtesy of Tim Buchanan.)

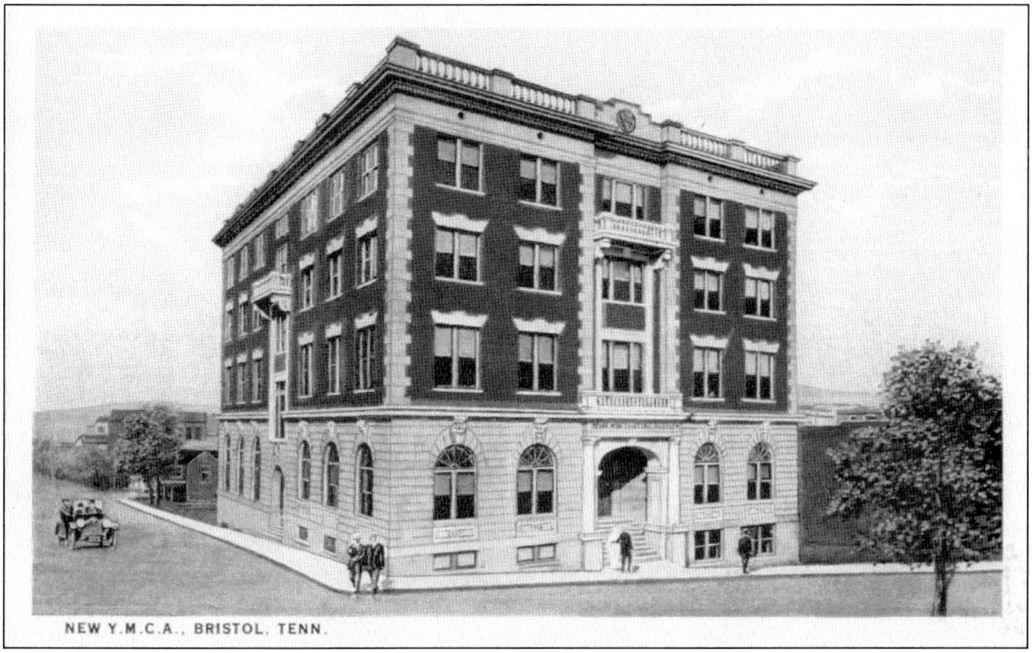

FUN TO STAY. This postcard showcased Bristol's "New Y.M.C.A." at Shelby and Fifth Streets. In 1911, the sender wrote: "Dear Mama, We came up here to Bristol this morning and are going back to J. C. in a little while. We had a fine automobile ride before dinner. I do hope I can come home Sunday, instead of Wednesday. Love to all from Amelia." (Courtesy of Shelby Edwards.)

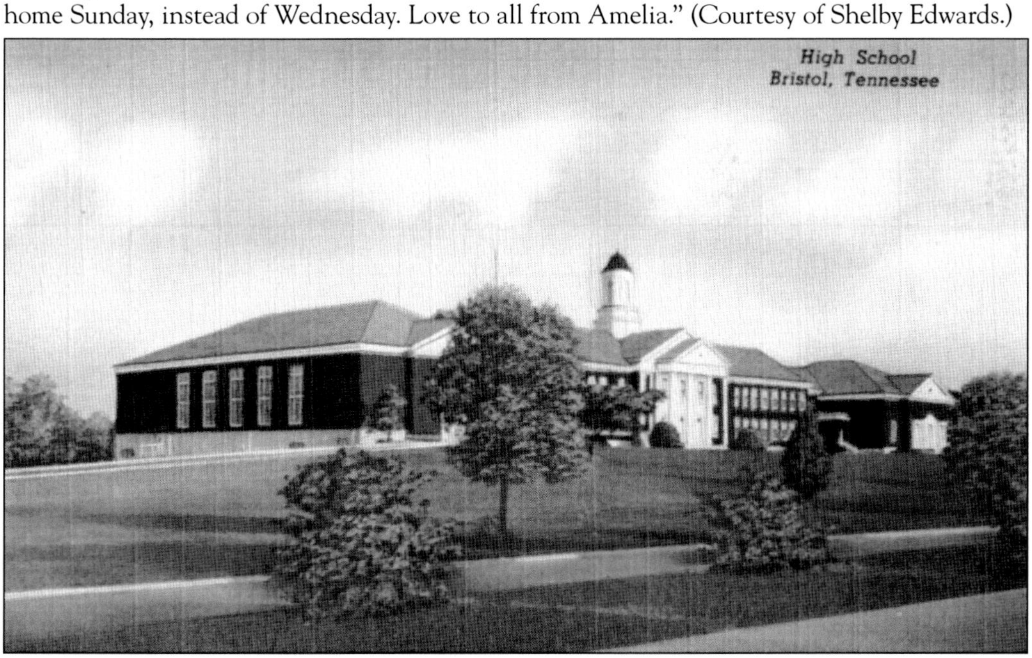

LEGENDARY SCHOOL. Built in 1939, the high school of Bristol, Tennessee, boasts many ghostly legends, including apparitions of a girl named Agnes, said to frequent the building. This 1940s-era postcard shows the campus before the 1981 addition of the Viking Hall Civic Center, which was built in the left foreground. Viking Hall has since attracted such performers as George Jones and Lynyrd Skynyrd. (Courtesy of Tim Buchanan.)

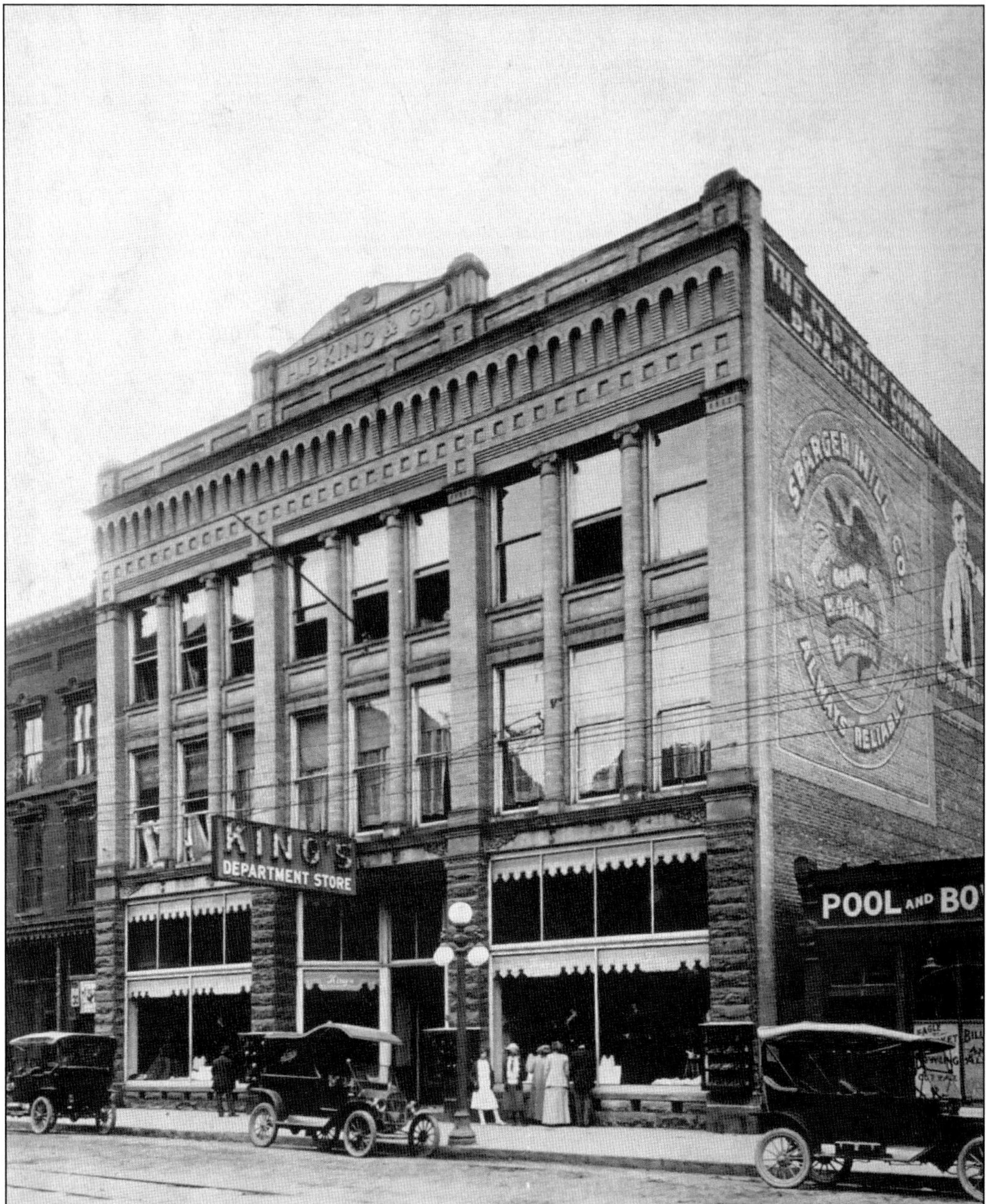

KING'S DEPARTMENT STORE. Nearly a century before any Wal-Mart opened in Bristol, King's Department Store was *the* place to shop. The proprietor, H. P. King (1862–1944), got his start in the retail world while clerking for his uncle, J. M. King, in nearby Piney Flats. Soon after, King opened his first Bristol store on the Virginia side of town in 1889. King moved operations and eventually settled on this Tennessee location in the 600 block of State Street by 1899. This photograph captures the operation in its heyday of the 1920s, when King's customers would come to Bristol on trains from all over the Appalachians. Once known as the largest department store between Roanoke and Knoxville, King's sold merchandise that ranged from clothes to furniture in more than 50 departments. The store closed in 1984. (Courtesy of Gary Rose.)

Four

KINGSPORT

The land was flat, and a river ran through it. So, naturally, this seemed like an ideal spot to build a town. Well, that happened in the early 1800s. But in the early 1900s, this town had to get started all over again.

On maps from the 18th century, this area was known as "Long Island" for a natural island at the center of the South fork of the Holston River. The Cherokee considered this a sacred place. But, in 1776, the area surrounding the island became bloody during the Battle of Long Island Flats, a skirmish that ended in a victory for the early settlers over the Native Americans.

From Long Island, Daniel Boone went west to the Cumberland Gap in 1775. From the north, about a generation later, William King came south down the North fork of the Holston River and arrived at a riverbank, where he established what became known as King's Boat Yard or King's Port. King mined the salt of Saltville, Virginia, and he used King's Port as a shipping station—a place where his boats could meet shuttles along the Wilderness Road.

In this vicinity, in 1822, a place called Kingsport was incorporated, but its township was short-lived.

Next came George L. Carter, John B. Dennis, and J. Fred Johnson. These men saw great opportunity in establishing a model city that would become a hub for industry and railroads. Kingsport acquired a new charter in 1917 and soon stretched beyond Sullivan County to part of Hawkins County, Tennessee.

At the dawn of the 21st century, Kingsport remains a retail destination for customers far beyond its borders. In return, as a thank-you gesture, the chamber of commerce has hosted a "Santa Train" since the late 1940s. Annually, city leaders ride the rails through Virginia in little towns like St. Paul, handing out gifts all along the way.

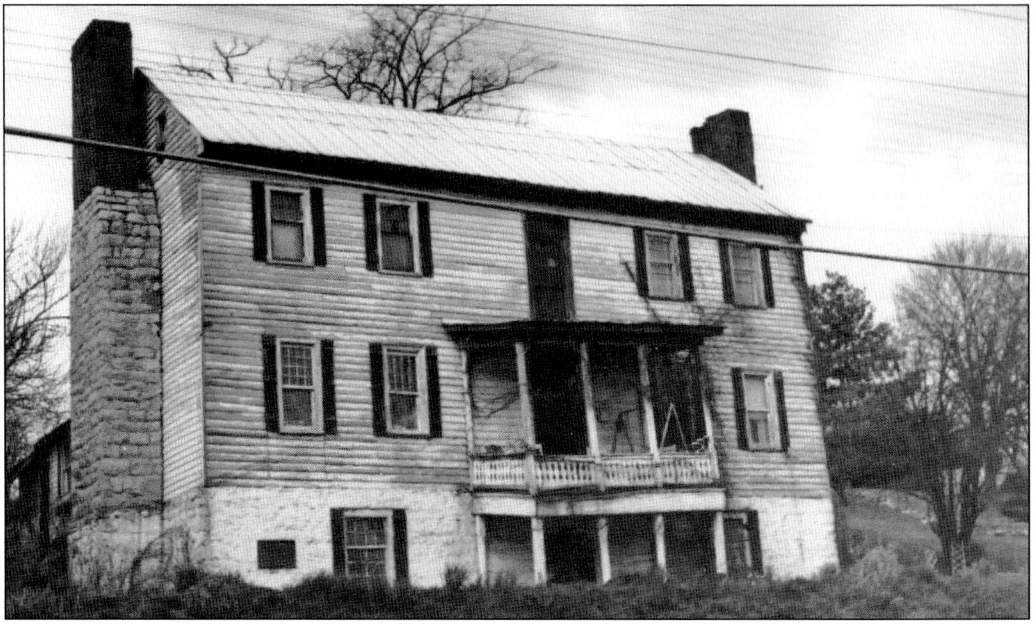

NETHERLAND INN. Richard Netherland's name became attached to the Netherland Inn in 1818 when he established the three-story structure as a stop for travelers on both riverboats and stagecoach shuttles. In 1962, when this photograph was made, Netherland Inn stood in need of a renovation. The front of the restored inn now features an elaborate set of porches. It is open to visitors. (Courtesy of Rocky Mount Museum.)

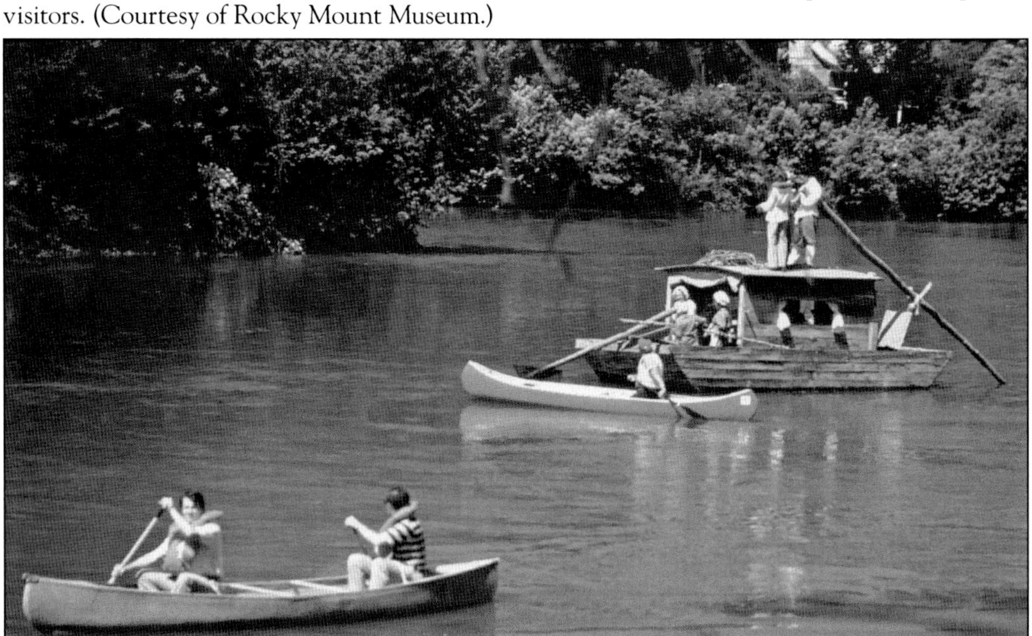

FLATBOAT BRIGADE. Three flatboats were used in 1976 to replicate the route of Col. John Donelson, who navigated the Holston River in 1779 with a flotilla of flatboats headed west to Middle Tennessee on a 1,006-mile journey. One of the flatboats used in 1976, called *Charlotte*, stands behind Kingsport's Netherland Inn as part of a museum complex. (Courtesy of the Kingsport Archives.)

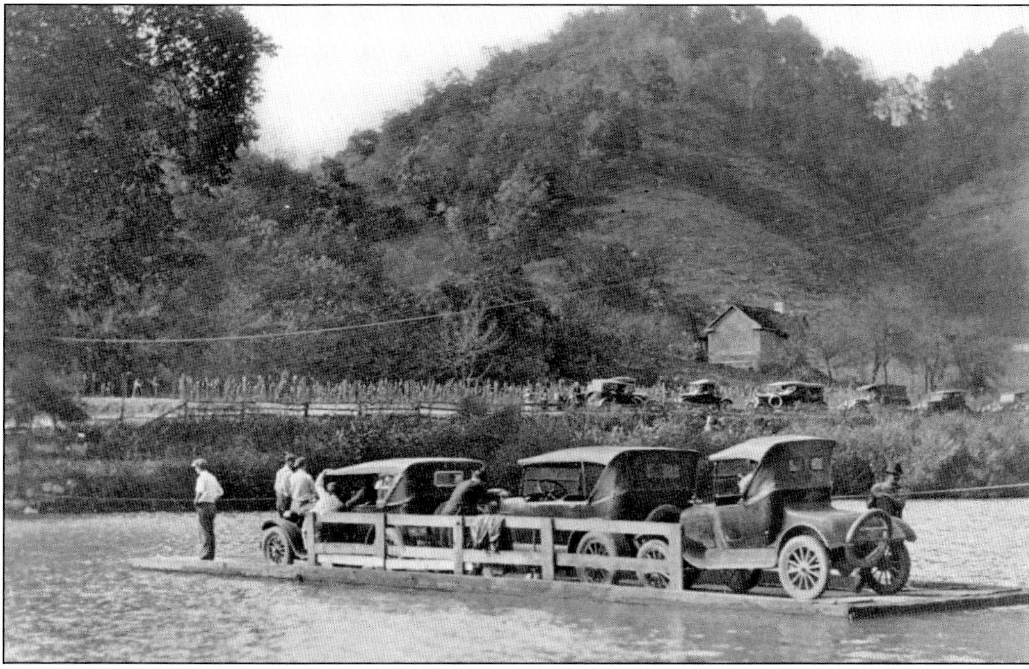

FERRY BOAT. Before bridges, ferries were once a common way for automobiles to cross the creeks and rivers of Sullivan County. This scene, *c.* 1922, was made in Kingsport on the Holston River near Long Island, a four-mile-long national historic landmark considered a sacred place to the Cherokee. (Courtesy of the Kingsport Archives.)

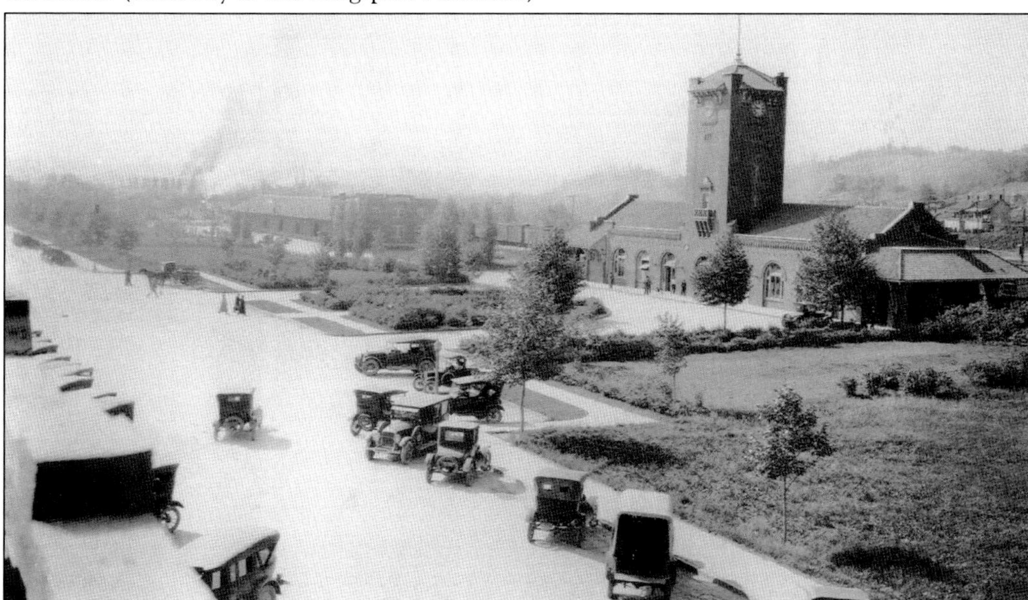

TRAIN STATION. Kingsport's passenger train station was built in 1916 for the Carolina, Clinchfield, and Ohio Railway, based on a design by New York architect Clinton McKenzie. Soon after, Kingsport's industrial boom began. Shown here in the 1920s, the train station has since been made into a bank, while the freight station, at far left, houses the Greater Kingsport Chamber of Commerce. (Courtesy of the Kingsport Archives.)

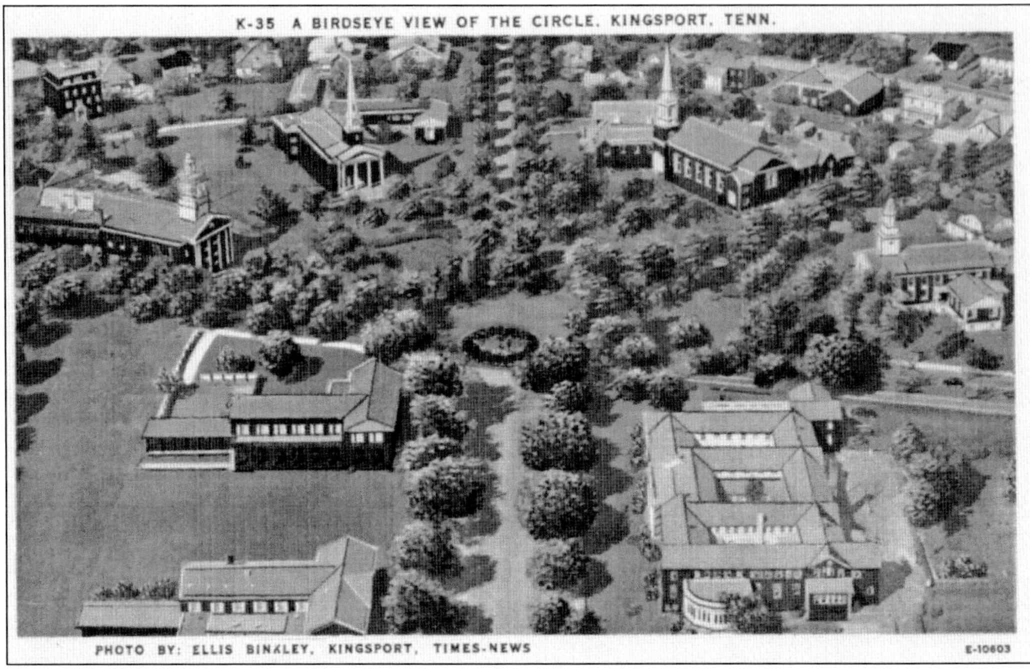

CHURCH CIRCLE. Houses of worship face each other with sharp steeples on Kingsport's Church Circle. In this postcard, the Kingsport Inn (no longer standing) is the building at lower right; the old post office (now the public library) can be seen at lower left. This postcard was made using a photograph by Ellis Binkley of the *Kingsport Times-News*. (Courtesy of Shelby Edwards.)

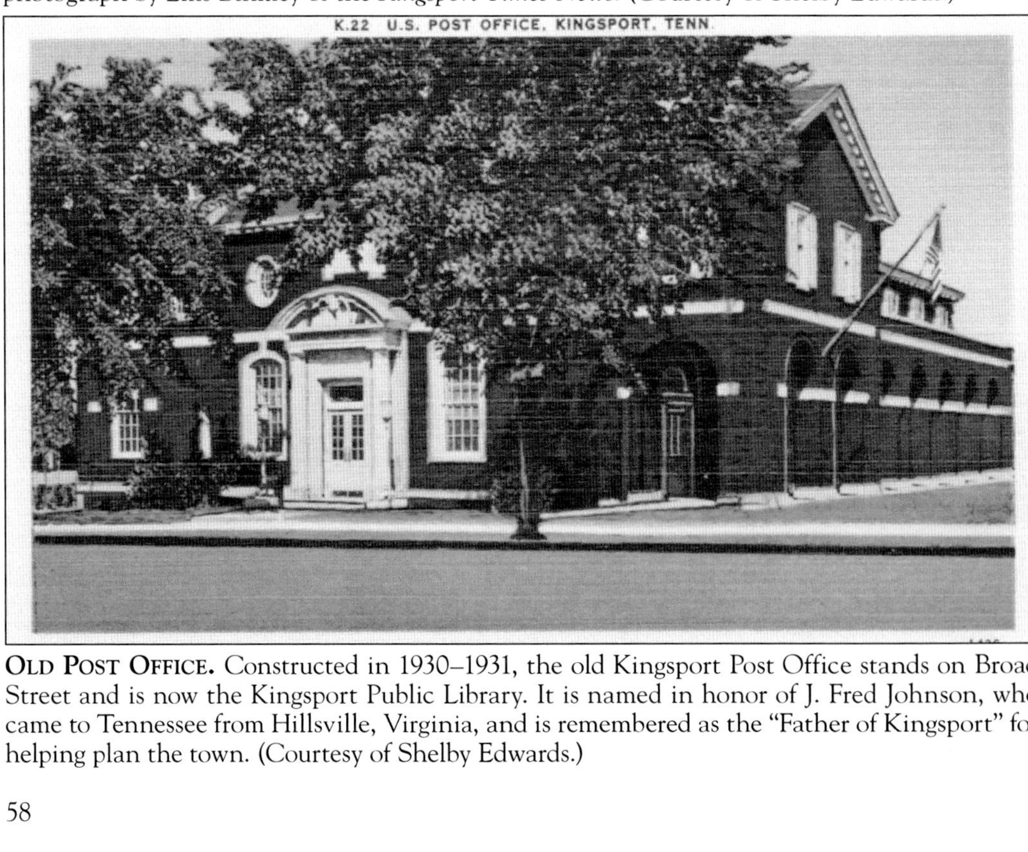

OLD POST OFFICE. Constructed in 1930–1931, the old Kingsport Post Office stands on Broad Street and is now the Kingsport Public Library. It is named in honor of J. Fred Johnson, who came to Tennessee from Hillsville, Virginia, and is remembered as the "Father of Kingsport" for helping plan the town. (Courtesy of Shelby Edwards.)

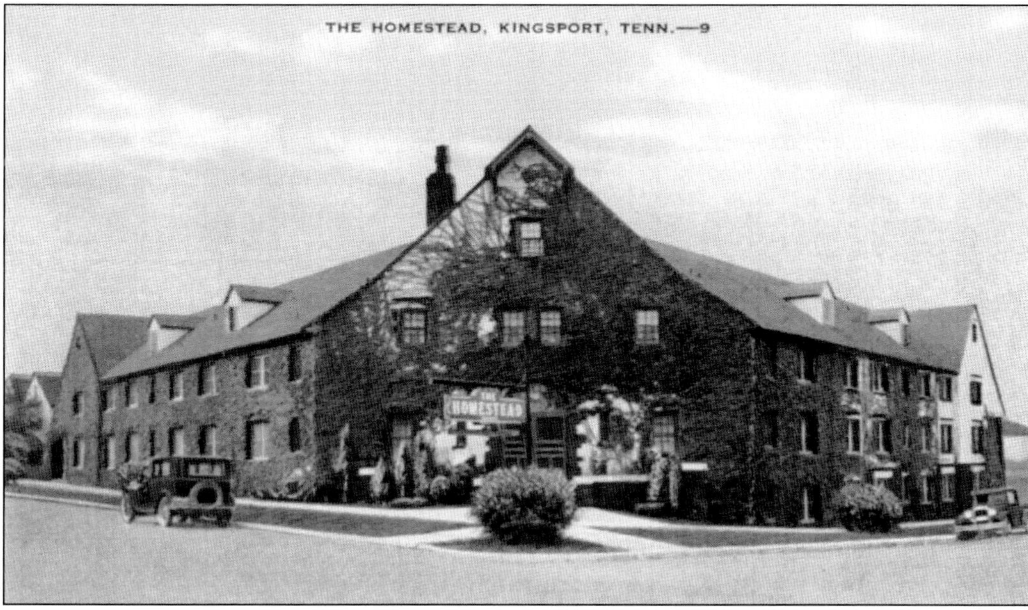

THE HOMESTEAD. Built in 1918, the Homestead welcomed overnight guests for years in Kingsport at the corner of Clay and Sullivan Streets. This postcard view shows the structure in its heyday of the 1920s and 1930s. (Courtesy of Shelby Edwards.)

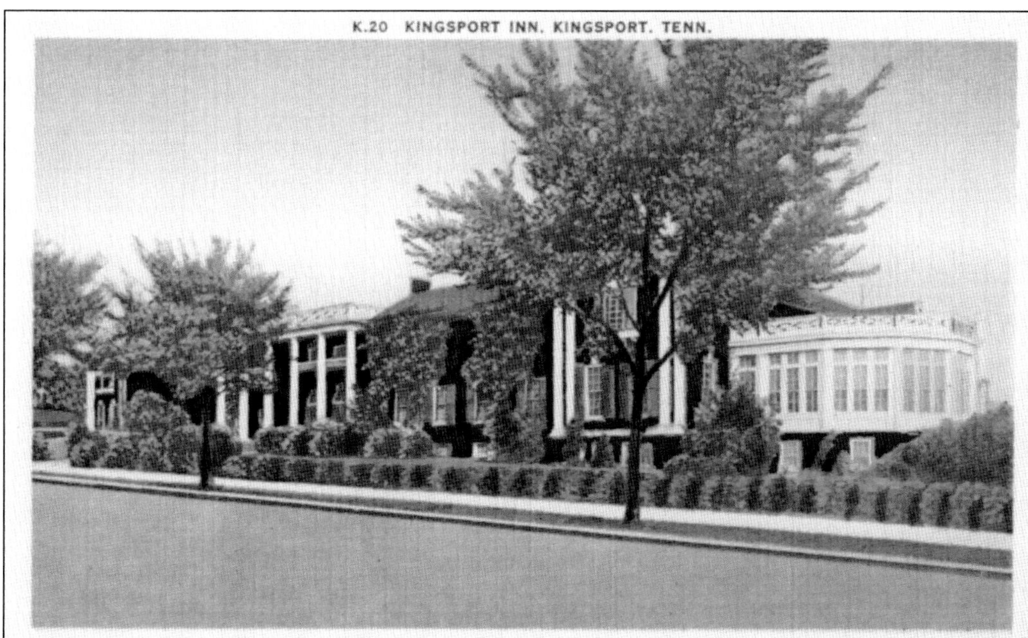

KINGSPORT INN. Noted for its well-landscaped grounds, the Kingsport Inn once stood on Church Circle at what is now the site of a bank. This 1930s-era postcard notes the inn as "a nationally-known stopping place for travelers" that "offers clean, comfortable rooms and excellent food at moderate rates." (Courtesy of Shelby Edwards.)

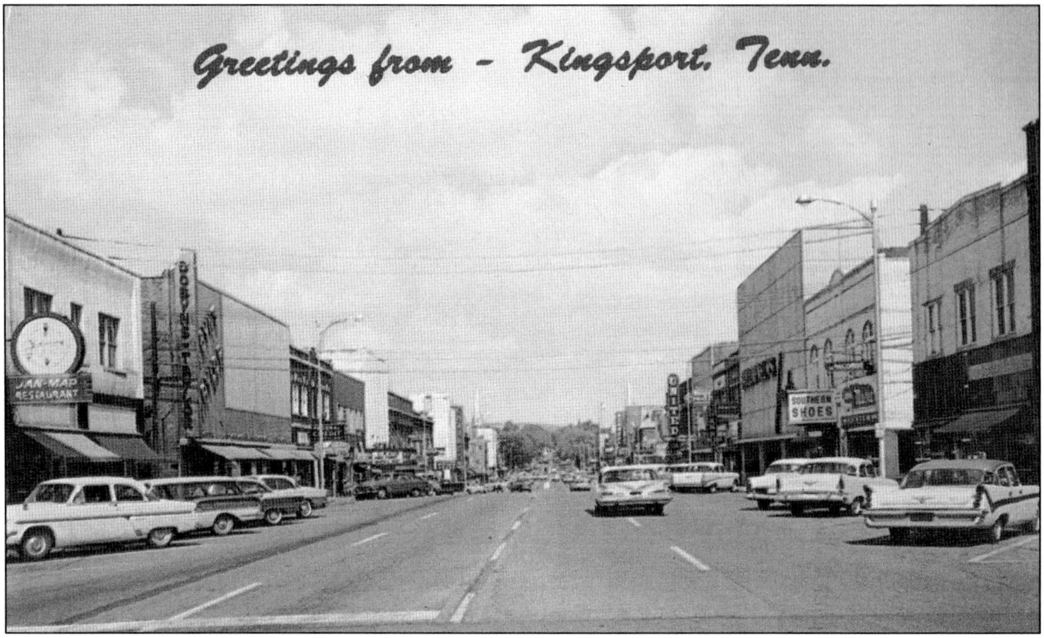

BROAD STREET. A 1960s postcard view of Broad Street shows the beloved cruising strip, as seen from the Main Street intersection. The Jan-Mar Restaurant, at left, was still standing in 2008 near the Dobyns-Taylor building, but Southern Shoes and the record store, at right, had become memories. A median and parking areas have since been built at Broad Street's center. (Courtesy of Shelby Edwards.)

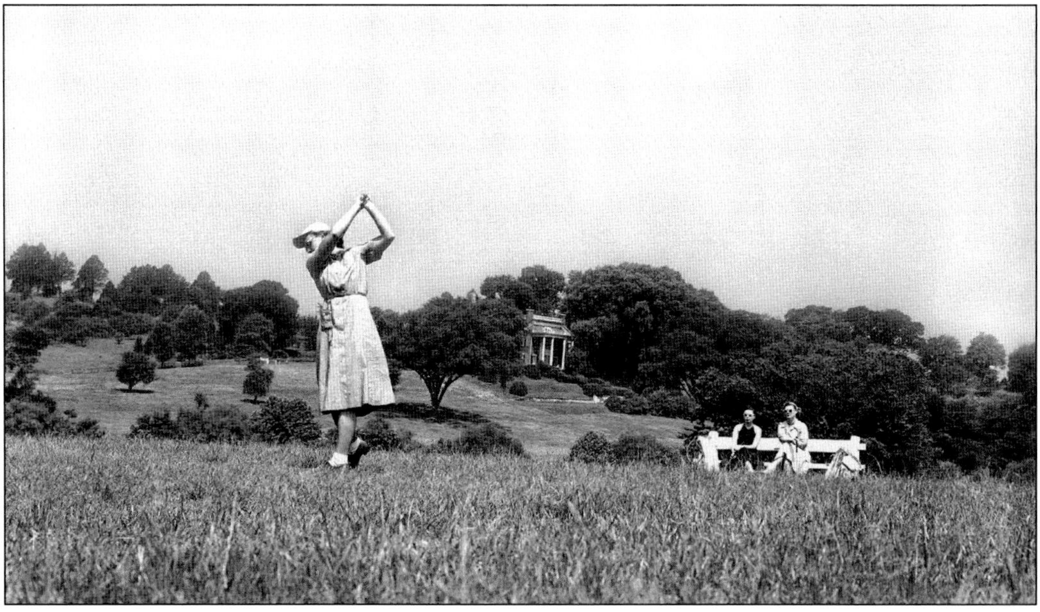

RIDGEFIELDS. Emily Jennings, left, tees off at the Ridgefields Golf Course in this 1949 photograph, which was used for promotional purposes when the course was built near the Sullivan-Hawkins county line. The house at rear right is the Rotherwood Mansion, a Kingsport landmark that is actually located in Hawkins County. Rotherwood was named for the home of a character in Sir Walter Scott's novel *Ivanhoe*. (Courtesy of the Kingsport Archives.)

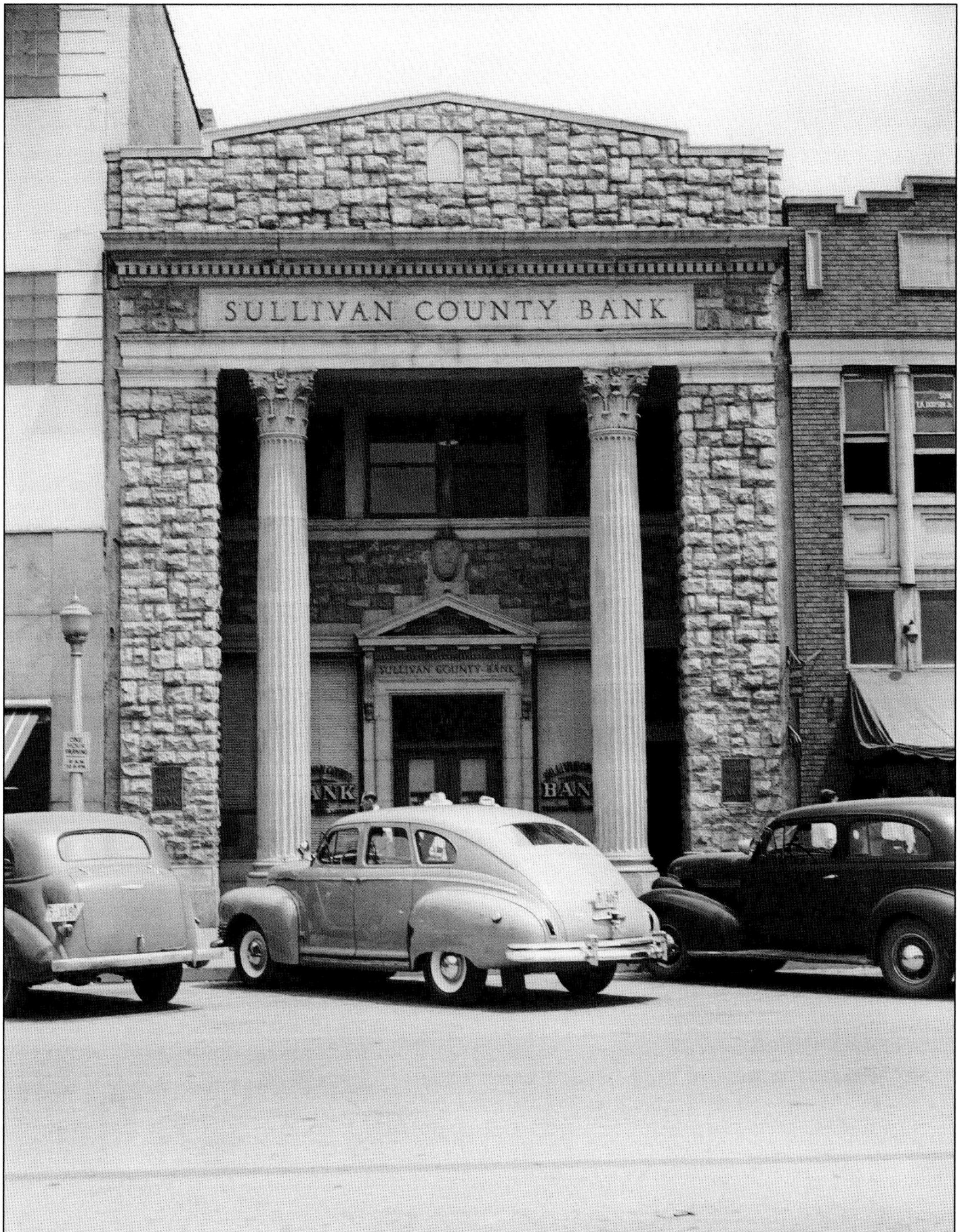

SULLIVAN COUNTY BANK. Several businesses in downtown Kingsport's Broad Street have experienced architectural face-lifts in recent decades. One of the most dramatic examples is the Sullivan County Bank building, shown here in 1946. The bank exited this location after a few years, and the building's columns were also removed. This building, located at 211 Broad Street, was practically unrecognizable by 2008, when it served as the office for attorney Frank D. Gibson. (Courtesy of the Kingsport Archives.)

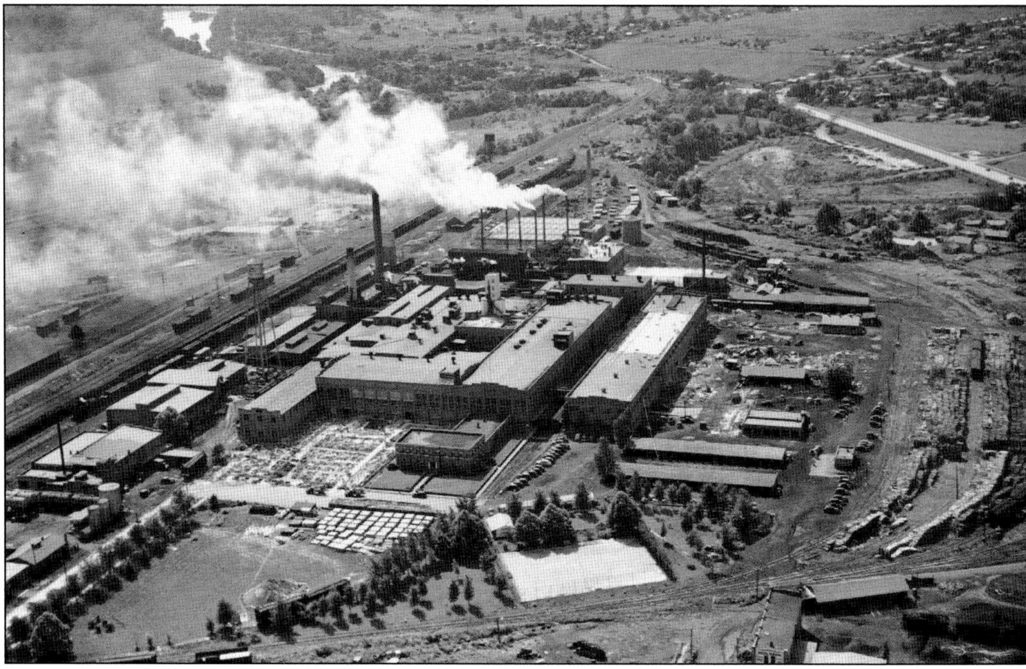

MEAD. Smoke rises above the sprawling factory of the Mead Corporation, noted as one of the largest industries in Kingsport when photographer Thomas McNeer Jr. shot this aerial view in 1946. Railroad tracks can be seen in the foreground. (Courtesy of the Kingsport Archives.)

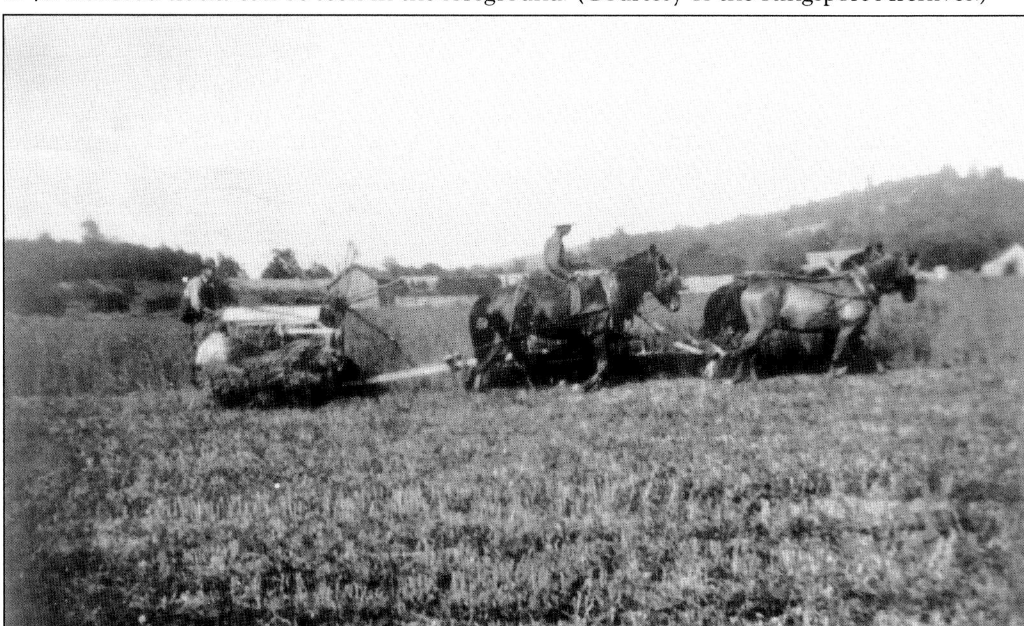

WHEAT HARVESTING. It is hard to believe where this scene is located today—at the corner of John B. Dennis Highway/Tennessee Route 93 and East Stone Drive/U.S. Highway 11 West—in one of the busiest commercial districts in Kingsport. This photograph shows wheat harvesting in the area in the 1920s, when much of Sullivan County remained rural and agricultural. (Courtesy of Shelia Steele Hunt.)

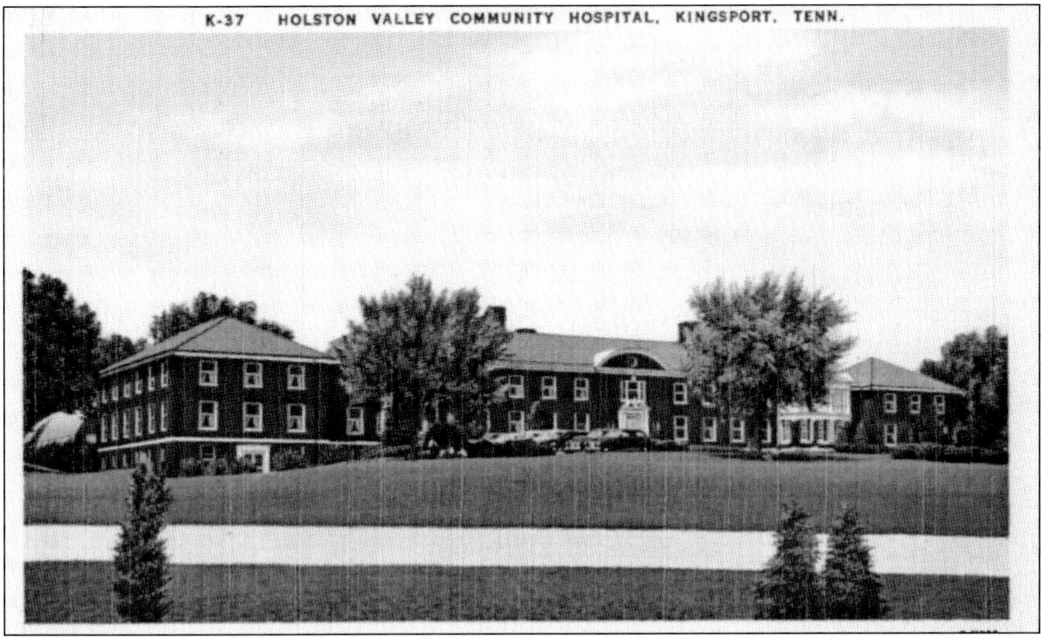

HOLSTON VALLEY COMMUNITY HOSPITAL. A leading health-care provider for Northeast Tennessee, the Holston Valley Community Hospital of Kingsport began serving patients in 1935. This postcard captures a scene soon after the hospital opened. (Courtesy of Shelby Edwards.)

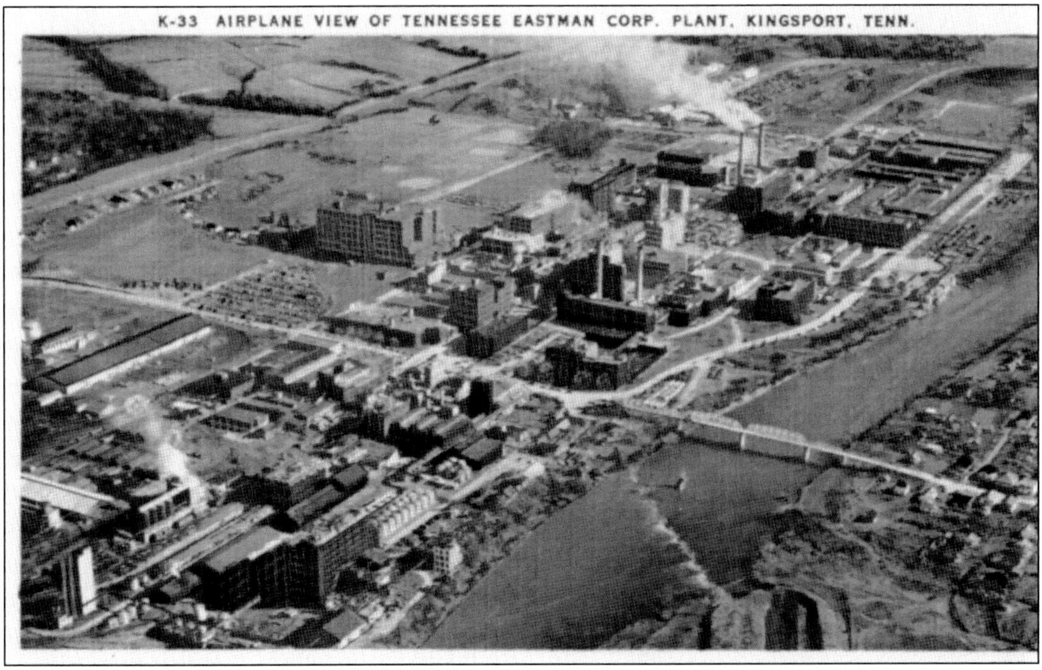

TENNESSEE EASTMAN. The sprawling plant of the Tennessee Eastman Corporation, later called Eastman Chemical Company, borders the banks of the South fork of the Holston River near the center of Kingsport. This aerial view postcard noted the operation as "one of the state's largest industrial units." It was named for George Eastman, founder of Eastman Kodak. (Courtesy of Shelby Edwards.)

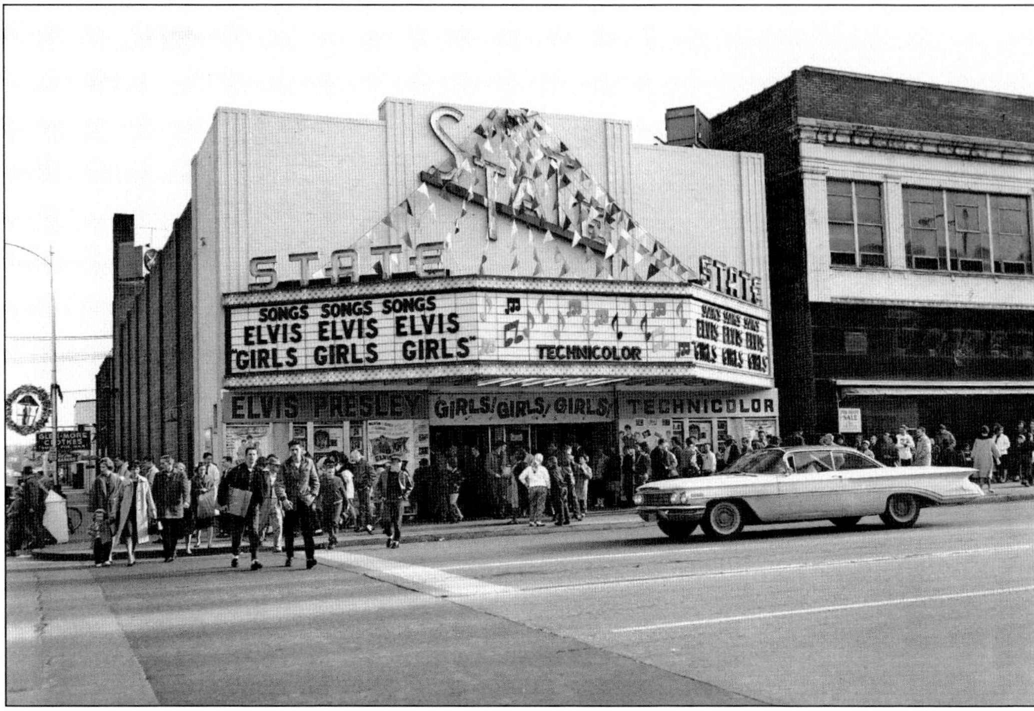

The King on Screen. The State Theater opened in 1936 at the corner of Broad and Market Streets. In 1962, the State showed the Elvis Presley musical *Girls, Girls, Girls*, featuring the hit "Return to Sender." A few years earlier, in 1955, Presley sang on stage in Kingsport at the city's civic auditorium. (Courtesy of the Kingsport Archives.)

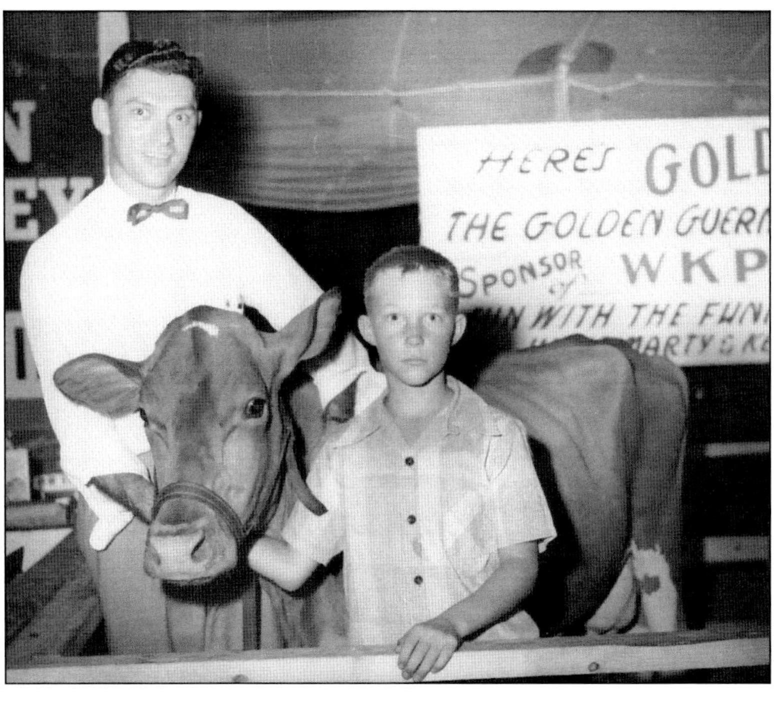

Fun with the Funnies. Longtime Kingsport disc jockey Marty Karant stands with his son Kenneth and a mascot named "Goldie," c. 1956. The father-and-son duo read comic strips on Kingsport radio station WKPT in a popular segment called "Fun with the Funnies." Originally from Chicago, Karant first broadcast on WKPT in 1942. Aside from a brief absence, he remained on the air for more than 50 years. (Courtesy of Charles Aesque.)

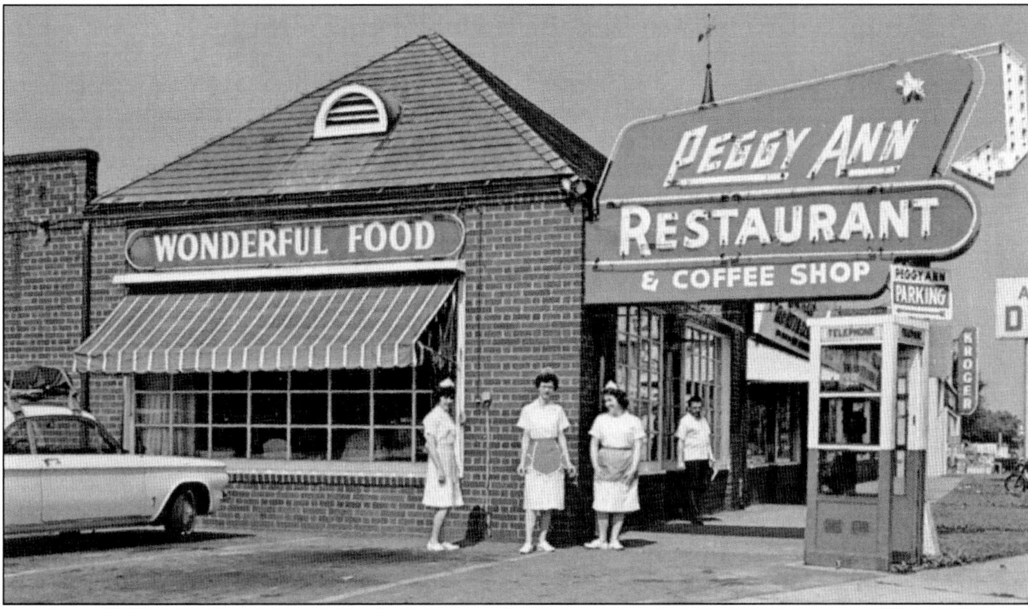

PEGGY ANN. A *c.* 1960s postcard view of the Peggy Ann Restaurant shows the beloved landmark at the corner of East Center Street and Fort Henry Drive. This building later housed the Hibbert Davis Coffee Gallery. The Kroger grocery store, at rear right, later became a Christian club named Fire Escape. The telephone booth, at front right, no longer stands. (Courtesy of the Kingsport Archives.)

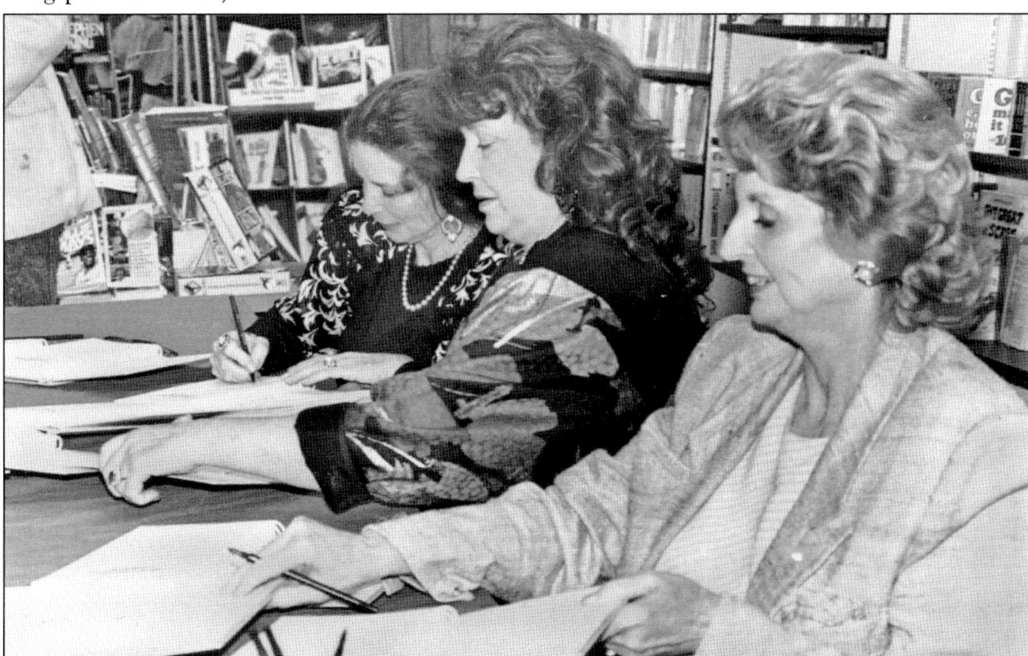

CARTERS IN KINGSPORT. Though they hailed from nearby Scott County, Virginia, the famous Carter Sisters were no strangers to Sullivan County. The singing siblings often visited Kingsport. Here the daughters of "Mother" Maybelle Carter meet the public, about 1989, at a Kingsport book signing. The sisters, from left to right, are June, Anita, and Helen. (Photograph by David McGee.)

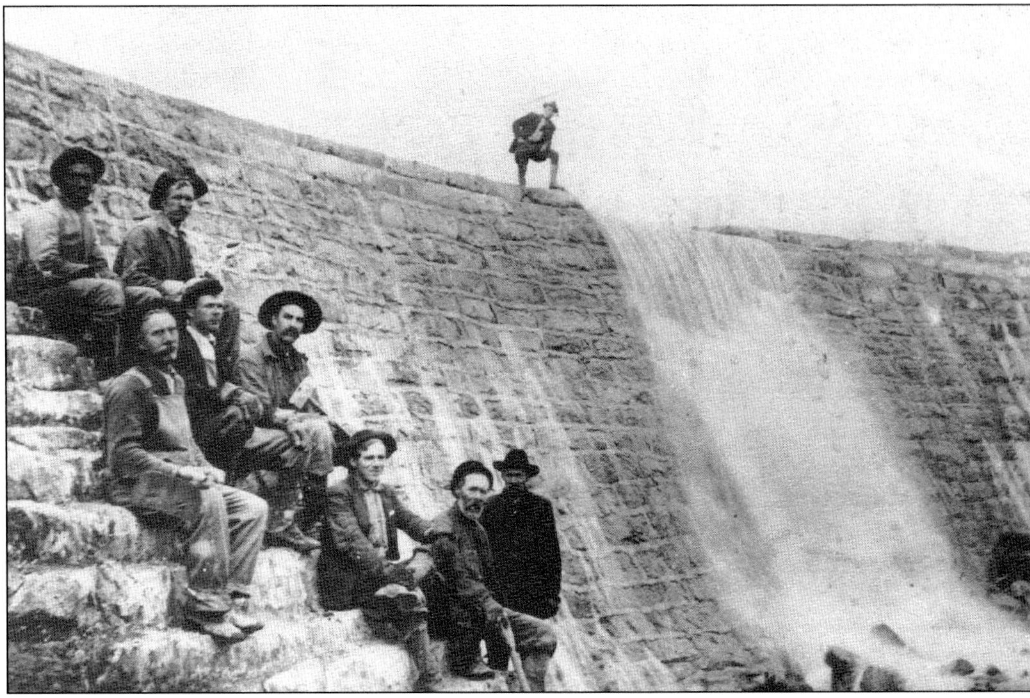

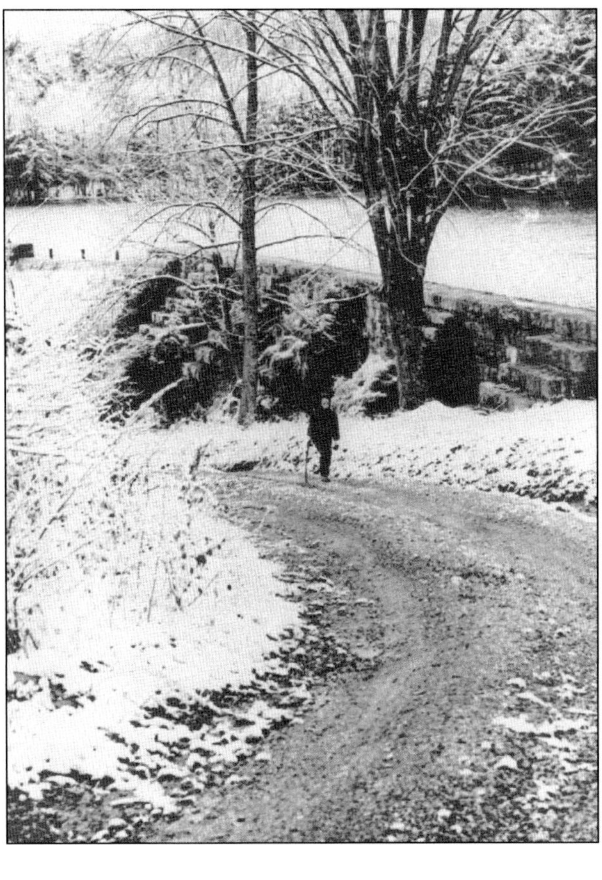

BUILDING BAYS MOUNTAIN PARK. Construction began on the concrete dam at Kingsport's Bays Mountain Park in 1916 and was completed the following year, forming a 44-acre lake. Pictured from left to right are (first row) John Quillen, Hiram Quillen, and George Fields; (second row) Joe Moore, Will Head, and Bill Hood; (third row) Matt Pierce and Sheb Hickman. The man atop the dam is William Slackhammer. (Courtesy of Bays Mountain Park.)

COLD CLIMB UPHILL. A pedestrian walks up the snowy road beside the dam at Bays Mountain Park. The recreation area features 25 miles of trails, using names like Sweet Gum, Indian Pipes, Food Plot, and Dolan Branch. (Courtesy of Bays Mountain Park.)

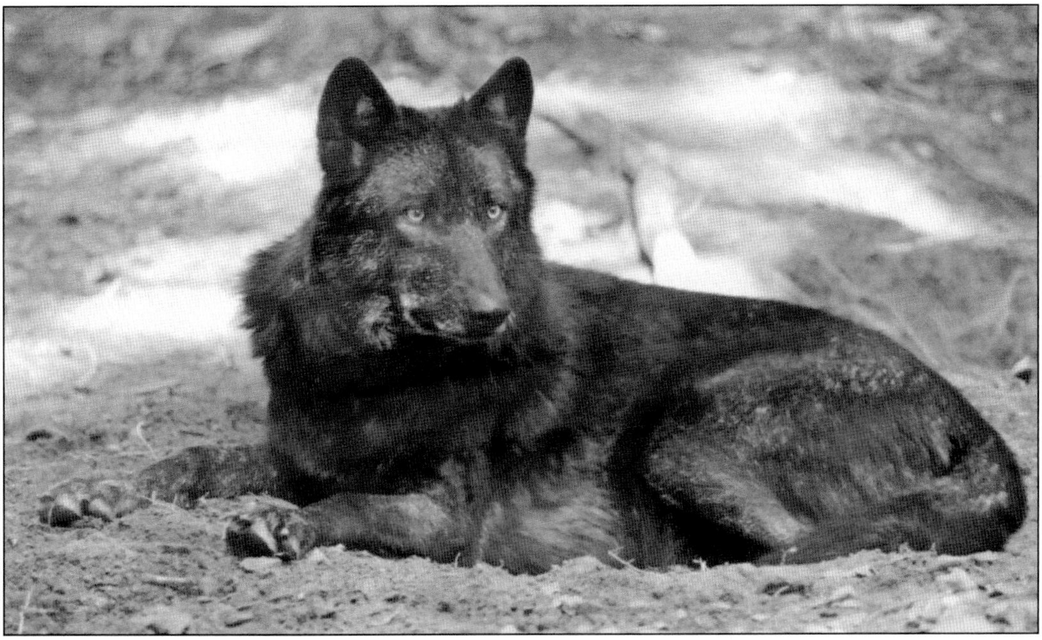

HOWL AT THE MOON. Since being established in 1992, the gray wolf population has become one of the most popular attractions at Bays Mountain Park in Kingsport. The wolves stay behind several layers of fencing, sleeping during the day and roaming at night. (Photograph by Earl Neikirk.)

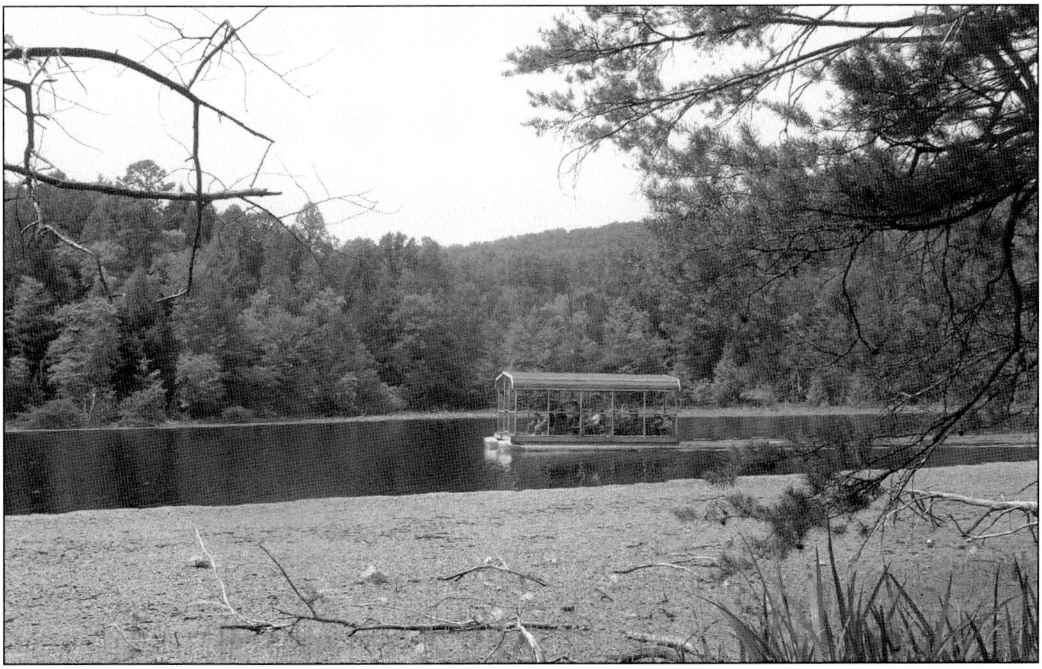

LAKE OF LILY PADS. Pontoon-boat tours are popular on Bays Mountain Lake, a reservoir used as the city's water supply until 1944. Several beavers call this water hole home and provide visitors a fascinating glimpse into their world of making dams with logs and mud. Barge rides are also offered at night, when deer can be seen eating brush amid a chorus of bullfrogs. (Photograph by Joe Tennis.)

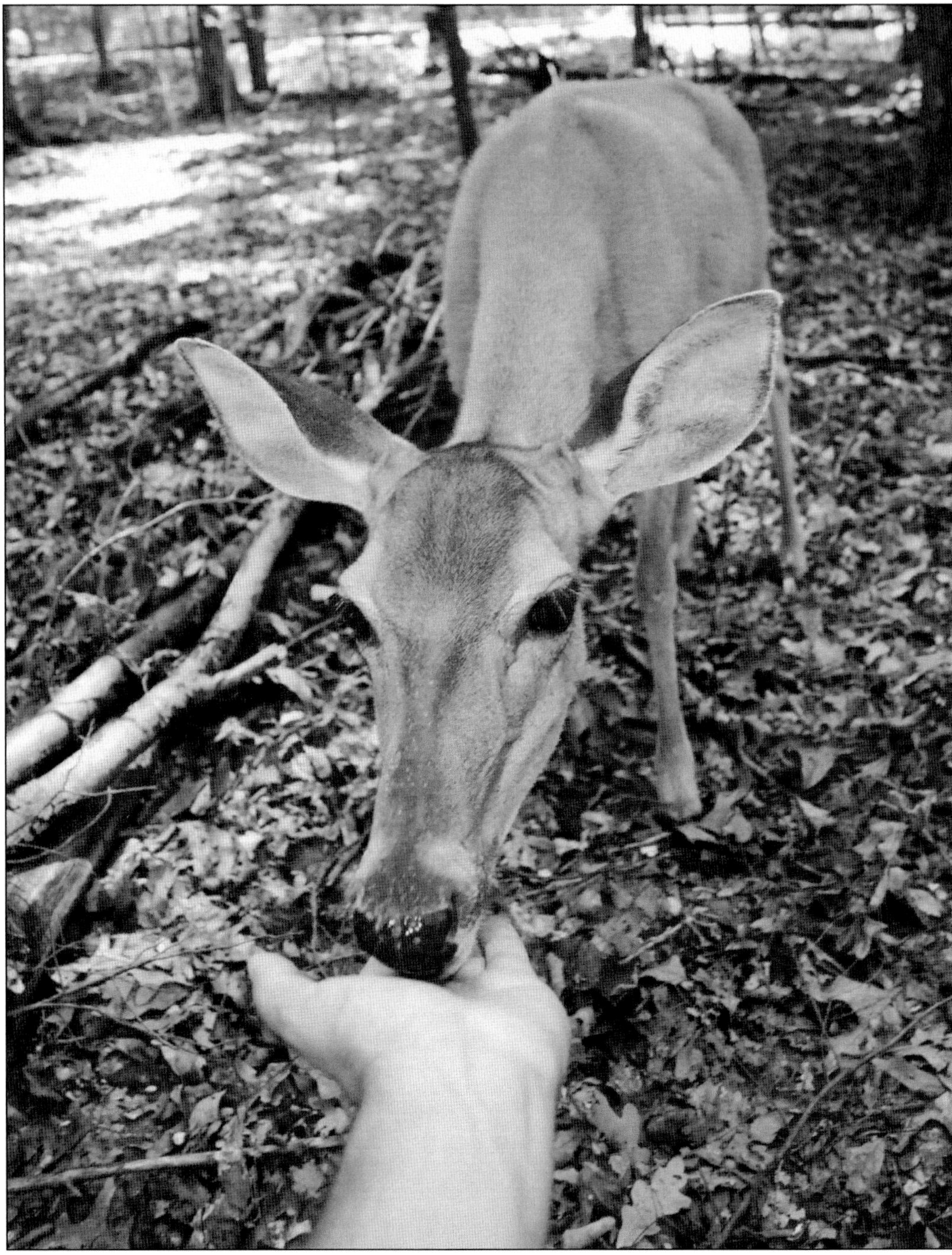

LOOKING FOR A HANDOUT. The deer of Bays Mountain Park are so famously tame that they are often known to eat from a visitor's hand. Dozens of deer roam the woods of the 3,500-acre sanctuary on Bays Mountain. Several deer also live in zoo-like habitats at the park, as do wolves, turtles, bobcats, and river otter. (Photograph by Earl Neikirk.)

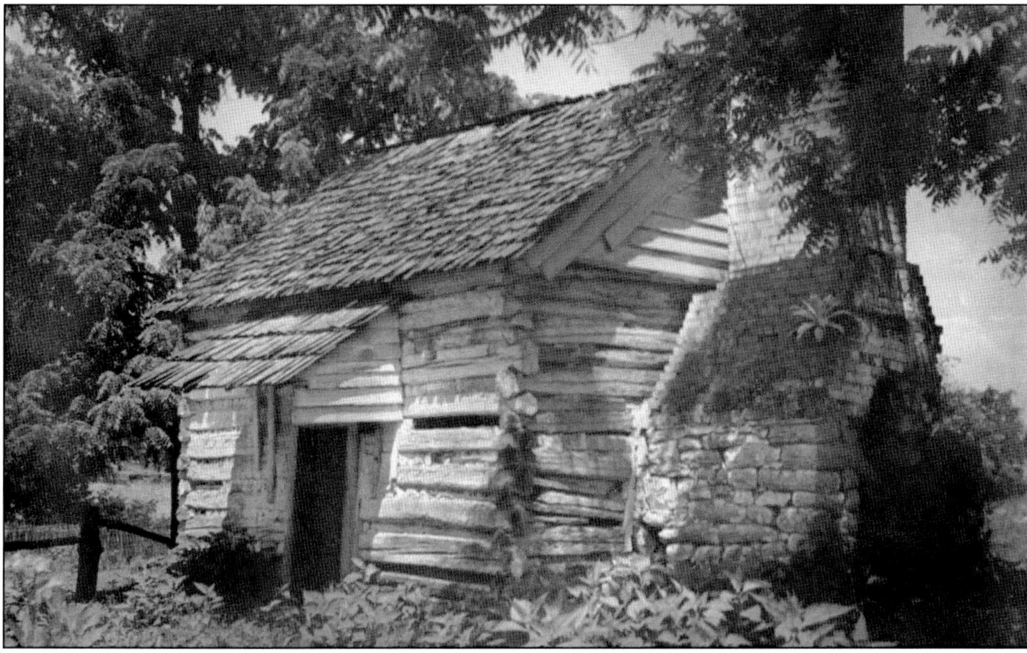

Long-Gone Landmark. The slave's cabin at the Exchange Place in Kingsport was about a century old when this photograph was made, *c.* 1940. The cabin was torn down sometime after 1970, when the Exchange Place was established as a living history farm and museum. A new cabin—a replica known as the "Cook's Cabin"—was built on the same foundation. (Courtesy of the Exchange Place.)

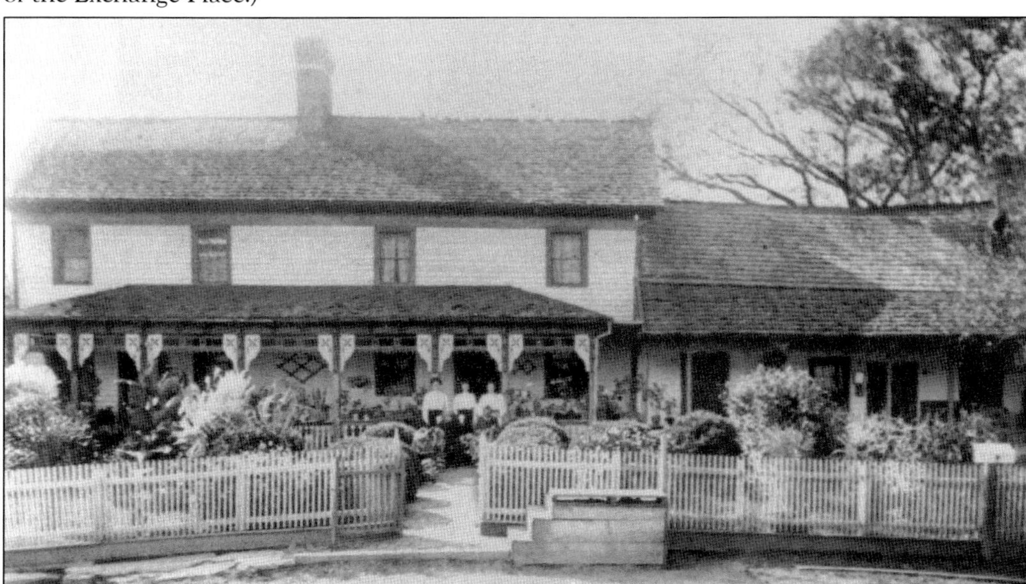

Roseland. Built in sections, with portions dating to the early 1800s, the sprawling mansion dubbed "Roseland" belonged to the Bachman, Steadman, and Shipp families and once stood on Shipp Street in the Kingsport area. It was moved in the early 1990s to the Exchange Place, a living history farm and museum near Orebank. The Exchange Place uses the home as a visitors' center. (Courtesy of Bays Mountain Park.)

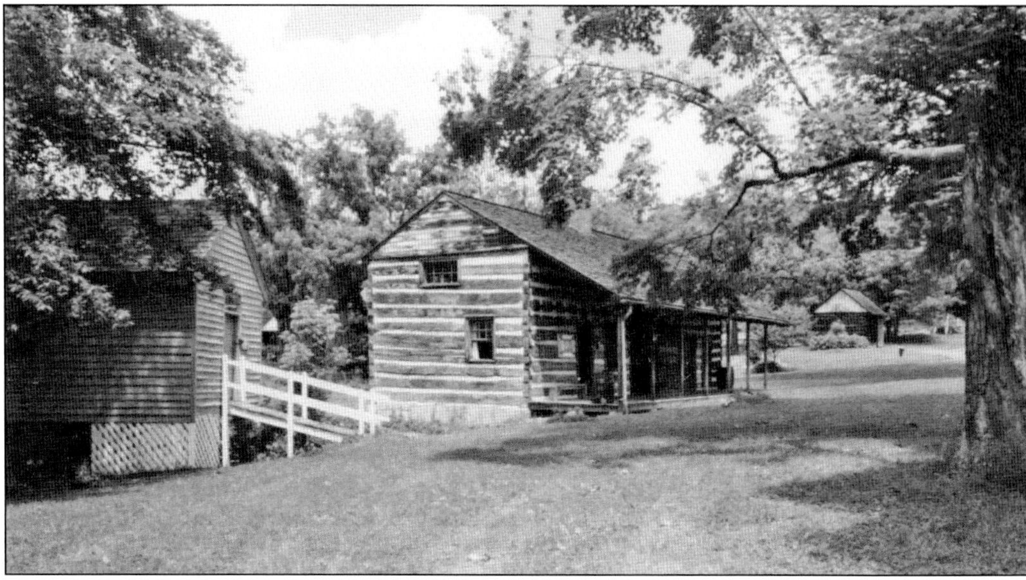

EXCHANGE PLACE. A modern look at the Exchange Place shows the tourist attraction in the 1990s. The building at the center, the cabin, was originally the main house, built about 1820. The springhouse, with an upstairs used as a schoolhouse, stands at left. The Exchange Place took its name from being a stagecoach stop where currency was traded. (Courtesy of the Exchange Place.)

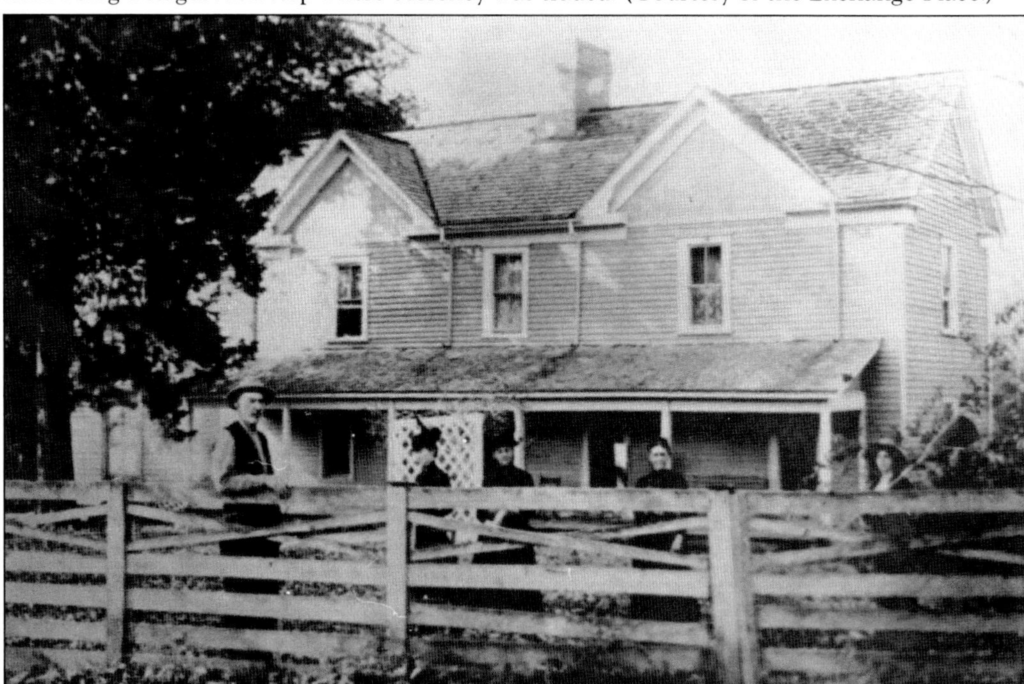

OLD HOME PLACE. John Preston, left, stands with his family about 1914, when a fence fronted the old home place that became known as the Exchange Place. The top level of this building was added to hide the log structure beneath during an era when log homes were seen as a sign of poverty. The springhouse, still standing, is on the left behind the tree. (Courtesy of the Exchange Place.)

Five

Piney Flats

Tall pines once towered over "The Forks," a place where the Watauga River meets the South fork of the Holston River. These pine trees and flat land naturally inspired the name "Piney Flats" for the surrounding community.

For a while, however, this unincorporated area was also known as "Shell's Crossing" or "Shell's Crossroads" for the Reverend Andrew Shell, a pioneer preacher who lived in the vicinity and served as postmaster in the 1850s. An effort, even, was made to officially change the name of the community to "Shell's Crossing," but the name "Piney Flats" persisted.

The modern four lanes of U.S. Highway 11 East cut through what looks like the center of this community. Still, the actual heart of Piney Flats lies on a parallel span, what is known as the "Old 11-E"—the road facing Mary Hughes School.

Far beyond, in outlying communities, much of Sullivan County also claims to be part of "Piney," reaching west to New Bethel Church and Rocky Springs.

Clearly, the most famous of all Piney Flats landmarks is Rocky Mount, a cabin that was once the capitol of the Territory of the United States South of the River Ohio. Called the "Southwest Territory" for short, this district predated the formation of Tennessee.

Rocky Mount, fully restored, stands in pristine condition. The home of William Cobb, it was built in the 1770s and used from 1790 to 1792, when William Blount served as governor of the Southwest Territory. Overnight guests have included the likes of Andrew Jackson.

This place is not only a historic treasure. It is also a popular point for elementary school field trips and is located just barely inside southern Sullivan County, near the Washington County, Tennessee, line.

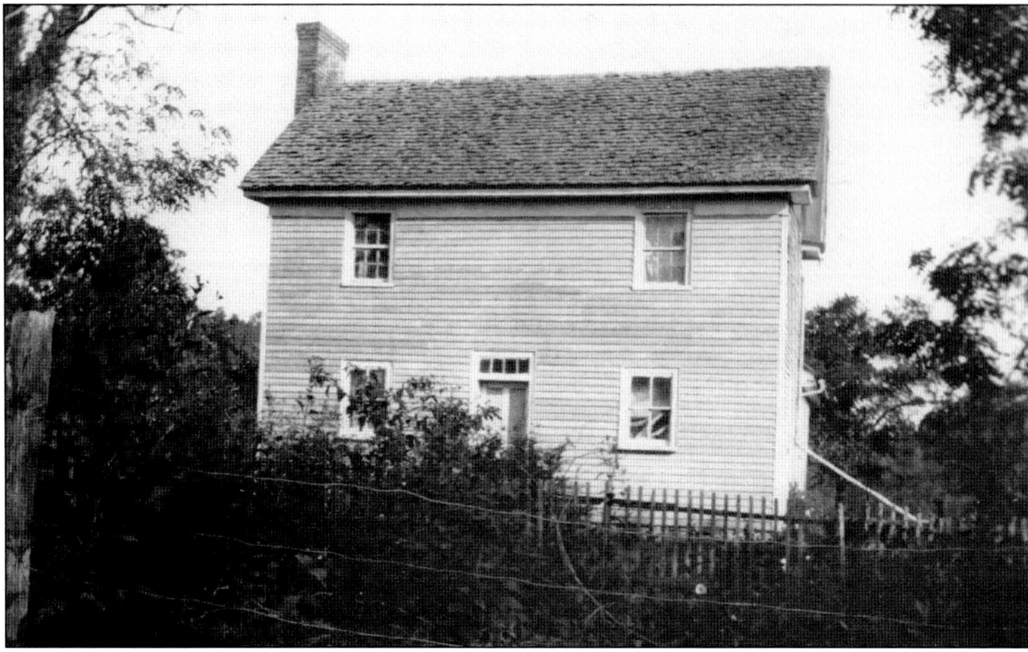

COVERED CABIN. The logs of the Cobb House were covered with siding when this photograph was made in about 1924. At the time, this 1770s home at Piney Flats belonged to the Massengills, and previously the girls in the family had told their father that they were ashamed to live in a log house. Unintentionally, or just because they wanted the exterior to be covered, these daughters actually helped preserve the original log structure. (Courtesy of Rocky Mount Museum.)

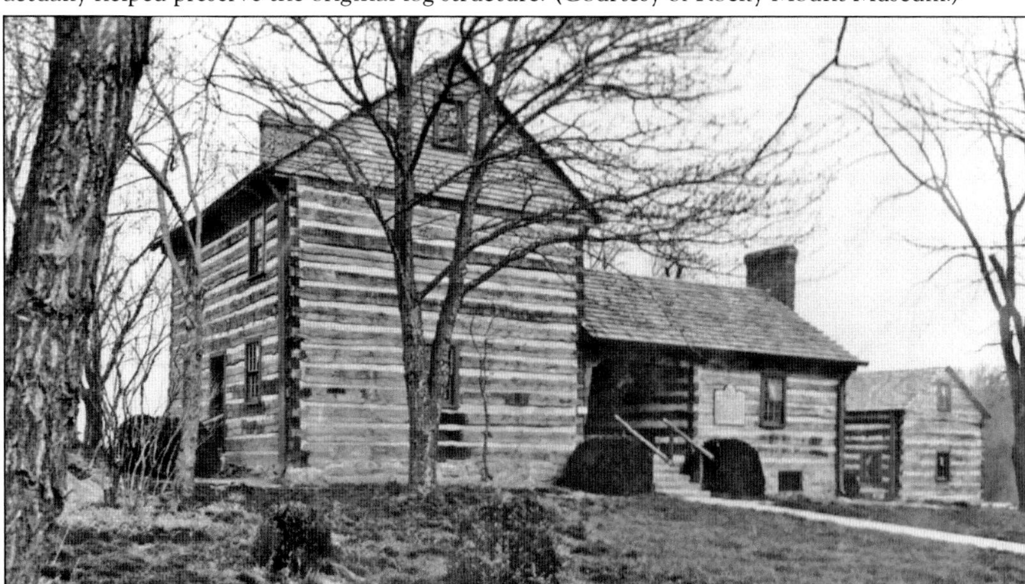

COMPLETE RENOVATION. The Rocky Mount Historical Association and the Tennessee Historical Commission completed an extensive renovation of Rocky Mount prior to the attraction opening for public tours in 1961. Located along an old stagecoach road between Abingdon, Virginia, and what is now Knoxville, Tennessee, this house served for two years as the capitol of a district commonly called the Southwest Territory in the 1790s. (Courtesy of Rocky Mount Museum.)

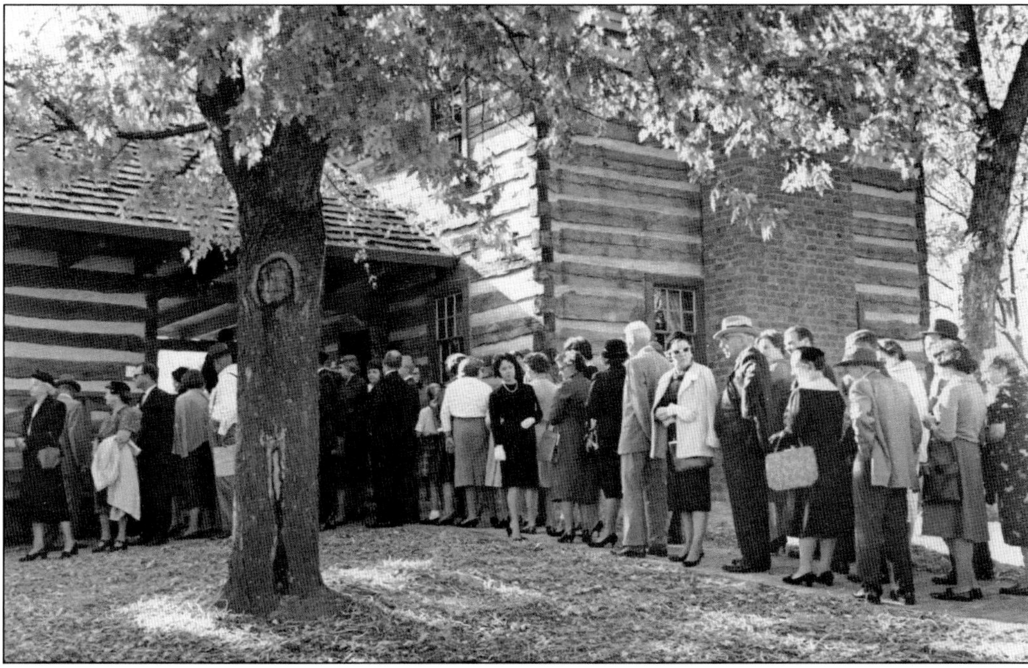

Opening Day. Only 500 people were expected, but at least 2,500 turned out for opening-day ceremonies at Rocky Mount on October 29, 1961. Walter Chandler delivered the dedication, saying the landmark now stood as "a challenge to all liberty-loving Americans to carry on as the founders of our state found it necessary to do in order that even we may be free." (Courtesy of Rocky Mount Museum.)

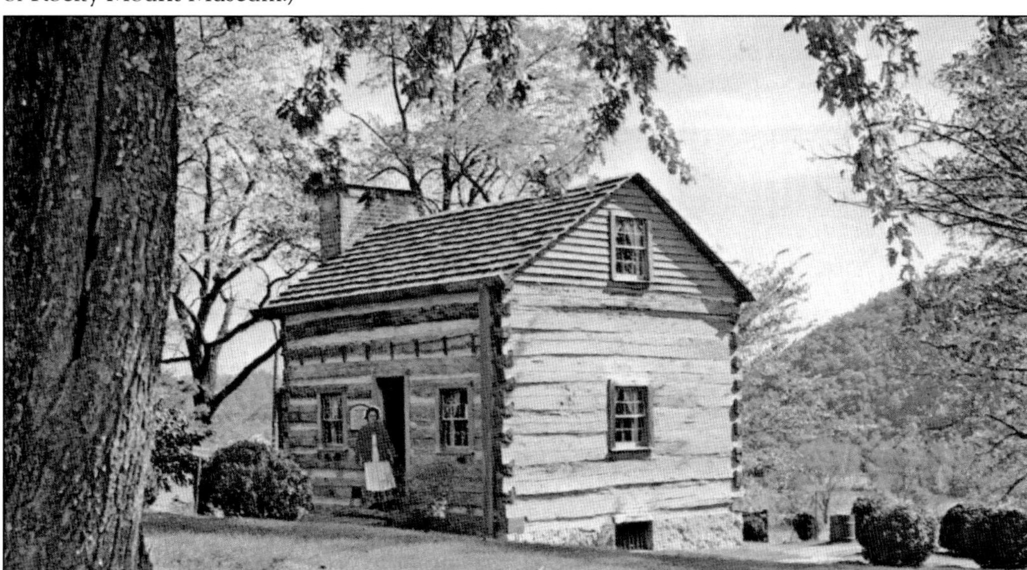

Kitchen Cabin. At the time this "Kitchen Cabin" postcard appeared about 1970, Rocky Mount was noted as one of Tennessee's top tourist attractions. Here costumed re-enactors guide visitors with an interpretation that never breaks from the idea that the year is 1791 and that Gov. William Blount is somewhere on the grounds, still in charge of the Southwest Territory. (Courtesy of Rocky Mount Museum.)

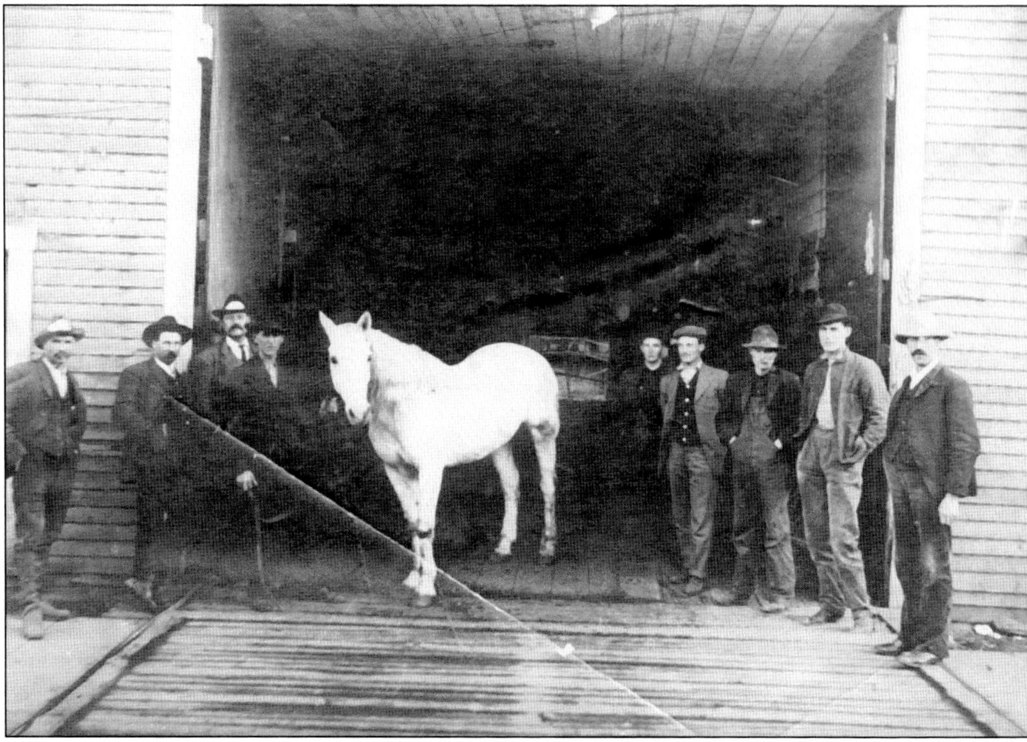

PINEY FLATS LIVERY. The Piney Flats Livery was an early business in the community, about 1900. The man fourth from right is Gentry Milhorn. Cleve Collins stands third from right. (Courtesy of Shelia Steele Hunt.)

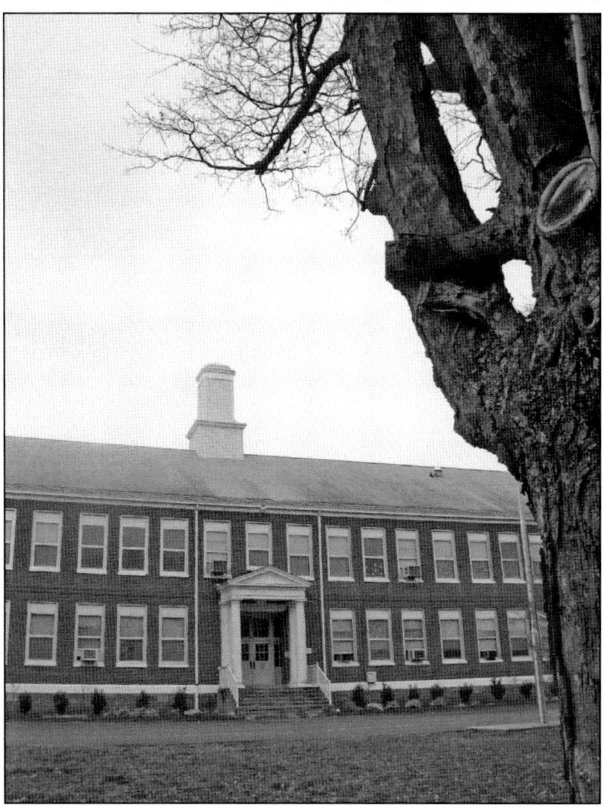

MARY HUGHES SCHOOL. The modern Mary Hughes School dates to 1942. It was named for the wife of Samuel Hughes, who gave land to establish a school in 1894. Hughes also helped make bricks to build the school but ended up catching a cold that developed into fatal pneumonia. The first school, called the Mary Hughes Institute, was completed in 1897 but was destroyed by fire in 1941. (Photograph by Joe Tennis.)

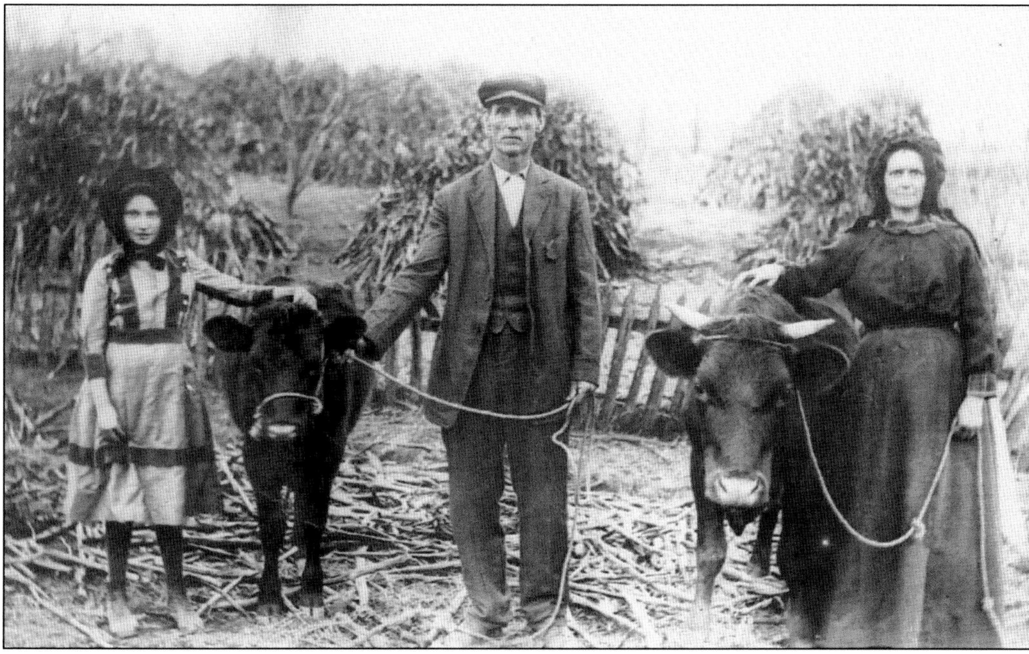

FAMILY PORTRAIT. Members of the Goforth family pose with their cows at Piney Flats about 1914. Daughter Pansy stands at left with her father, John Lafayette Goforth (1867–1947), (center) and mother, Martha Oliver (1872–1951). (Courtesy of Shelia Steele Hunt.)

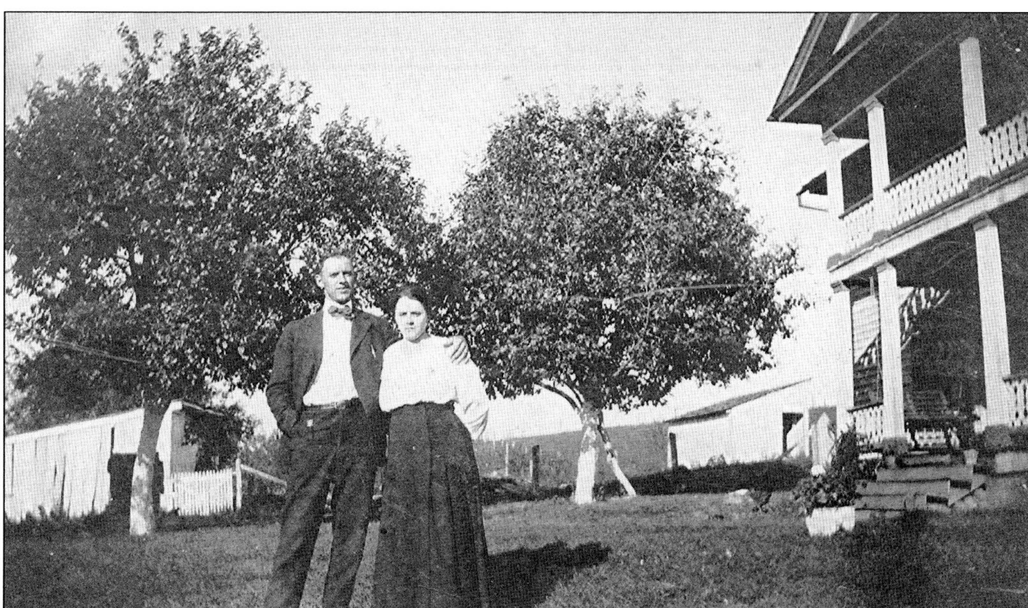

BROTHER AND SISTER. Twins Gordon Frank McKenry and Martha McKenry St. John, born August 13, 1888, posed for this photograph near Piney Flats in about 1910. Martha graduated from the Martha Washington College of Abingdon, Virginia, and married George Washington St. John, the owner of a large dairy farm in the Piney Flats area. (Courtesy of Shelia Steele Hunt.)

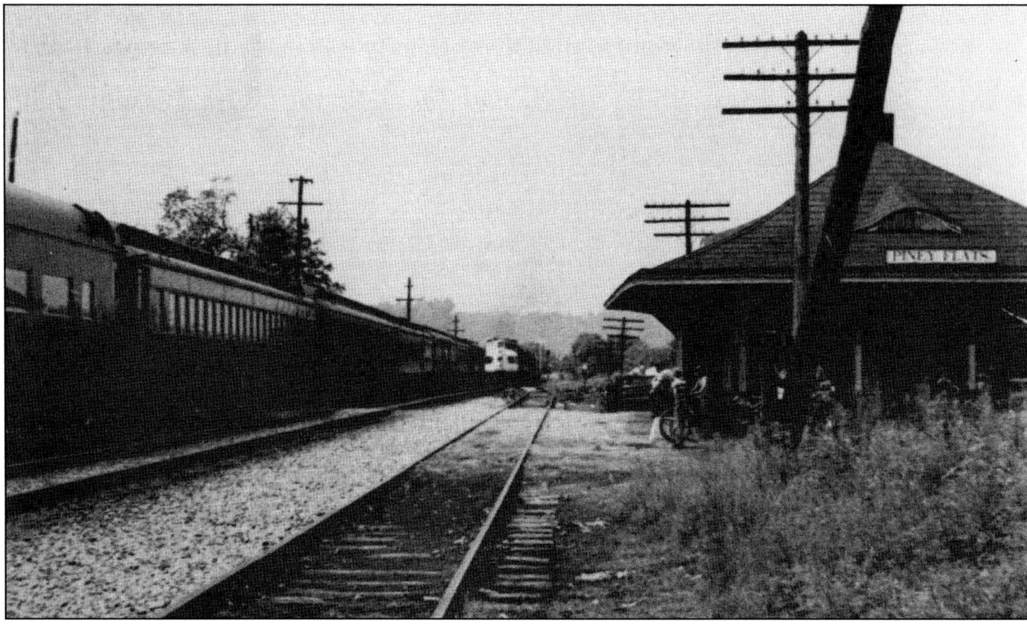

PINEY FLATS DEPOT. Passengers once boarded the train at the Piney Flats Railroad Station when passenger service was still common in the early 1900s. The first depot at Piney Flats was built in the late 1850s. Piney Flats was a stop along the Southern Railway, just south of Bluff City. (Courtesy of the Bluff City Public Library.)

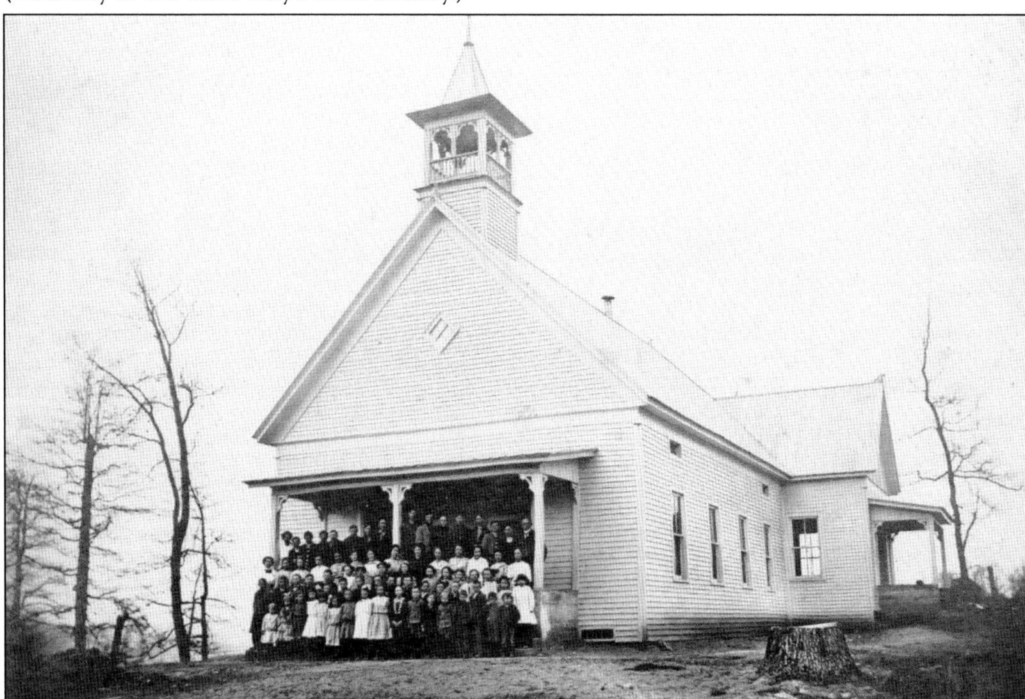

NEW BETHEL CHURCH. A congregation gathers outside the New Bethel Church near Piney Flats about 1905. The Reverend Samuel Doak founded this church in 1782. The present sanctuary was built in 1873 and was renovated in 1968. (Courtesy of Shelia Steele Hunt.)

Seven

County Crossroads

From Bloomingdale to Buncombe, crossroads called Beechnut City and Rock City lie across the hills and valleys of Sullivan County. Never mind that an address says Kingsport, Bristol, or Bluff City. Residents retain pride in distinguishing Possum Creek from Hickory Tree, and Silvacola from Central Heights.

At one time, dozens of post offices operated in Sullivan County, leaving maps with names derived from prominent churches, schools, landowners, families, early postmasters, and just plain people. The place named Akard, for example, comes from J. Craft Akard Sr., who served as the superintendent of Sullivan County Schools from 1915 to 1923.

In the far southwestern corner of the county, the sparsely populated Blair's Gap community takes its name from a natural gap in Bays Mountain. On the opposite side of Sullivan County, the Offset community simply takes its name from a weird case of geography. In this place, Sullivan County juts into Virginia, just south of Damascus, in a line that does not look like it belongs. Various reasons explain why this "offset" exists; some say it was drawn around the moonshine stills of mountaineers who wanted to remain in what is now Tennessee.

Avoca, now part of Bristol, was once its own town with a post office name originating from landowner A. R. Ordway; he came from a town called Avoca in Pennsylvania. Nearby, the Vance community was named for brothers John and Thomas Vance, who gave railroad officials a right-of-way across their property in the 1850s.

What flows atop the ground naturally lent its name to Indian Springs, a place where many Native American relics have been found. The same watery inspiration goes for Double Springs, an area known as a mustering ground for Revolutionary War troops.

What grows atop the ground, meanwhile, served as inspiration for Hickory Tree, a place that took its name from an actual hickory tree that no longer stands.

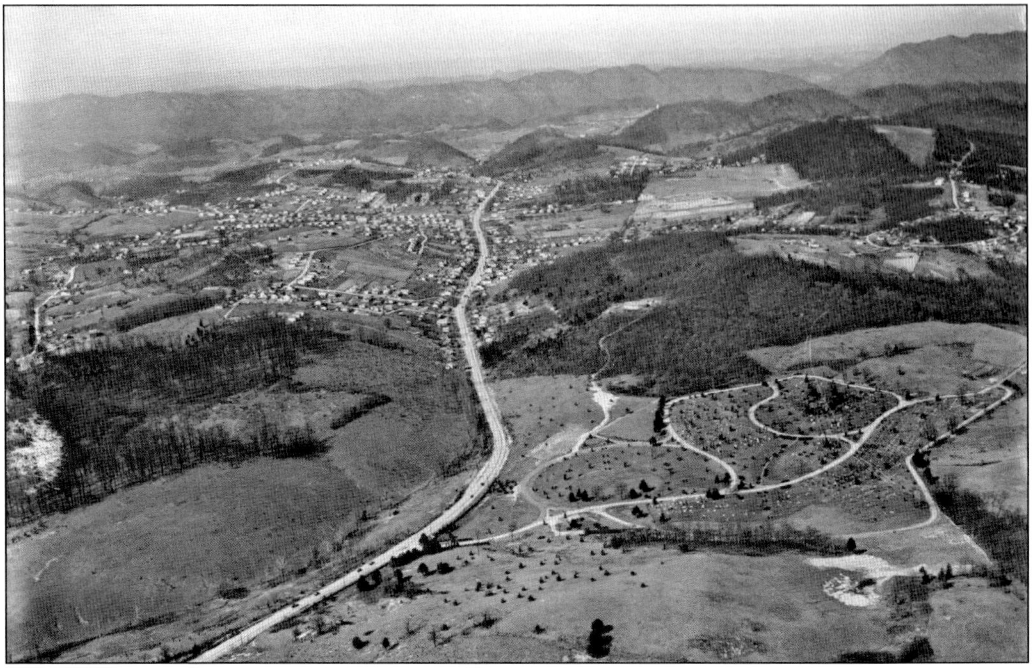

LYNN GARDEN. A 1948 aerial shot of the area north of Kingsport shows the Lynn Garden community bordering Scott County, Virginia. The mountain in the upper right corner is the Virginia portion of Clinch Mountain and shows the "Moccasin Gap" that separates the towns of Weber City and Gate City—both economically and socially tied to the Kingsport community. (Courtesy of the Kingsport Archives.)

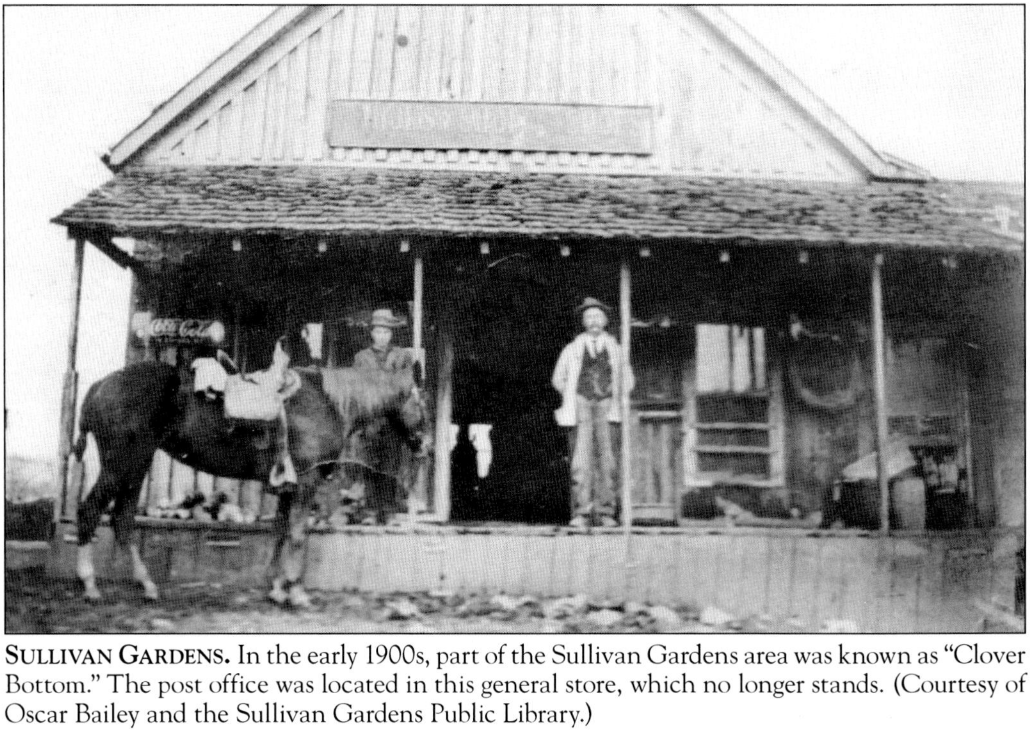

SULLIVAN GARDENS. In the early 1900s, part of the Sullivan Gardens area was known as "Clover Bottom." The post office was located in this general store, which no longer stands. (Courtesy of Oscar Bailey and the Sullivan Gardens Public Library.)

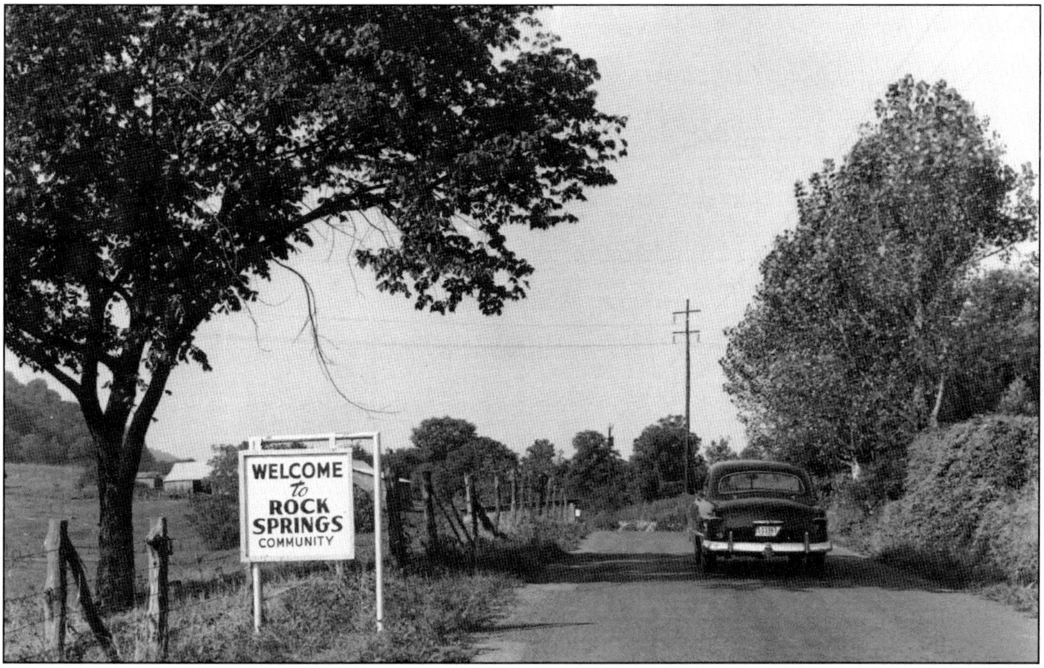

ROCK SPRINGS. Located near Kingsport, Rock Springs can be easily confused with other similarly named places, such as Rock City, Rock Hill, Rocky Mount, and Rocky Springs in Sullivan County. In the 1950s, the Rock Springs Community Club regularly sponsored agricultural fairs at the old Rock Springs School. This scene shows the area along Rock Springs Road in 1952. (Courtesy of the Colonial Heights Public Library.)

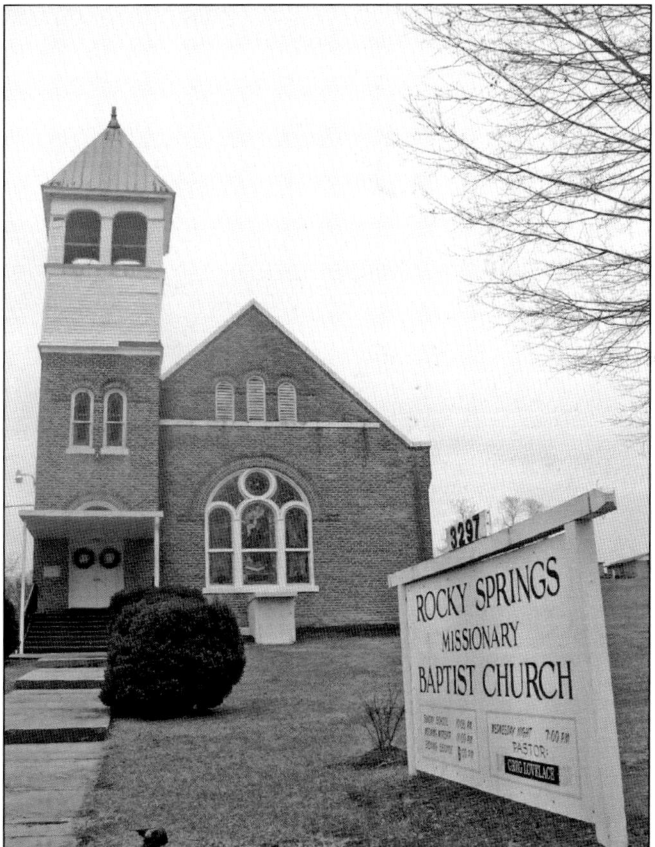

ROCKY SPRINGS. The Rocky Springs Missionary Baptist Church was constructed in 1906 with bricks made on-site near Piney Flats. Col. Nathan Gregg (1835–1894) and his wife, Catherine Morrell Gregg (1834–1902), donated land to build the church and a nearby school at Rocky Springs. Colonel Gregg was a Confederate veteran and also a sheriff of Sullivan County. (Photograph by Joe Tennis.)

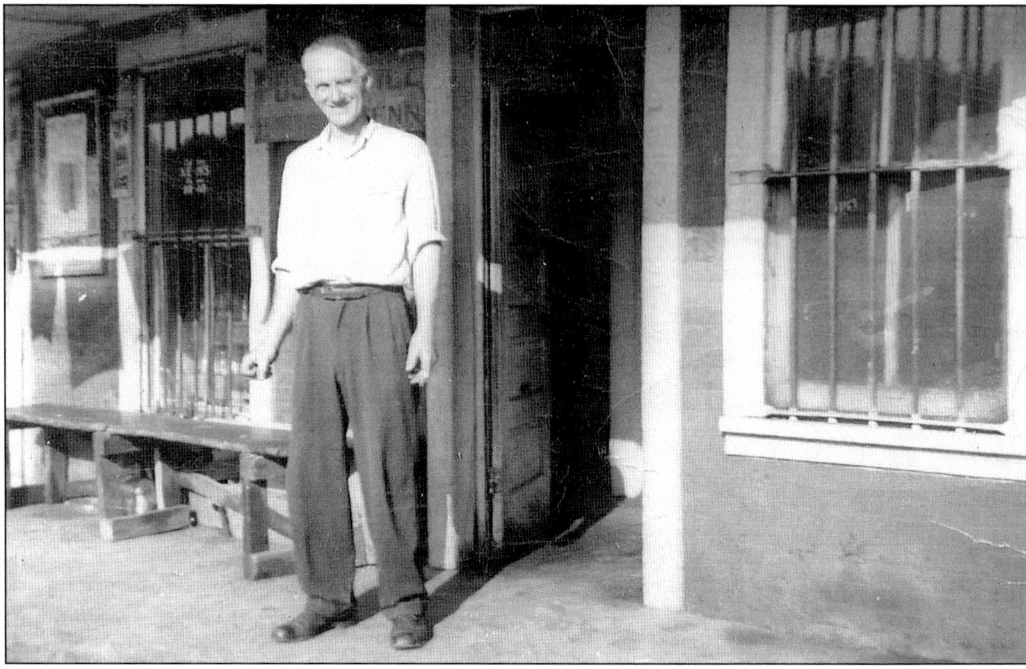

FORDTOWN. Ray Irvin served as the postmaster of the now-closed Fordtown Post Office when this photograph was made in 1954. Located south of Kingsport, Fordtown took its name from several Ford families living in the area. (Courtesy of Shelia Steele Hunt.)

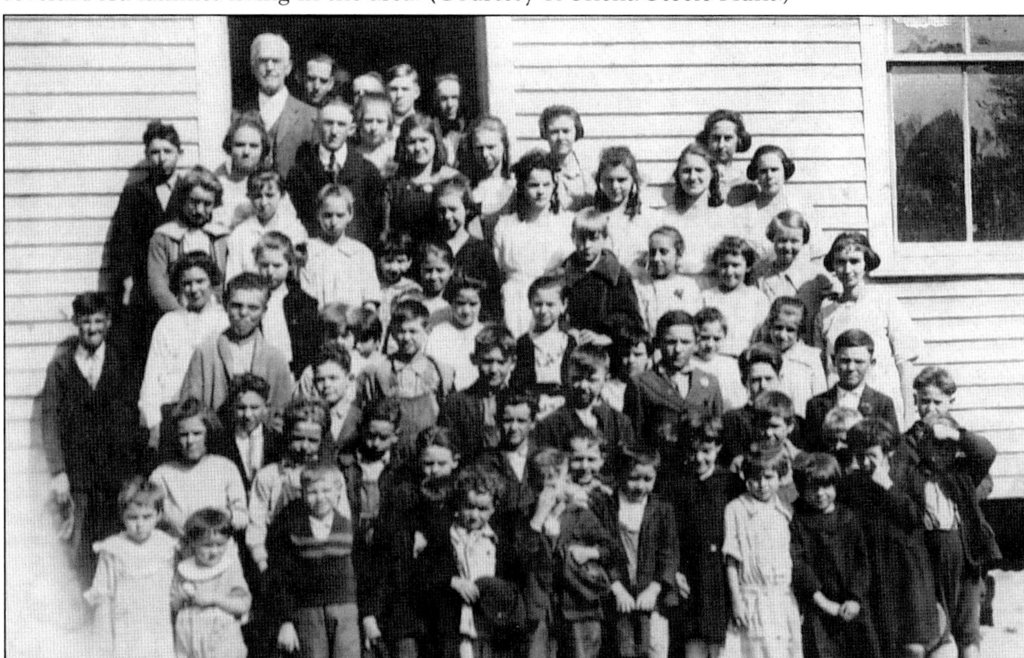

HORSE CREEK. A 1921 photograph shows children posing at the old Horse Creek Academy. This school was located near Sullivan Gardens in southwestern Sullivan County. Standing in the lower left corner are Jessie Fields (left) and Louise Fields. (Courtesy of Oscar Bailey and the Sullivan Gardens Public Library.)

Colonial Heights. Roma Hill served for 10 years as Colonial Heights' first librarian, starting in 1962 when the branch library was open two days a week for three hours a day and was inside a room at the Colonial Heights Presbyterian Church. A native of Rochester, New York, Hill attended Dobyns-Bennett High School in Kingsport. She also became the "football queen" and traveled with the team. (Courtesy of the Colonial Heights Public Library.)

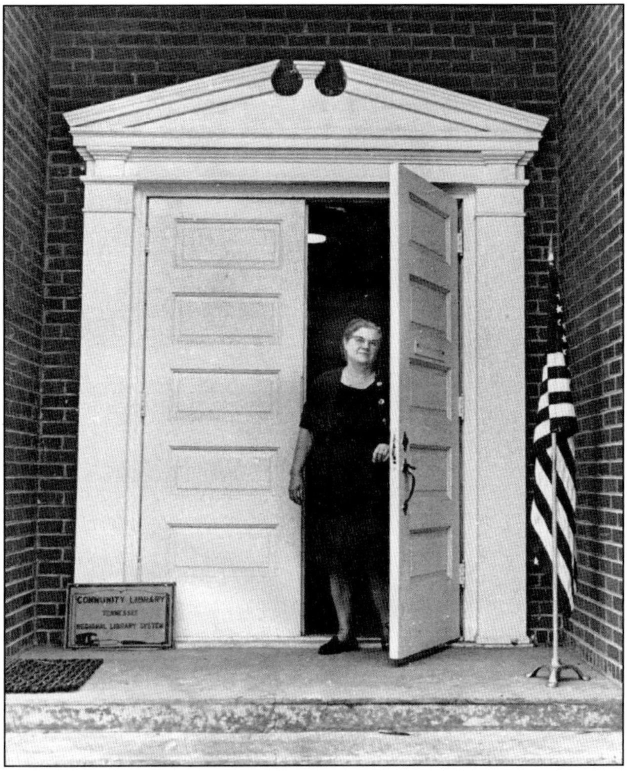

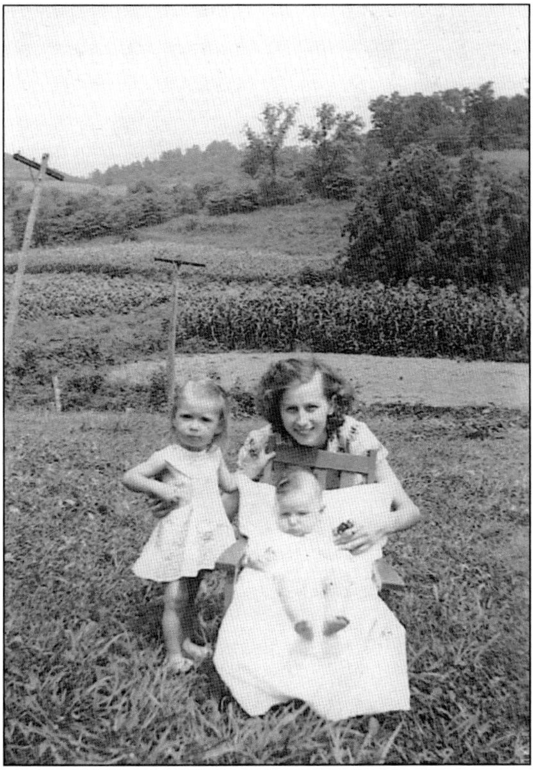

Holly Springs. Azel Olinger poses with her infant daughter, Mary Innis Olinger, and a family friend, Rachel Margaret Robinette (left), near Holly Springs in 1941. Azel grew up at nearby Indian Springs, where her father, Kenneth Monroe Smith, served as the postmaster in the 1950s. The cornfield in the background of this scene has since been made into Bloomingdale Pike, with houses now standing on the ridge. (Courtesy of Mary Olinger.)

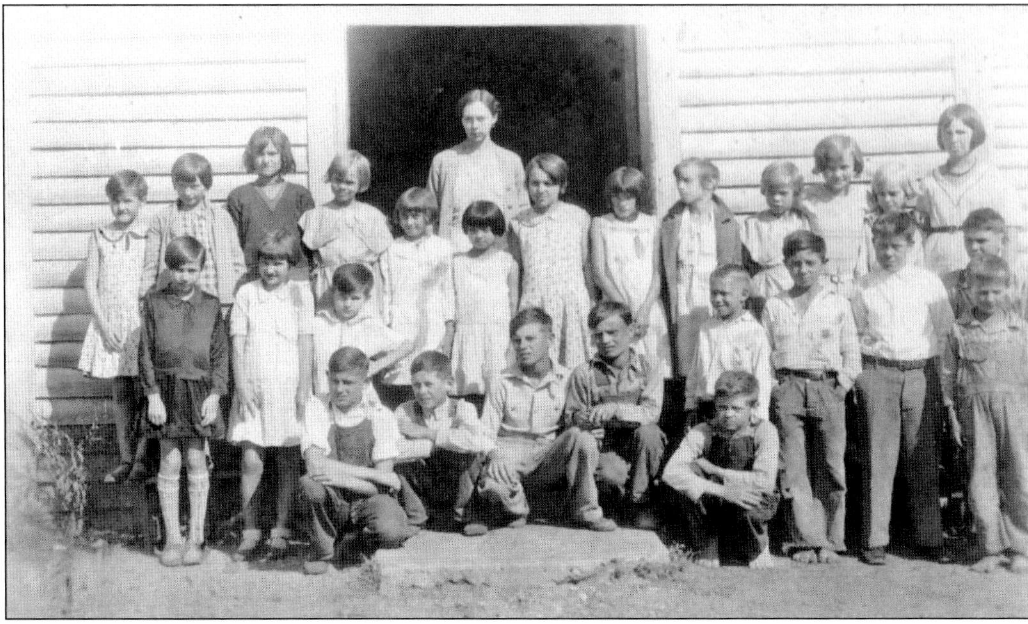

BLOOMINGDALE. Built at Bloomingdale about 1911, the old Kingsley School took its name from the old Kingsley Seminary, built in 1877 by Joseph Ketron and named for Bishop Calvin Kingsley. The Kingsley School primary class posed for this photograph in the 1931–1932 school year, a few years before the school was destroyed by fire. It was later rebuilt. Teacher Lela Whitaker stands in the doorway. (Courtesy of Ethel Ketron.)

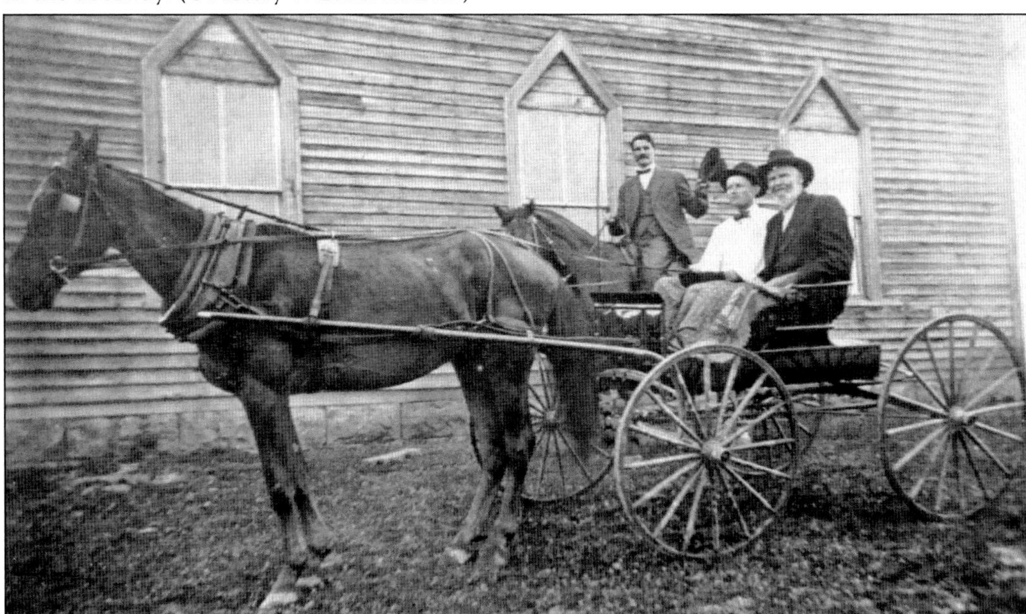

ARCADIA. The plantation home of Thomas Fain, called "Arcadia," lent its name to a community along Reedy Creek and referenced a region of ancient Greece regarded as an ideal of rural simplicity and contentment. Local landmarks have included the Reedy Creek Academy, or "Temperance Hall." Stopping a buggy outside the academy about 1900 are Thomas Hicks, left, and his grandfather Wesley Hicks. The horseback rider is unknown. (Courtesy of Shelia Steele Hunt.)

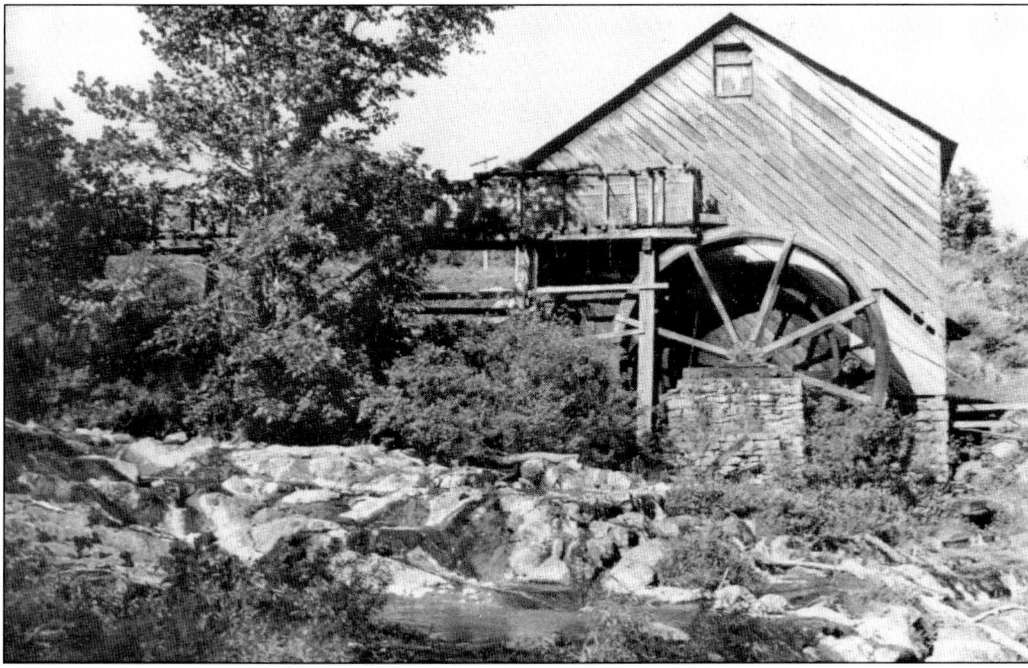

BOOZY CREEK. Shown in about 1940, the Lessley (or "Leslie") Mill was built on the natural cascades of Boozy Creek and took its name from early landowner Andrew Leslie. This creek, also spelled "Boozie," runs into Virginia's Scott County. Local tradition says the name comes from booze spilt by moonshiners who would try to get rid of evidence as law officials approached them. (Courtesy of Shelia Steele Hunt.)

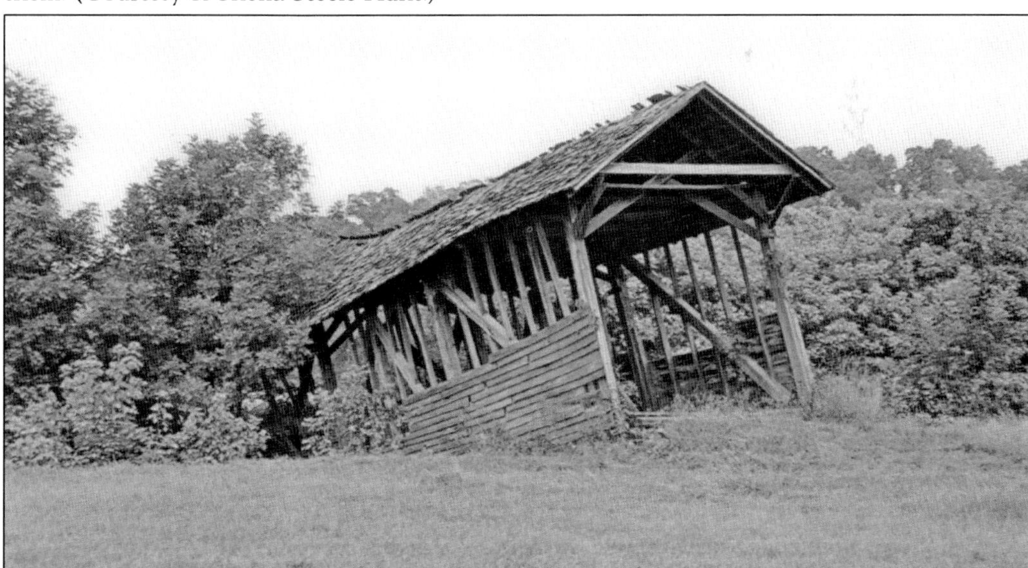

REEDY CREEK. The Bloomingdale Covered Bridge was located over Reedy Creek just north of U.S. Highway 11 West. Standing on a private road, the bridge had a 44-foot span and was built in about 1880. This postcard, issued by L. D. Thompson, shows the bridge's dilapidated condition in 1965. The community of Reedy Creek, surrounding the bridge, was named for natural reeds growing along the creek banks. (Courtesy of Tim Buchanan.)

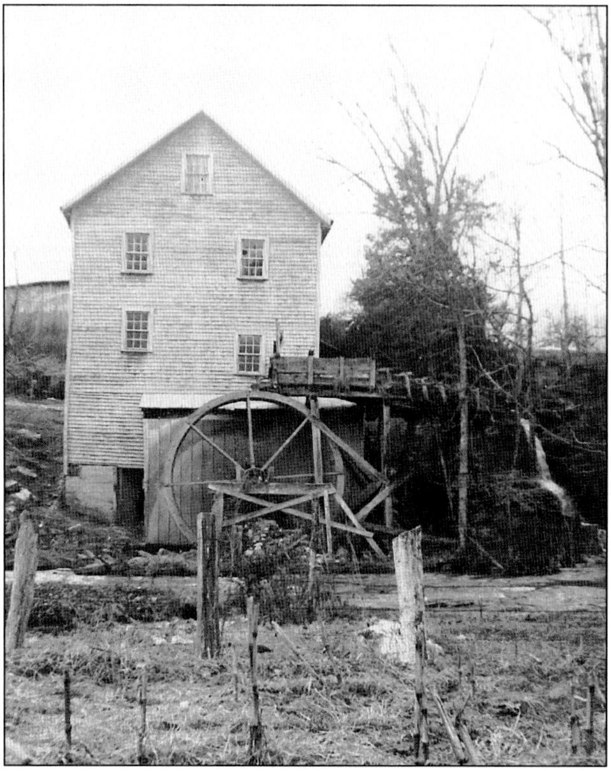

SHAVER MILL. The Shaver Mill was built along Muddy Creek near its confluence with the South fork of the Holston River. It took its name from a local Shaver family and, in turn, provided maps with the Shaver Mill name. (Courtesy of Shelia Steele Hunt.)

GUNNINGS. Acuff Chapel dates to 1786, and it became the first Methodist Episcopal church built in what is now Tennessee. It takes its name from Timothy Acuff, who gave land along the Great Stage Road to erect the chapel. Bishop Francis Asbury often preached at this cabin. It stands in the Gunnings community, a place named for a local Gunning family. (Photograph by Joe Tennis.)

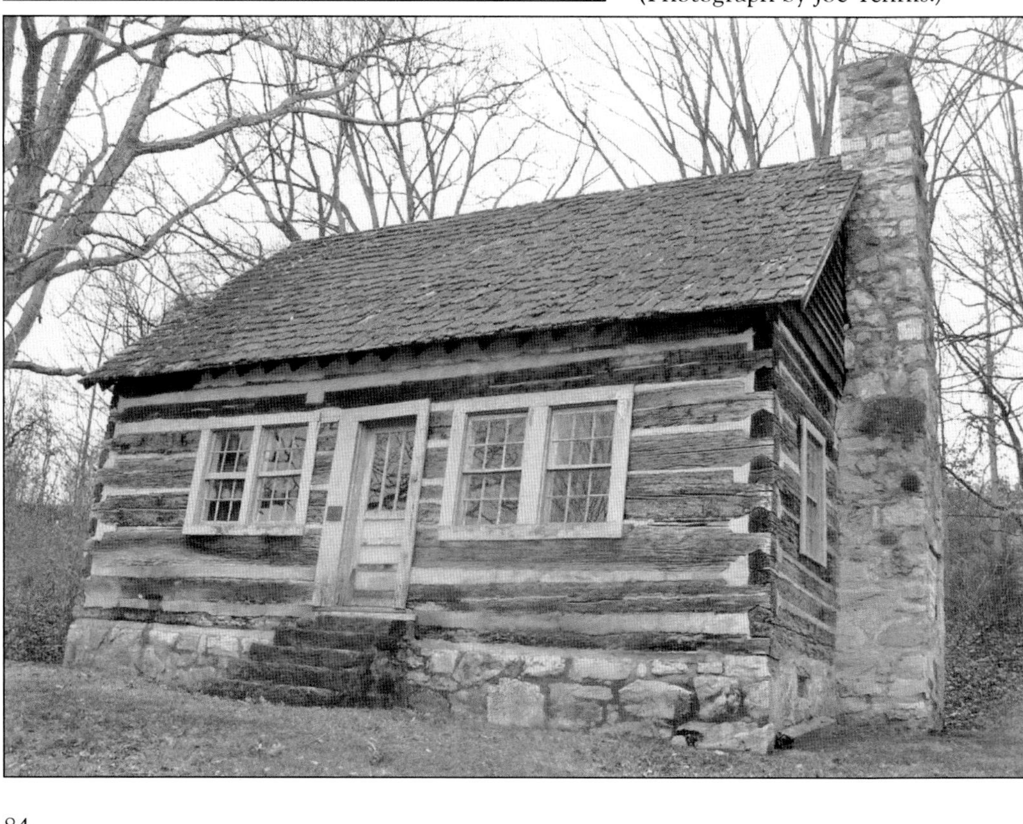

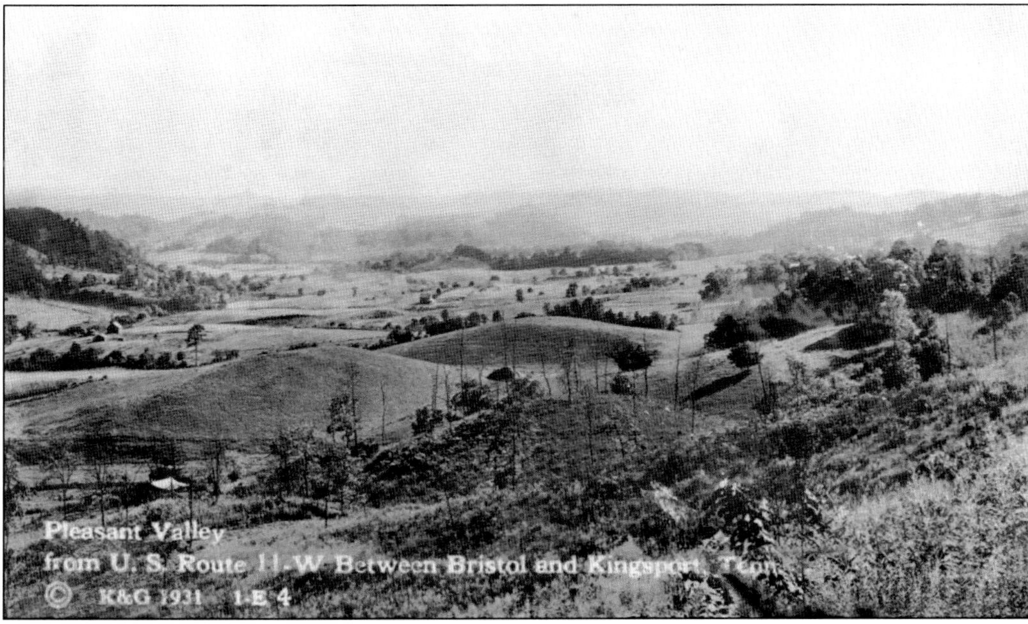

PLEASANT VALLEY. This 1931 postcard shows a "Pleasant Valley" near the communities of Cooks Valley and Bridwell Heights on the old U.S. Highway 11 West, which generally followed the path of Tennessee Route 126 between Indian Springs and Kingsport. Houses now cover the round hills in the forefront of this scene, photographed by Robert R. McIlwaire of Bristol-based Kelly and Green. (Courtesy of Tony Marion.)

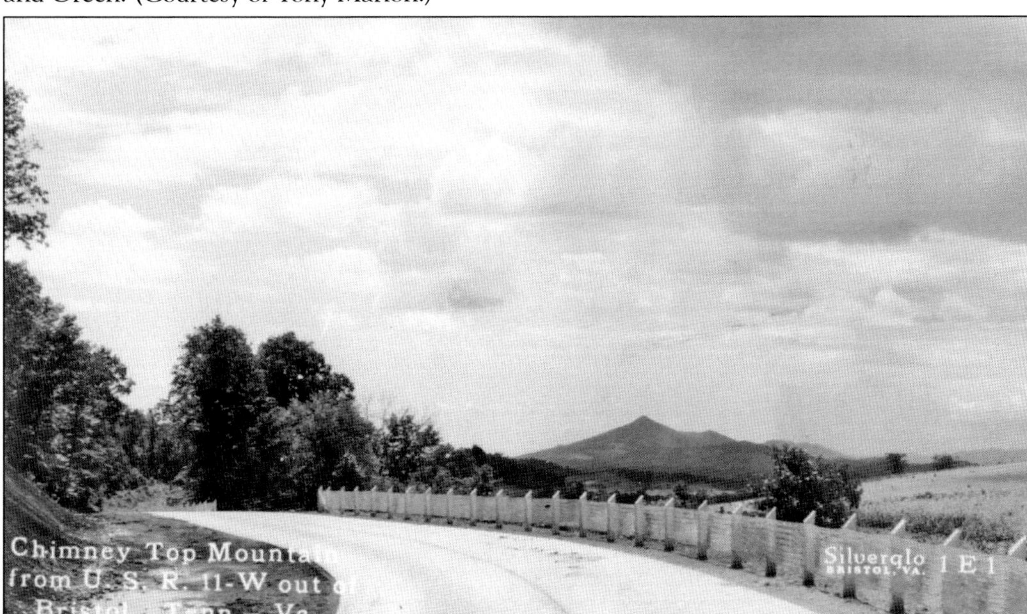

OVERLOOKING CHIMNEY TOP MOUNTAIN. The old U.S. Highway 11 West between Bristol and Kingsport produced a stellar view of Chimney Top Mountain, seen popping out of the lower right corner of this 1930s postcard. Chimney Top is not located in Sullivan County but actually stands farther south in Tennessee, along the line between Hawkins and Greene Counties. (Courtesy of Shelby Edwards.)

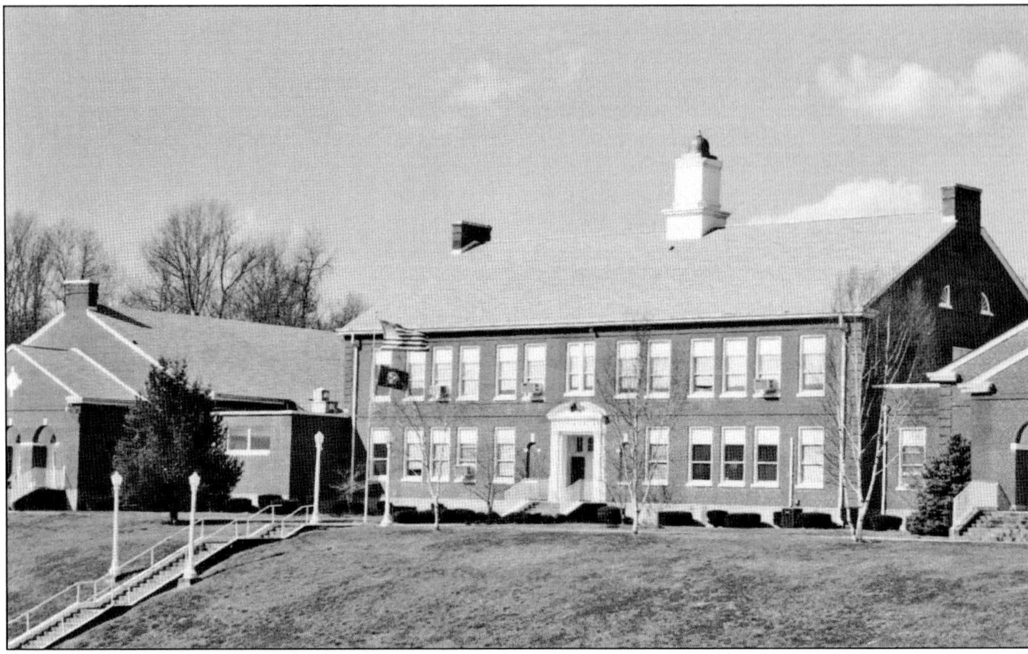

VINEGAR HILL. Opened in 1936, the Holston Valley Middle School was originally built as a high school near a place called Vinegar Hill. According to legend, Vinegar Hill got its name from a farmer who lost his wagonload of apple cider vinegar while trying to pull the wagon up the area's steep hill. (Photograph by Joe Tennis.)

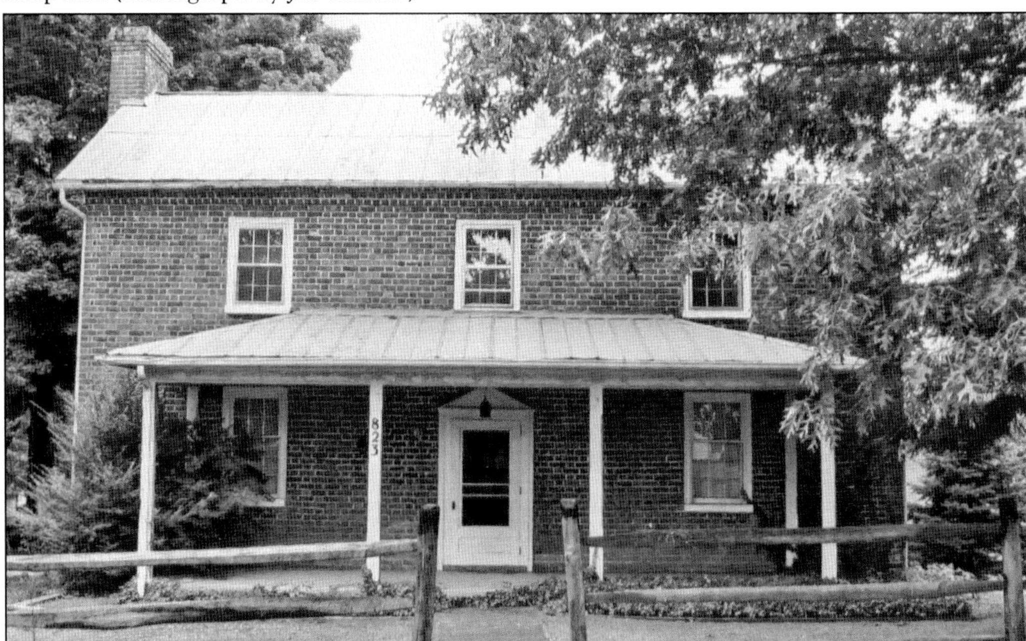

STOP. The privately owned Steele-Barker-Seneker House stands near neighborhoods called Walnut Hill and Maple Hill between Bristol and Blountville. Located along the Great Stage Road, this was once the site of one of the oddest names in Tennessee history—Stop—when a post office was located in a small building near the main house in the early 1900s. (Courtesy of Bud Phillips.)

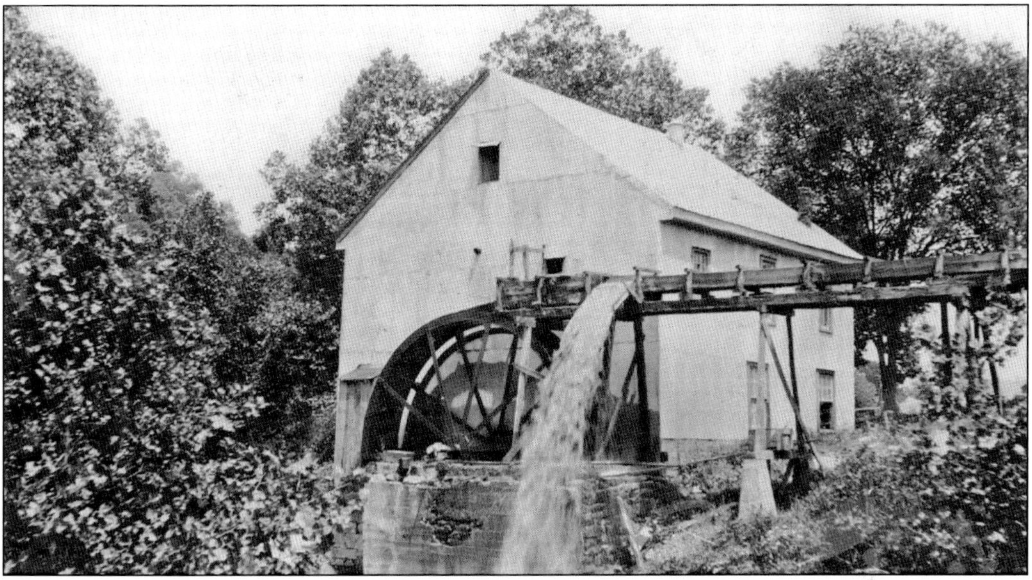

WEAVER BRANCH. This 1928 photograph shows the Massengill Mill, once located on the Weaver Branch of the South fork of the Holston River. Felty Devault Massengill owned the mill until his death in 1894. It was torn down in the early 1950s to construct Boone Lake. (Courtesy of Rocky Mount Museum.)

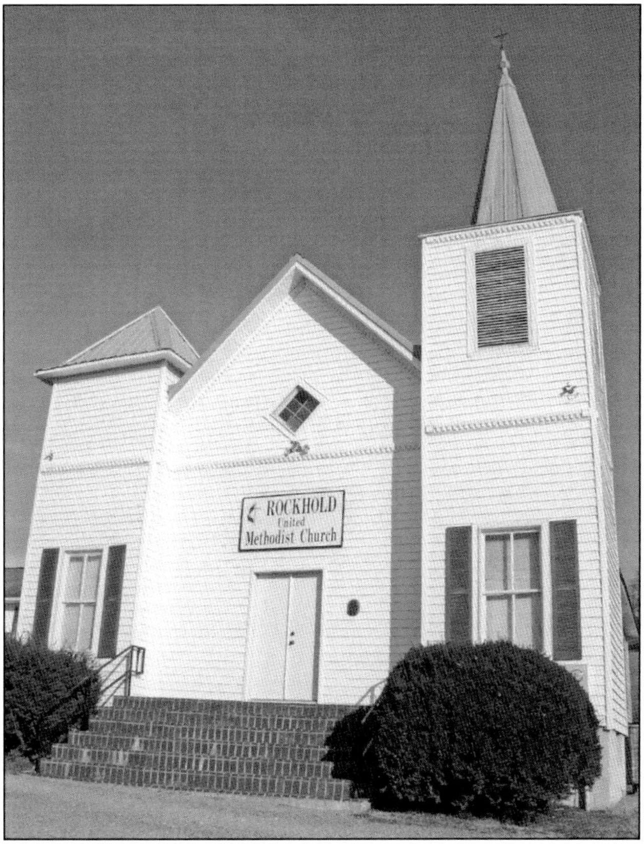

ROCKHOLD CHURCH. Methodist campground meetings have been held since the mid-1800s at the site of the Rockhold United Methodist Church, overlooking the South fork of the Holston River near Bluff City. This church took its name from plantation owner William Rockhold, a son-in-law of Richard Netherland, the owner of Kingsport's Netherland Inn. William Rockhold donated land to build this church. (Photograph by Joe Tennis.)

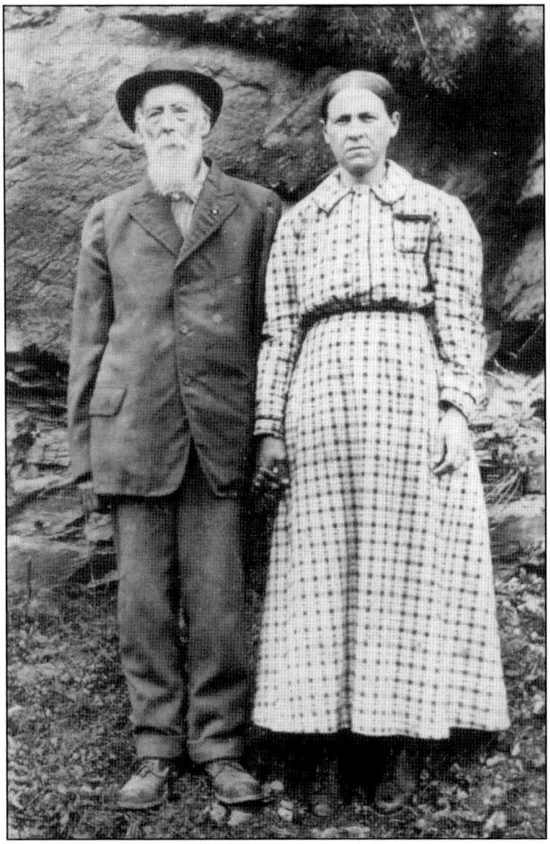

BUNKER HILL. Born in 1845, William Perry and his second wife, Nellie Goodman, stand near their home, about 1900, at Bunker Hill on the southeastern side of Sullivan County. The Bunker Hill community is located near Chinquapin Grove, which takes its name from the area's small, shrubby chinquapin trees. (Courtesy of Shelia Steele Hunt.)

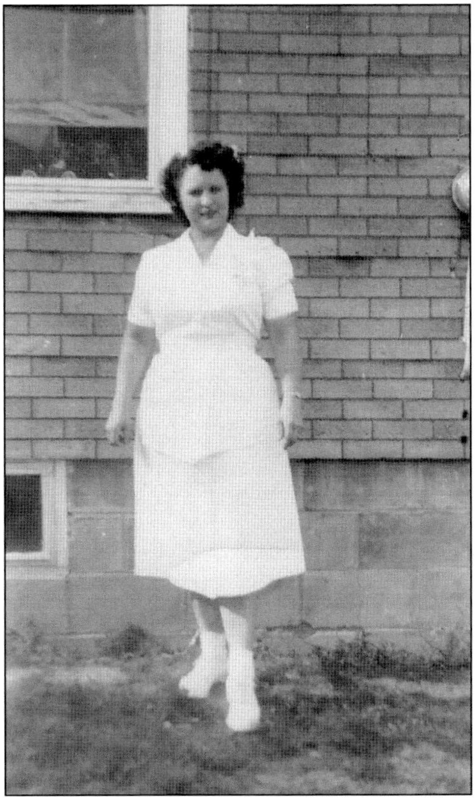

RIDGEWOOD. Grace Reynolds Proffitt (1917–2003) served barbecue for years at the Ridgewood, a restaurant in the Rock Hill community. A native of Easley, South Carolina, Proffitt opened the restaurant in 1948 with her husband, Jim, and named their business for the Ridgewood Inn of Daytona Beach, Florida. Once known as a roadhouse, the Ridgewood has since built a loyal following for its smoked pork. (Courtesy of Larry Proffitt.)

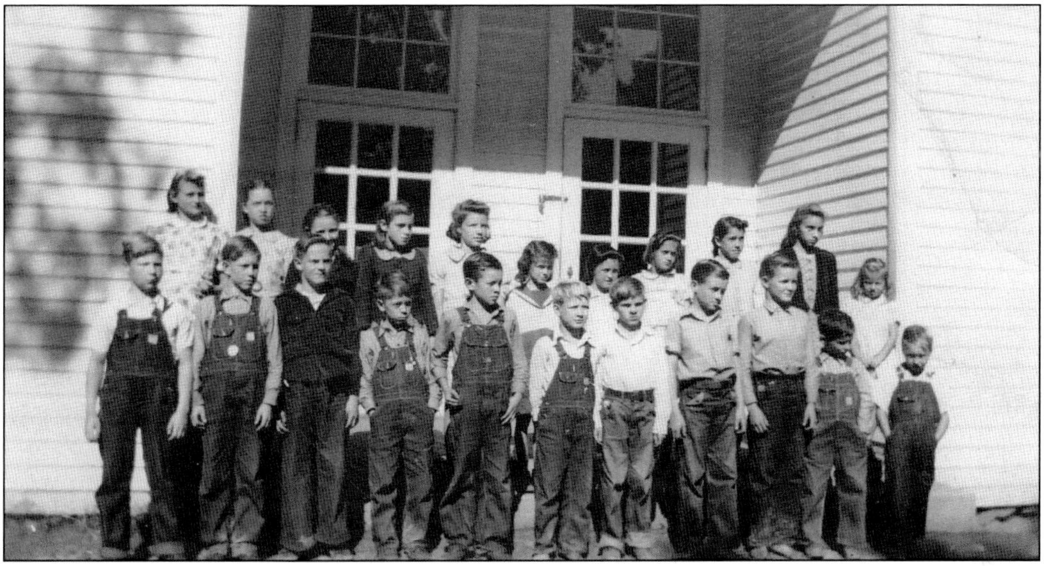

Friendship. In 1942, the honor roll pupils posed at the old Friendship School, a building that had to be relocated in 1950 after the creation of South Holston Lake. Jack Gross, standing in the middle of the front row, later operated Jack's Gross'ry along U.S. Highway 421 on Holston Mountain in the 1970s. (Courtesy of Jack Gross.)

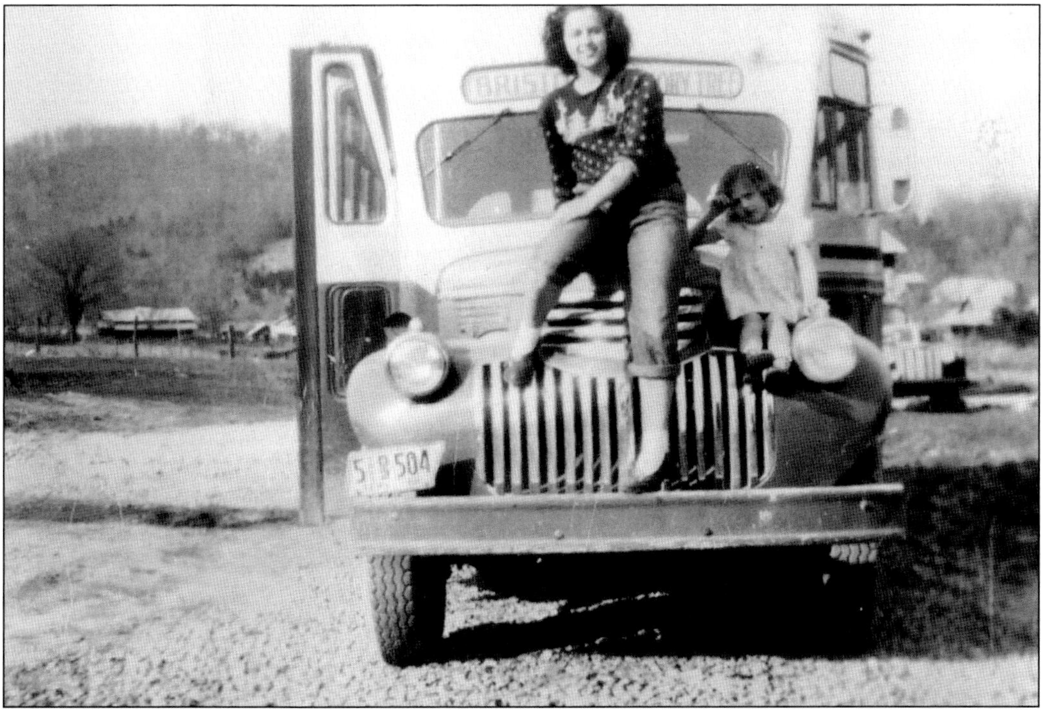

Hickory Tree. Betty Lou Hayes Nelson, left, and her baby sister, Carol Hayes Gouge, climb atop a bus belonging to their father, Dave Hayes, the operator of the Hickory Tree Bus Lines, in 1950. Betty Lou, in 1952, graduated Bluff City High School, where she was a cheerleader and was voted "Best Looking." Both Betty Lou and Carol later became schoolteachers. (Courtesy of Carol Gouge.)

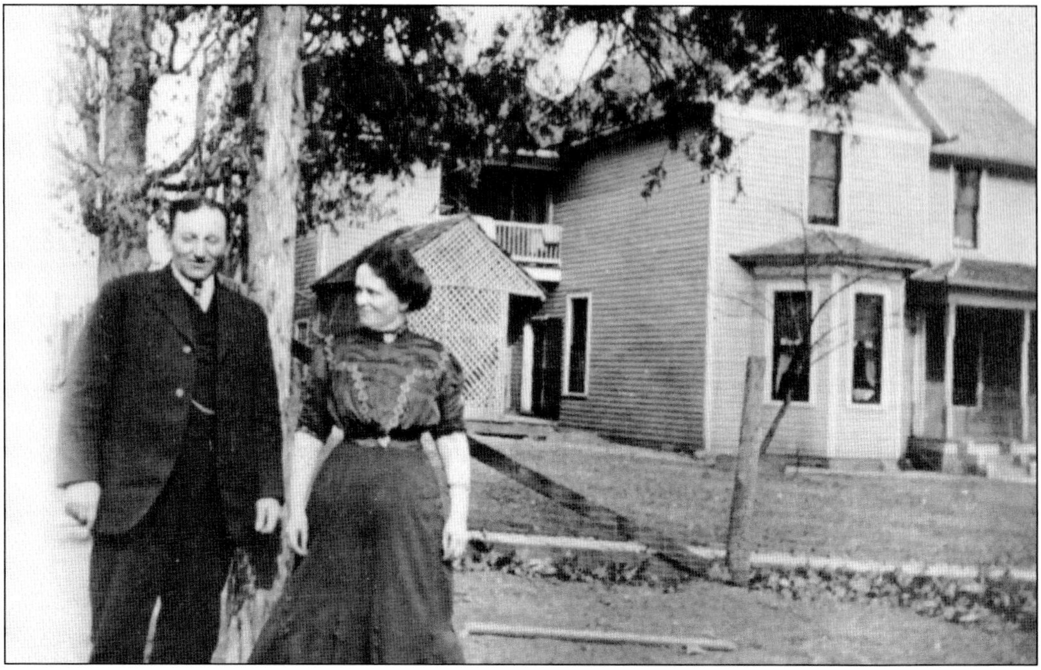

HOLSTON VALLEY. Dr. Charles Warren Fleenor Sr. (1870–1936) grew up in Benhams, Virginia, and married Josephine St. John, right, of Chilhowie, Virginia, in 1906. The couple lived at Forest Knoll Farm, a large home built in 1900 at the center of the Holston Valley community. In 1930, Dr. Fleenor established a nearby resort called Fleenora, now under the waters of South Holston Lake. (Courtesy of Mary Lou Fleenor.)

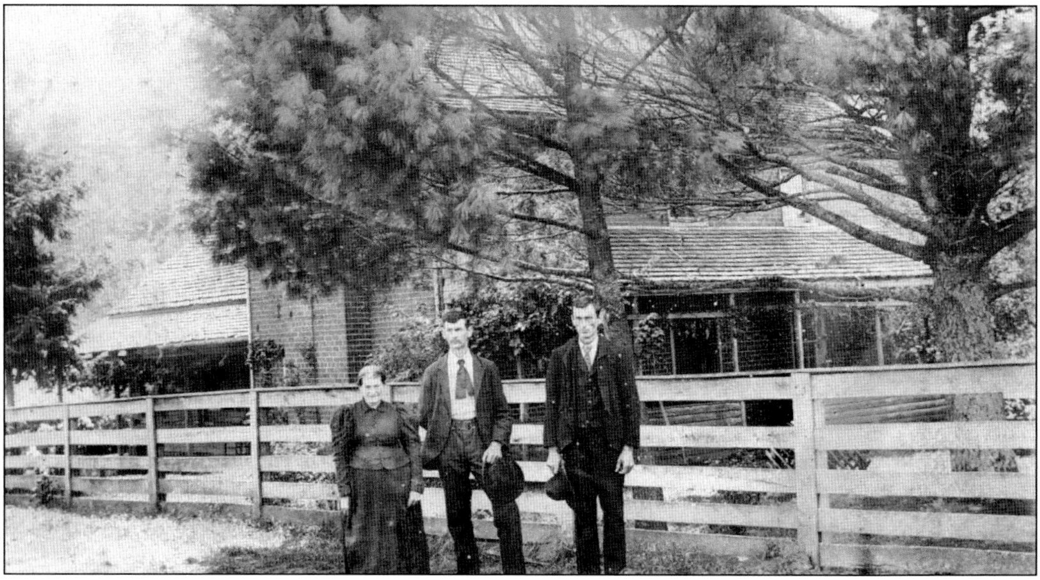

HOME ON THE BORDER. David O. King built this brick home in 1846 just three feet below the Virginia line. The house took its name, Painter Place, from Jonathan F. Painter, who also helped name nearby Painter Spring and Painter Creek. Jonathan's widow, Caroline, a daughter of David O. King, stands at left, about 1910, with her sons Phillip (center) and David. (Courtesy of Bud Phillips.)

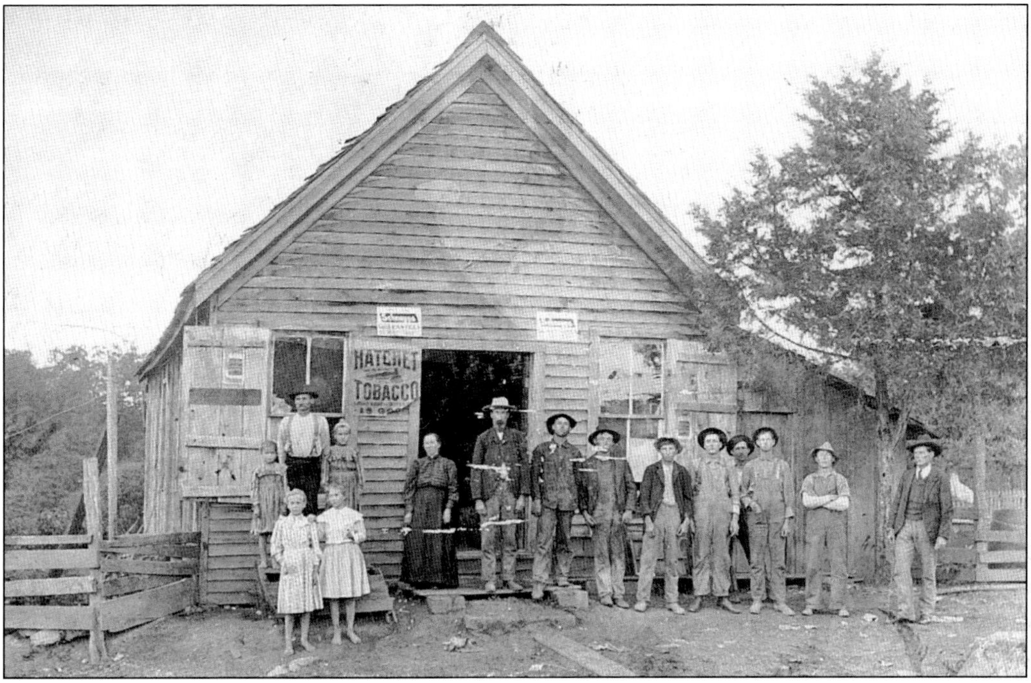

RUTHTON. For years, a local landmark of Ruthton was a general store that sold such products as Hatchet Tobacco. Standing at the door, right, is David K. Montgomery. Ruthton is located between Paperville and Emmett. (Courtesy of Shelia Steele Hunt.)

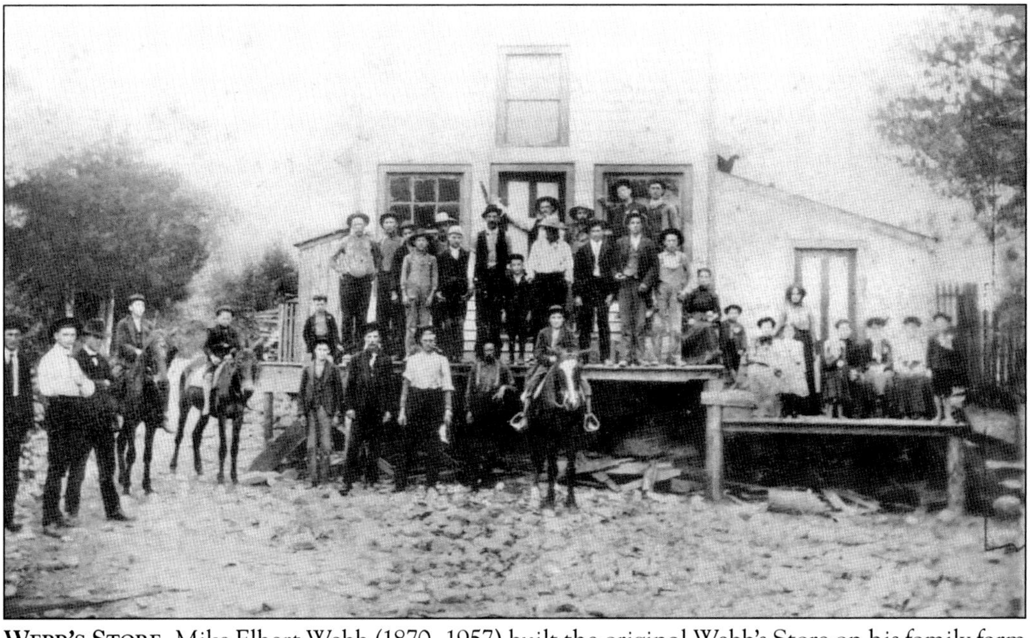

WEBB'S STORE. Mike Elbert Webb (1870–1957) built the original Webb's Store on his family farm in 1895 near what is now the corner of Hickory Tree and Possum Creek Roads. The mercantile became a stopping point for travelers between Bluff City and Hickory Tree. A newer Webb's Store, made of cinder blocks, was built in 1962 and remained in the Webb family until 1991. (Courtesy of Webb's Store.)

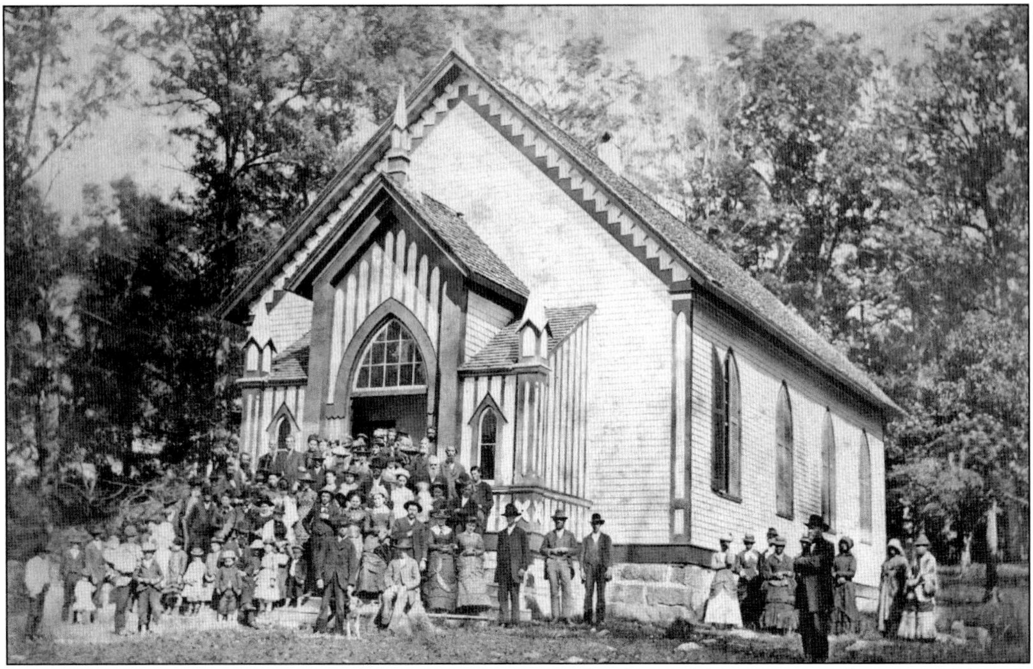

COLD SPRING. A group of worshippers gather outside the Cold Spring Presbyterian Church about 1885. This handsome church was built in 1880 at a cost of $1,012, replacing an earlier structure, built in 1841 at a cost of $333. The founder of King College, James King, served as the first minister at Cold Spring in 1841. (Courtesy of Bud Phillips.)

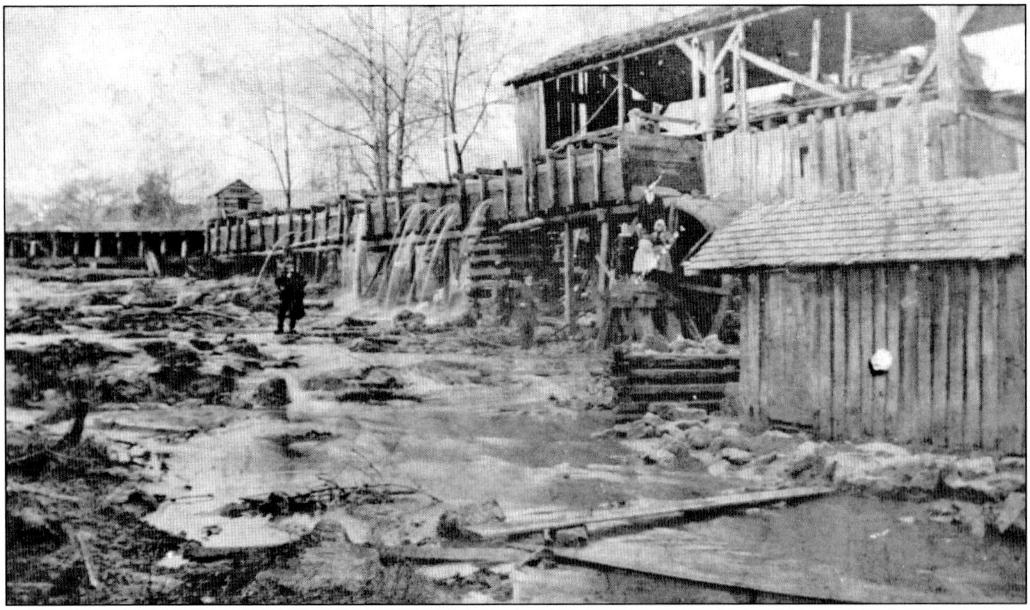

PAPERVILLE. Originally called Greenfield, Paperville took its name from a paper mill operated by George Burkhart on Sinking Creek in the mid-1800s. The community also became known for its Paperville Inn, built in the early 1800s by Alfred Hammer along a stagecoach route between Abingdon, Virginia, and Jonesborough, Tennessee. This photograph captures the sometimes-muddy nuances of running a sawmill at Paperville about 1900. (Courtesy of Shelia Steele Hunt.)

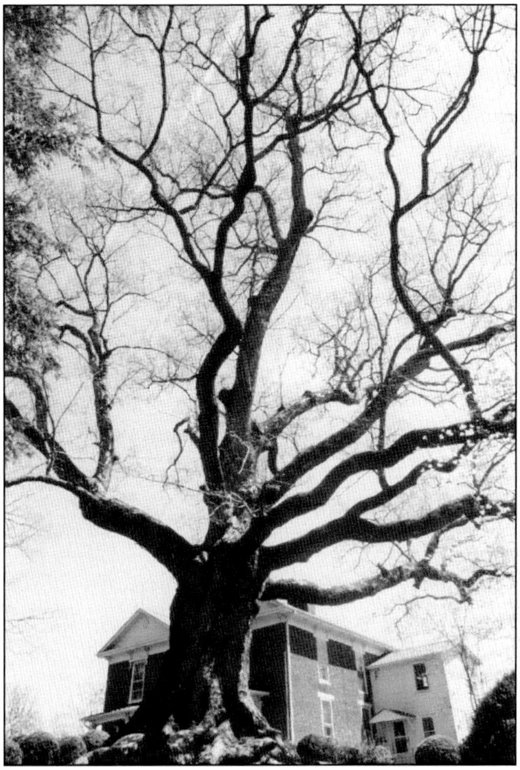

PEMBERTON OAK. Sullivan County's most famous tree, the Pemberton Oak, stood just outside the 19th-century Pemberton Mansion. Local tradition says Col. John Pemberton rallied troops at this spot on September 24, 1780, as men from Virginia and North Carolina (now Tennessee) marched to South Carolina to defeat British major Patrick Ferguson at the Battle of King's Mountain. (Courtesy of the *Bristol Herald Courier*; photograph by Toby Tobler.)

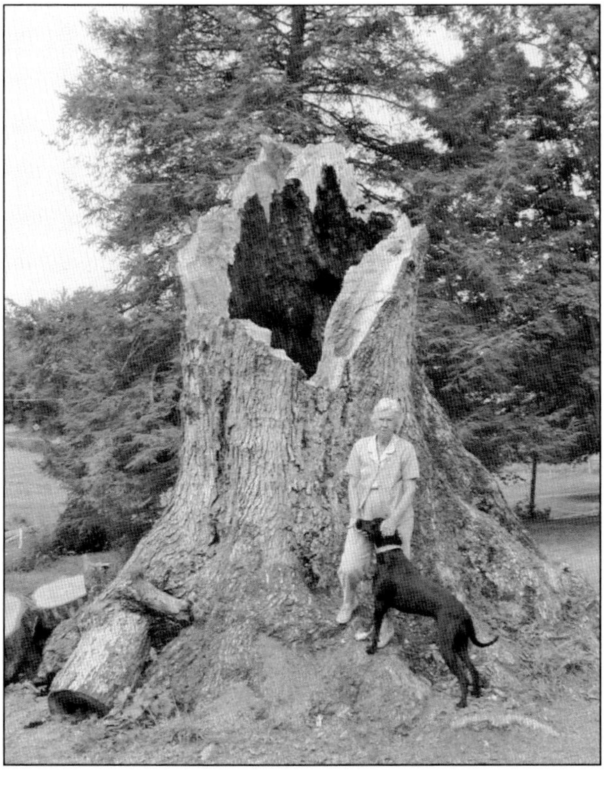

FALLEN TREE. The mighty Pemberton Oak reduced itself to a monstrous stump on August 1, 2002. Just a few days later, homeowner Sue Pemberton Vaughan stood with her newly adopted puppy in front of the fallen landmark as limbs stretched all across her lawn. Experts at the time estimated the tree to be as much as 500 years old. (Courtesy of the *Bristol Herald Courier*; photograph by Joe Tennis.)

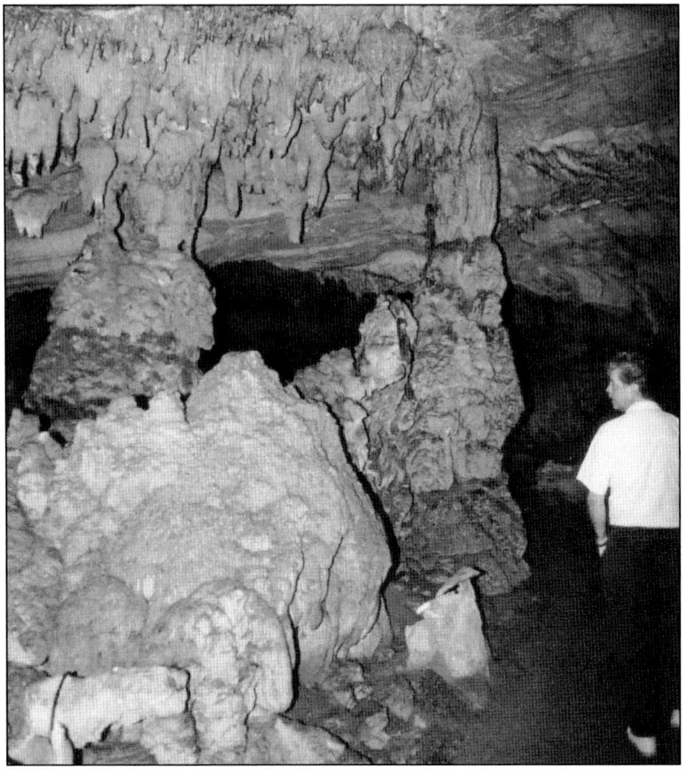

APPALACHIAN CAVERNS. Once known as the "Linville Cave" for a pair of Linville brothers, the Appalachian Caverns stretch for miles beneath the center of Sullivan County, with ceilings standing as high as 135 feet tall. In 1991, early caverns promoter Bob Joyner, far right, led a tour about a month before the attraction opened to the public. (Courtesy of the *Bristol Herald Courier*; photograph by Toby Tobler.)

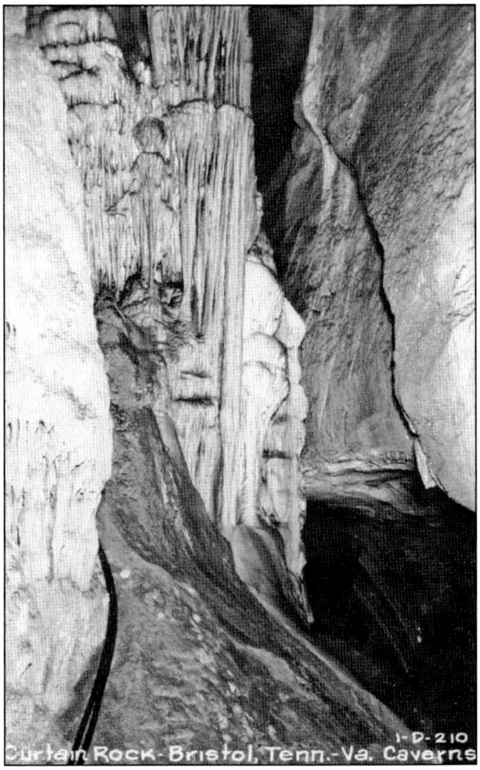

CURTAIN ROCK. A drapery-shaped formation, once called "Curtain Rock," showed up on this 1950s postcard promoting the Bristol Caverns. This tourist attraction, developed in the 1930s, was once known as "Bishop's Cave," a name alluding to the love-triangle tragedy of Betty Bishop, whose dead body was found inside a cave opening. (Courtesy of Shelby Edwards.)

BRIDAL VEIL FALLS. A subterranean room overlooks Bridal Veil Falls, a waterfall-style formation in Bristol Caverns. This room has been used for several weddings. In turn, Bridal Veil Falls has shown up on T-shirts promoting the attraction, located about halfway between Bristol Motor Speedway and South Holston Dam. Formations like this are believed to be more than 200 million years old. (Courtesy of Shelby Edwards.)

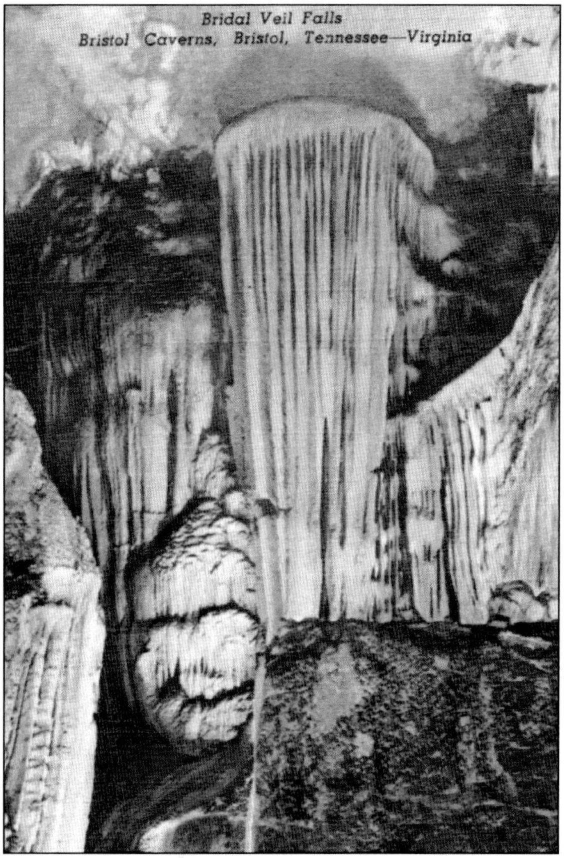

BRISTOL CAVERNS. A group of schoolchildren visiting Bristol Caverns in 1959 stop at the well-known Indian Head landmark sign to show off various souvenirs, including a corncob pipe and tiny Confederate flags. Bristol Caverns always makes a great refuge during the heat of summer. Temperatures inside the caverns stay about 57 degrees year-round. (Courtesy of Bristol Caverns.)

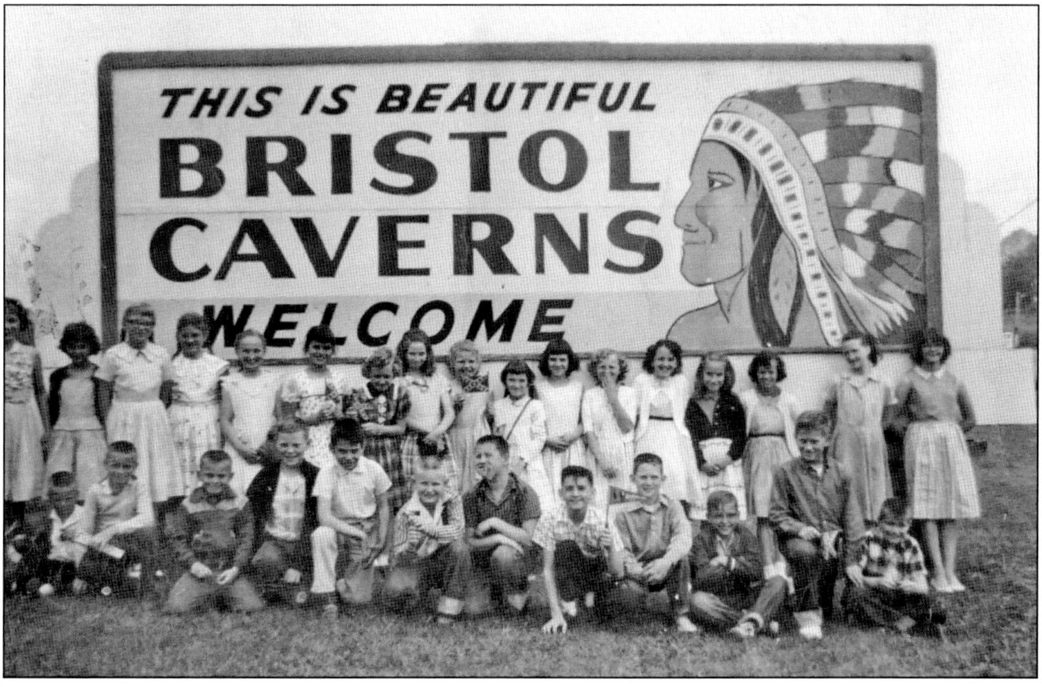

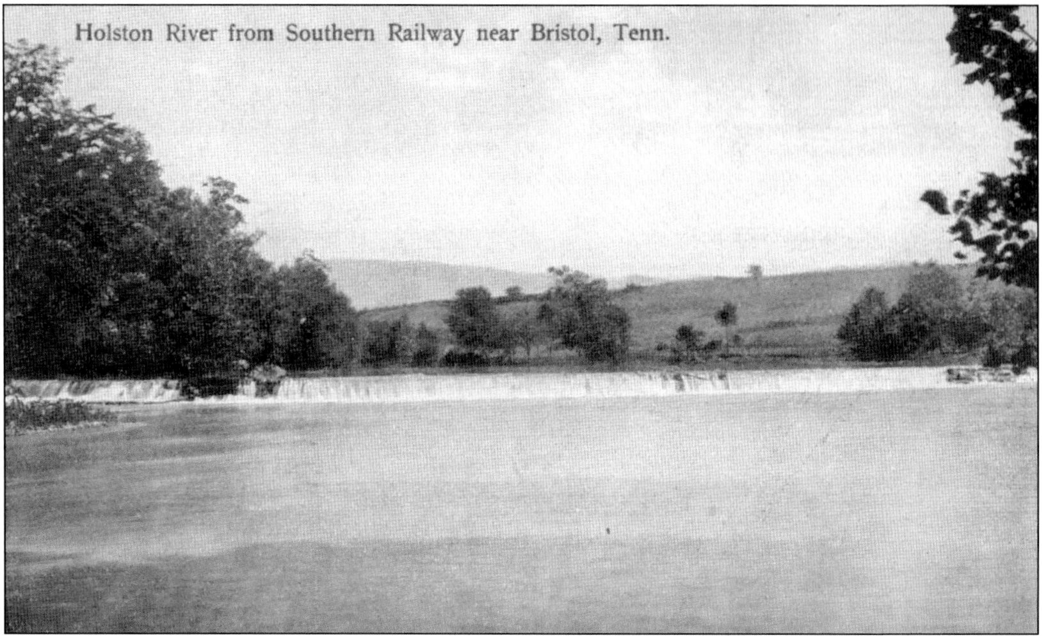

HOLSTON MOUNTAIN AND THE RIVER. The South fork of the Holston River provided the inspiration for many postcard scenes of Sullivan County in the early 1900s. The International Post Card Company of New York published the above view. Below, a dusting of snow covers Holston Mountain in a view from the county's east side, where Holston Mountain looms above neighborhoods like Riverside, Emmett, and what is now South Holston Lake. (Both courtesy of Shelby Edwards.)

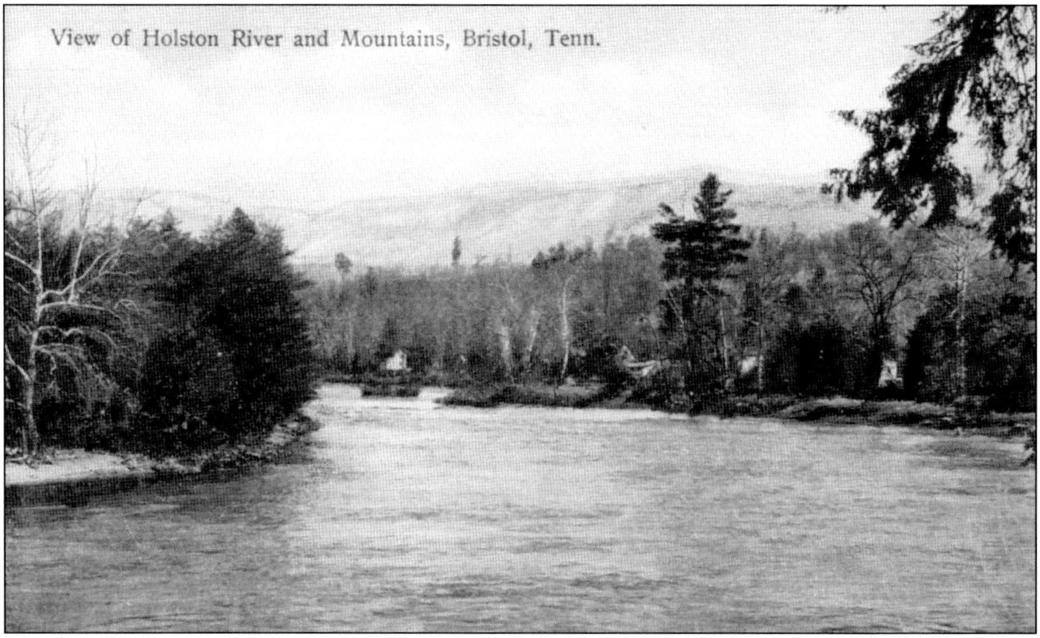

Seven

Cherokee National Forest

Marching north from Springer Mountain, Georgia, the Appalachian Trail cuts across the Great Smoky Mountains and edges along the North Carolina–Tennessee border.

Then the famous footpath winds its way into Sullivan County. The trail largely follows the spine of Holston Mountain, a hump standing 4,000 feet above sea level on the county's eastern skyline. Mile after mile, the Appalachian Trail teeter-totters atop this mountain and straddles the Sullivan County border shared by Carter and Johnson Counties. Along the way, the Appalachian Trail provides access to the vast Cherokee National Forest.

Named for the Cherokees who once inhabited the Appalachian Mountains, the forest encompasses thousands of acres timbered in the early 1900s by operations like the Willie Boom Lumber Company. In these remote woods, tiny trains once loaded logs. More timber rolled down the South fork of the Holston River.

Over time, train lines evolved into logging roads, which, in turn, now double as trails, cutting swaths across the forest's sanctuary for deer, bear, and wild turkey. Motorists, too, can cut through this wilderness on U.S. Highway 421, which crosses Holston Mountain between Shady Valley and South Holston Lake.

Lined with crushed gravel, the Flatwoods Auto Tour cuts south from U.S. 421 and provides another view. This remote road snakes its way between South Holston Lake and the base of Holston Mountain. Ultimately, it leads to the Little Oak Recreation Area, reaching out to South Holston Lake with a campground, trails, and a boat ramp. Along the way, more footpaths weave into the woods, providing access to trout hangouts and somewhat-secret shorelines.

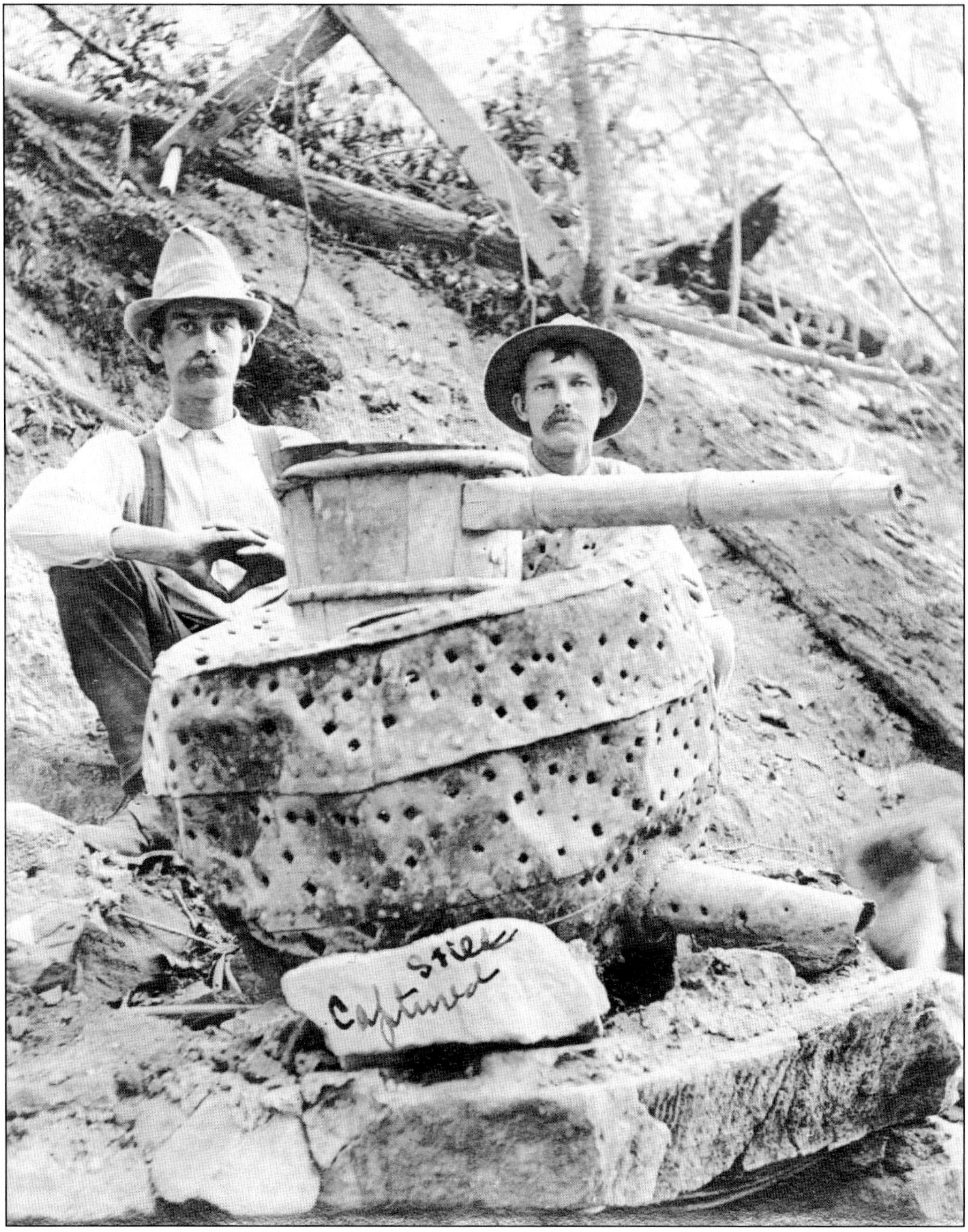

TENNESSEE MOONSHINE. No tale of the Tennessee mountains would be complete without a jug of the original "mountain dew," and moonshine stories are quite common in the Holston Mountain range of the Cherokee National Forest. Making moonshine often helped keep families fed when crops fell flat or a local sawmill shut down. In this *c.* 1920 photograph, a couple of men, possibly sheriff's deputies or revenue agents, pose by a captured moonshine still believed to have been taken from the vicinity of what is now the Cherokee National Forest near Sharps Creek. Notice the still has been riddled with dozens of bullets. (Courtesy of Bud Phillips.)

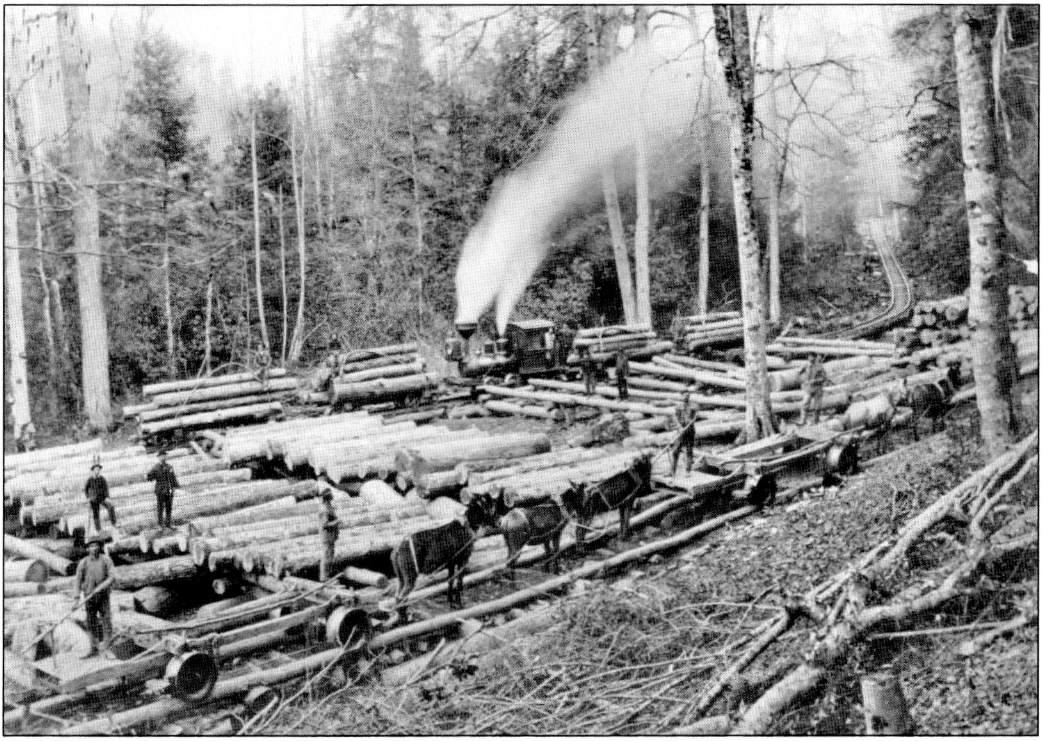

LOGGING AT FISH DAM. Soon after the completion of a railroad to Bristol in the 1890s, a series of timber trains hauled virgin timber off the sides of Holston Mountain at Fish Dam. This area, adjoining the Cherokee National Forest, was flooded in 1950 with the creation of South Holston Lake. (Courtesy of James Thomas.)

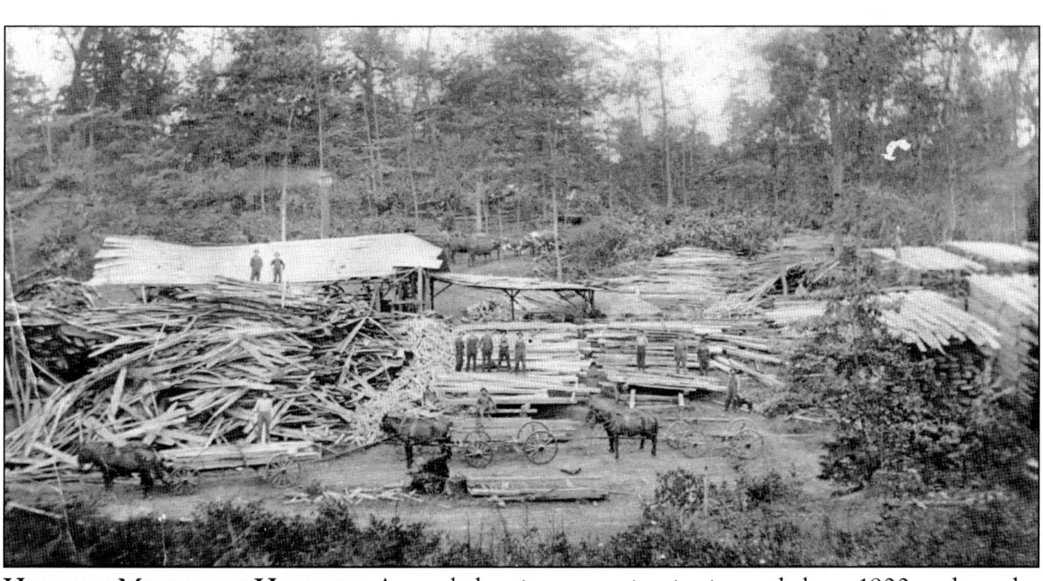

HOLSTON MOUNTAIN HARVEST. An early logging operation is pictured about 1900 to show the extensive lumber available on Holston Mountain. Notice the horse-drawn wagons used to pull logs out of such huge harvests. (Courtesy of Bud Phillips.)

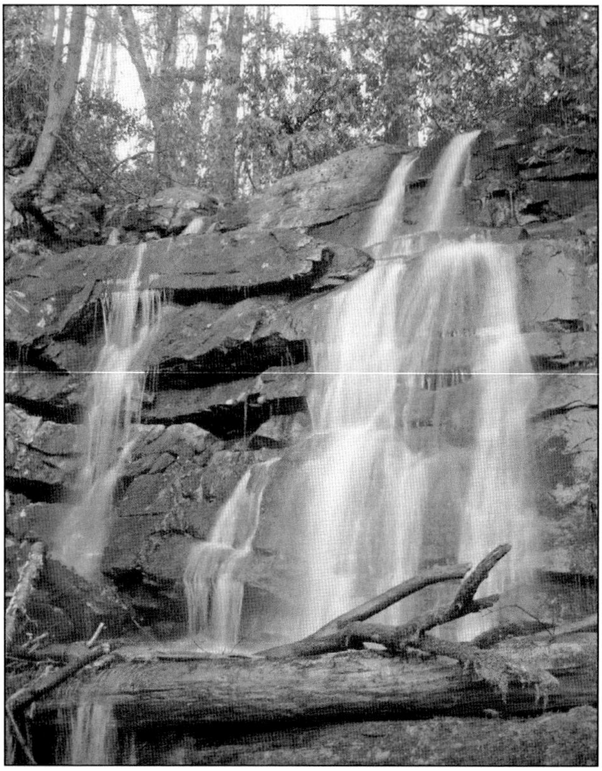

Sulphur Springs Falls. The little-known falls of the Sulphur Springs Branch (left) take a tumble of about 25 feet on Holston Mountain. The branch then drops again, over a ledge of nearly 10 feet, (below) to form a broken but beautiful cascade in Sullivan County's portion of the Cherokee National Forest. No formal trail leads to this hard-to-find jewel, tucked into a landscape lushly lined with fallen logs, mossy rocks, and rhododendron. But the waterfall can be reached through an off-trail hike following the creek bed and by finding passage around tree limbs and rock slides. From this waterfall, Sulphur Springs Branch courses down Holston Mountain for another two miles before finally emptying into South Holston Lake. (Photographs by Joe Tennis.)

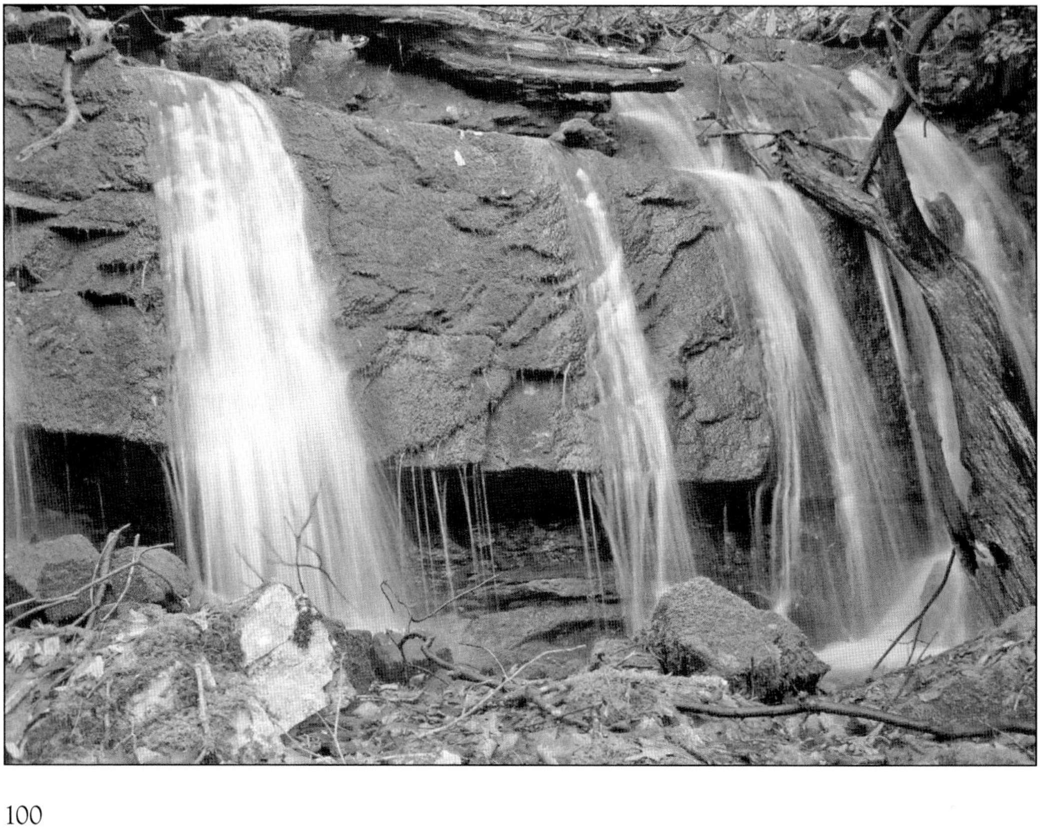

Eight

South Holston Lake

Before the 1940s, the Holston River was wild—a breeding ground for trout, which leapt up the rapids of the South fork beside sandbars and tiny islands, cutting past little homes and farms. Those trout disappeared into webs of ice-cold creeks, reaching deep into a maze of mountains.

Then came the Tennessee Valley Authority (TVA). To prevent flooding and to produce electricity, the South fork of the Holston River landed on the TVA's to-be-tamed list by 1941. That year, just before Christmas, TVA officials moved into downtown Bristol and set up offices at the First National Bank. Officials then began work on what was called Big Creek Dam. Along the way, TVA announced that the community of Big Creek would disappear into the depths of its future lake once a giant dam was thrown across the river near the mouth of Riddle Creek.

Work began on the dam in 1942. About 300 families in Tennessee had to be moved, and cemeteries were relocated.

By the time the reservoir was complete in 1950, Sullivan County's Friendship community watched its school site be swallowed by water. A nearby place, Fish Dam, was simply wiped off the map. The lake also took Rooty Branch, a place named for the proximity of a tree branch that was practically nothing but roots.

In later years, the county gained Observation Knob Park, plus boat ramps, marinas, and even the legends told in William Hill's *Dawn of the Vampire*, a horror novel with a plot set on South Holston Lake.

Creating this new lake also inspired a series of postcards in the 1950s. One bragged that South Holston Lake was "one of the newest and most beautiful of the TVA lakes." Another called the lake "a veritable paradise for fishermen, boat enthusiasts, and other water-sport loving visitors."

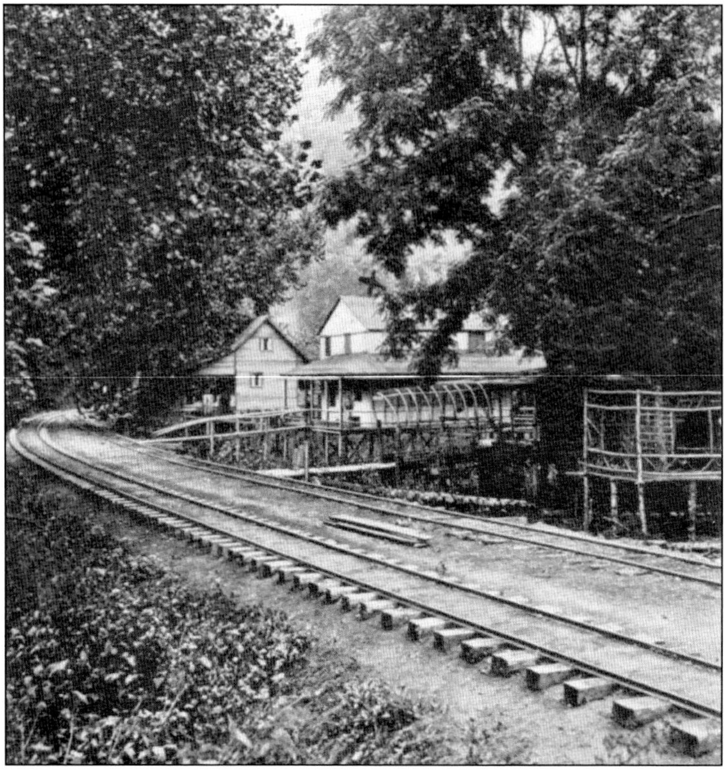

RESORT COMMUNITY. A 1906 penny postcard shows railroad tracks leading to Big Creek, a resort community where visitors would splash in cool mountain streams. Many years later, work on what was once called "Big Creek Dam" in 1942 employed 1,200 people working three shifts, day and night, to make way for the South Holston Reservoir at this site. (Courtesy of Tim Buchanan.)

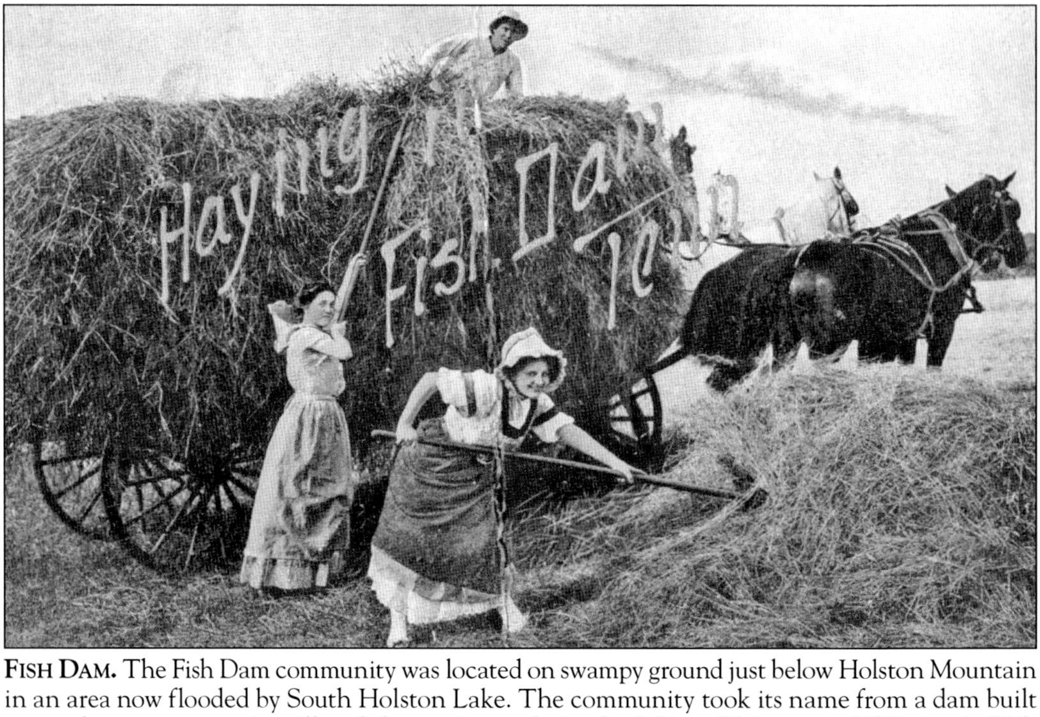

FISH DAM. The Fish Dam community was located on swampy ground just below Holston Mountain in an area now flooded by South Holston Lake. The community took its name from a dam built to supply water to a grain mill and the area's popularity for fishing. This comical "Haying in Fish Dam, Tenn." postcard dates to about 1909. (Courtesy of Shelby Edwards.)

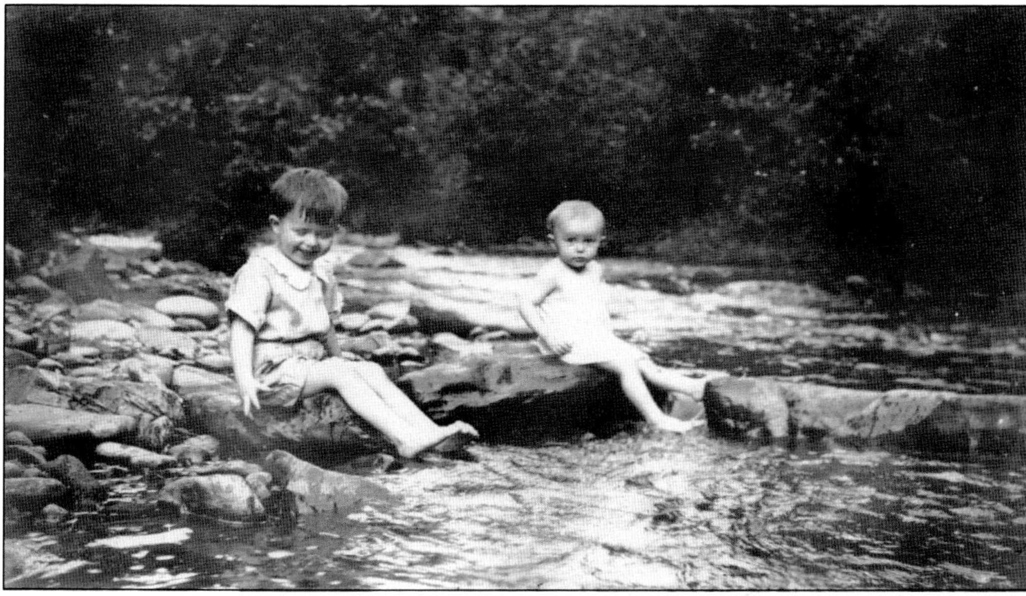

BIG CREEK. Siblings Richard "Dick" Burk, left, and Joyce Burk Slagle dip their toes in the water of Big Creek in September 1931. Dick later became a teacher at Bristol Tennessee High School, and Joyce helped operate Lake View Dock with her husband, Joe. The place where this photograph was made, however, would become lost at the bottom of South Holston Lake. (Courtesy of John and Julie Slagle.)

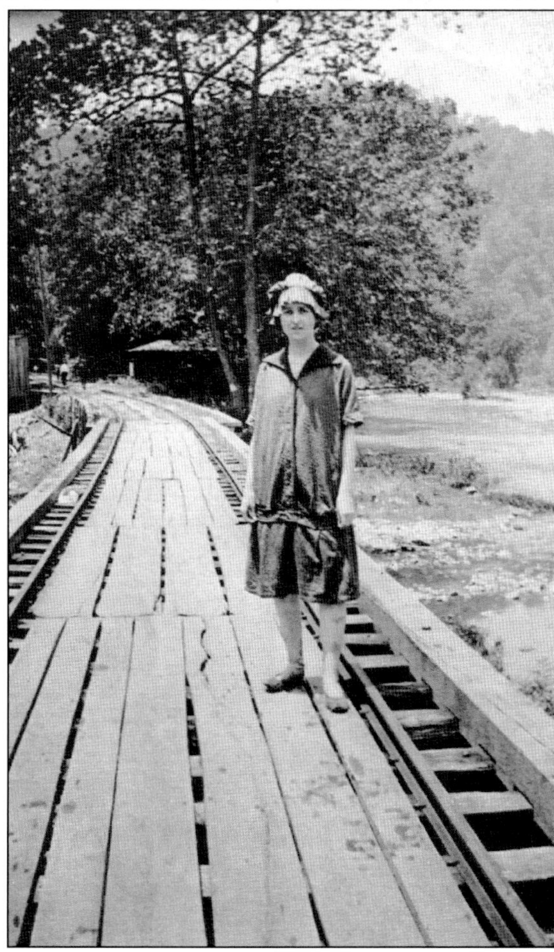

ON THE TRACKS. Bertha Tomlinson Faivre, known as "Aunt Burrie," stands in her bathing suit on the railroad tracks near Big Creek about 1916. This area near Holston Mountain was once known for its swimming hole and fishing spot at Buffalo Rock. But, in 1941, Tennessee Valley Authority officials announced that Big Creek would be flooded forever. (Courtesy of John and Julie Slagle.)

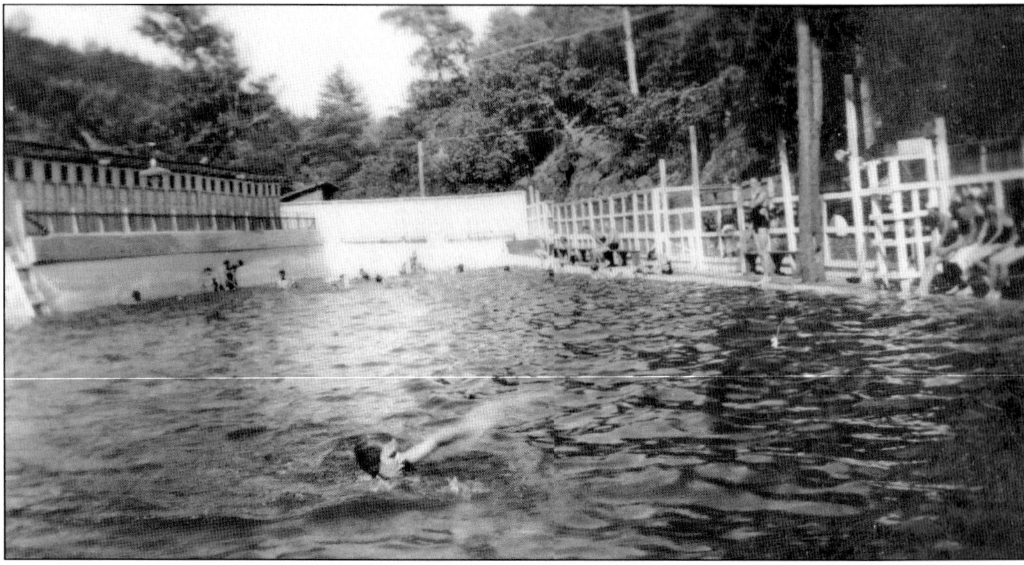

FLEENORA PARK. Dr. Charles Warren Fleenor Sr. established Fleenora Park in 1930 with resort cabins along Jacob Creek. Water to fill the park's 120-foot-long swimming pool came from a mountain stream, and football players from local high schools served as the pool's lifeguards. Dances were held at a pavilion, and ice was kept in sawdust at a hillside dugout. Dr. Fleenor's son, Warren, sold advertisements on the dressing room walls behind the pool by calling on various Bristol businesses, including Goode Motor Company, Live and Let Live Shoe Shop, Twin City Welding Company, Bunting's Drug Store, and the Gen. Shelby Garage. The Fleenors sold the property in 1938, and in 1950, the park was lost beneath the waters of South Holston Lake at Jacob Creek, a stream named for a pioneer settler, Jacob Thomas. (Courtesy of Mary Lou Fleenor.)

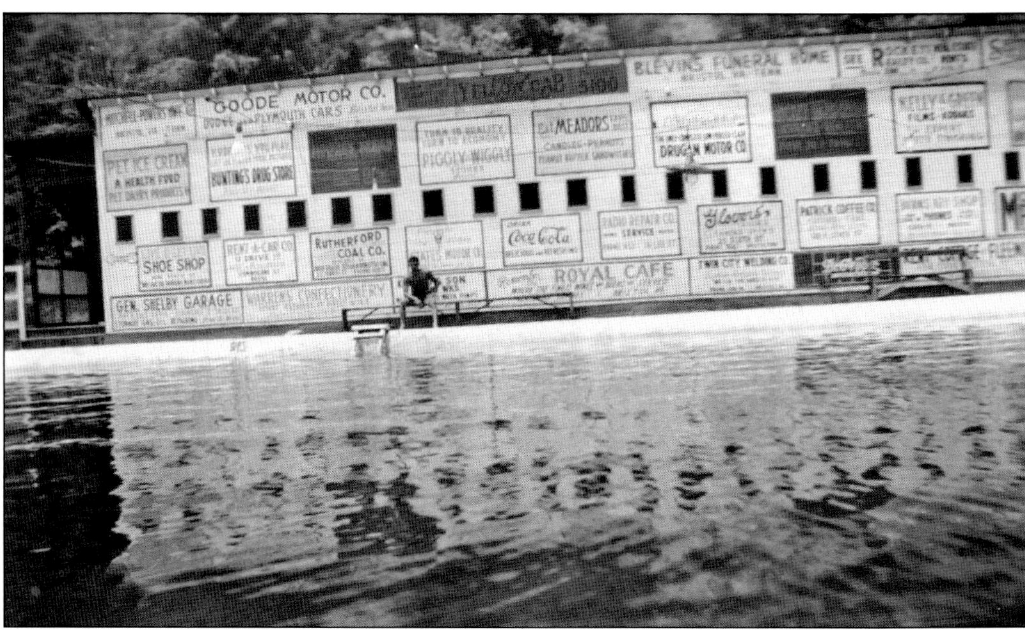

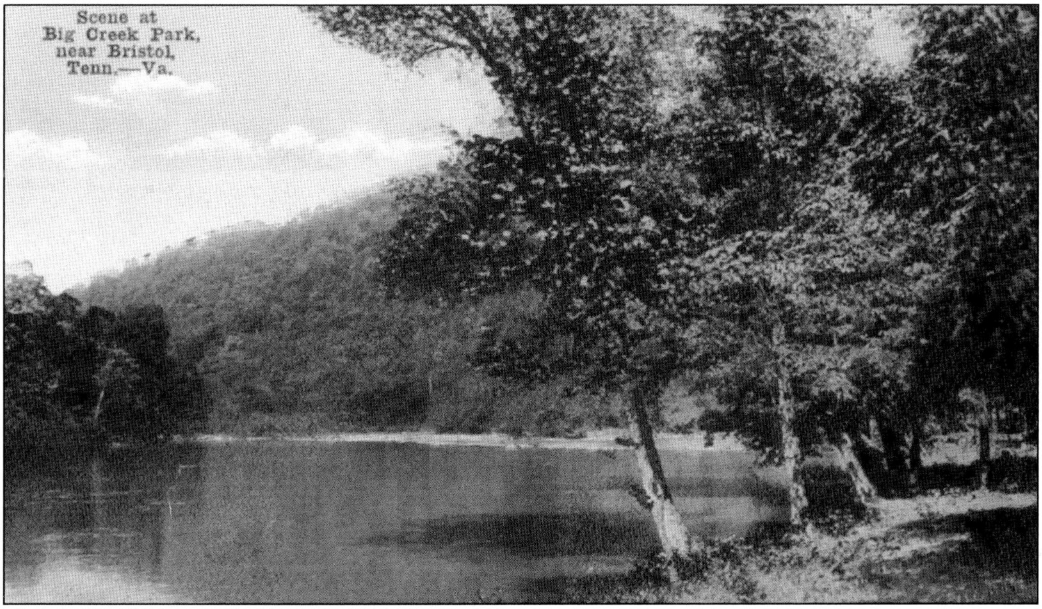

BIG CREEK PARK. By 1904, the Holston Valley Railroad Company regularly transported passengers to Big Creek, where people vacationed in summer cottages in the shadow of Holston Mountain. Known by many for its moonshine operations, the remote community found fame in 1930 when it became the setting for Anne W. Armstrong's novel *This Day and Time*, which included character depictions of real-life Big Creek residents, including "Big" Dave Boling, the operator of a general store, and Rosy Duncan as the novel's heroine. Along the way, the community's Big Creek Park appeared on a series of postcards in the early 1900s, displaying railroad tracks running along the mountainside creek. (Courtesy of Shelby Edwards.)

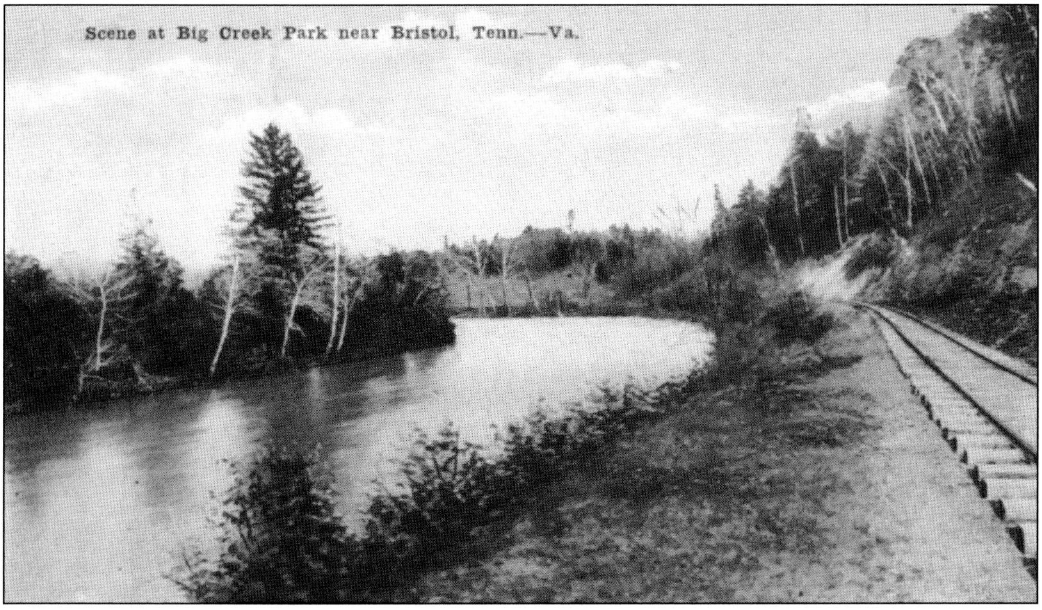

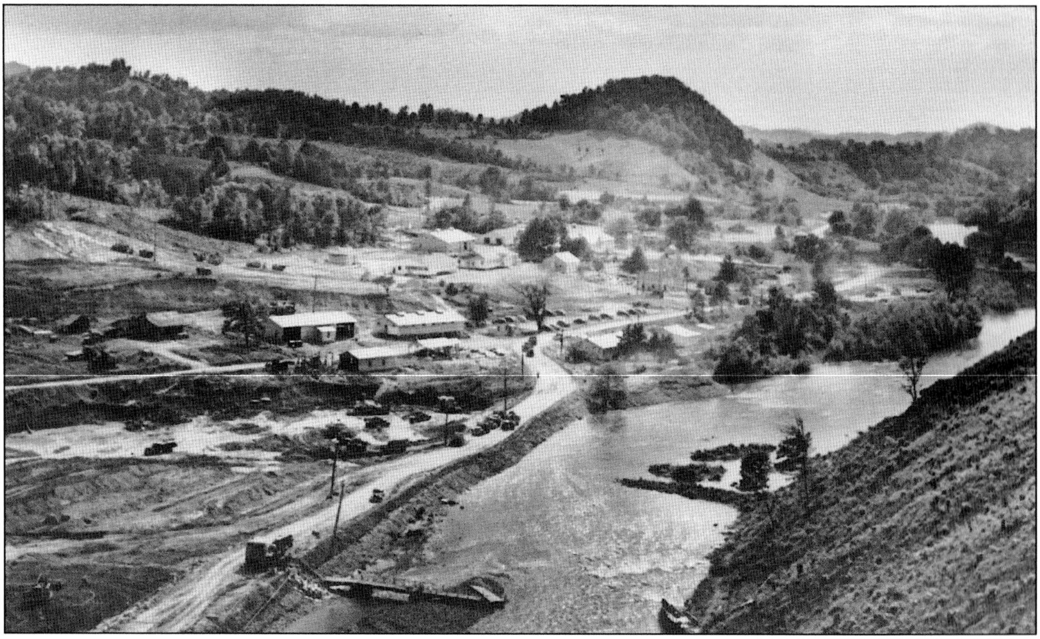

Early Construction. This 1940s view shows continuing construction at the South Holston Dam site, looking downstream toward Emmett and Osceola Island. In this remote country, killing snakes in the 1940s became an everyday occurrence as hillsides were leveled. One crew, while building a tunnel to divert the flow of the river, reportedly killed a nest of 23 copperheads. (Courtesy of John and Julie Slagle.)

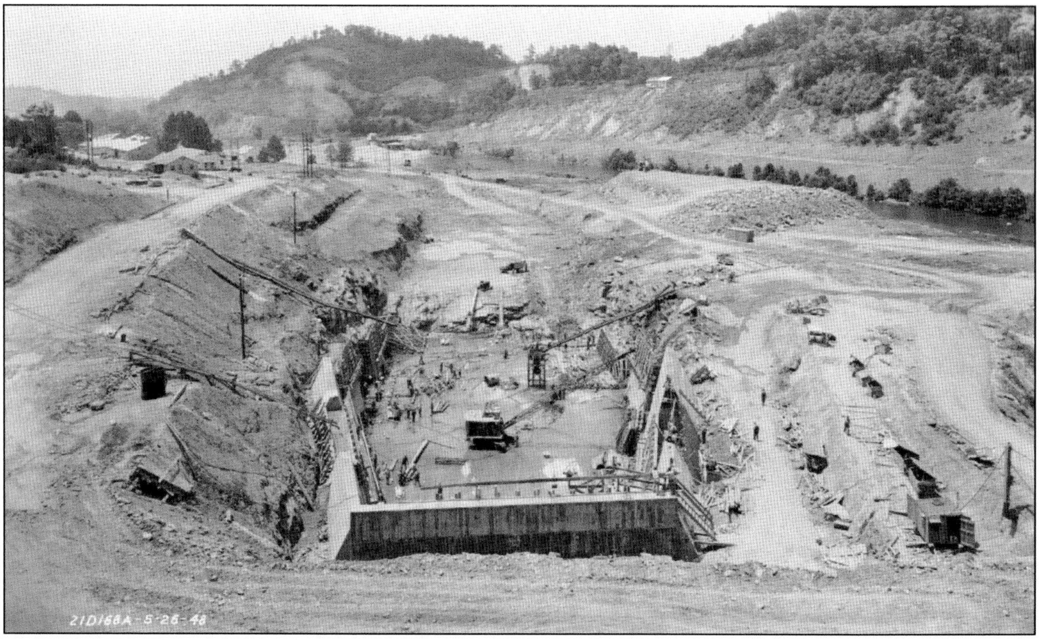

Building the Dam. Work on South Holston Dam was suspended after 1942 because of the effort of World War II. When construction began again in 1947, the work site formed a small community—with dormitories, a post office, a recreation room, and a cafeteria. This May 1948 photograph shows ongoing construction of the dam. (Courtesy of the National Archives.)

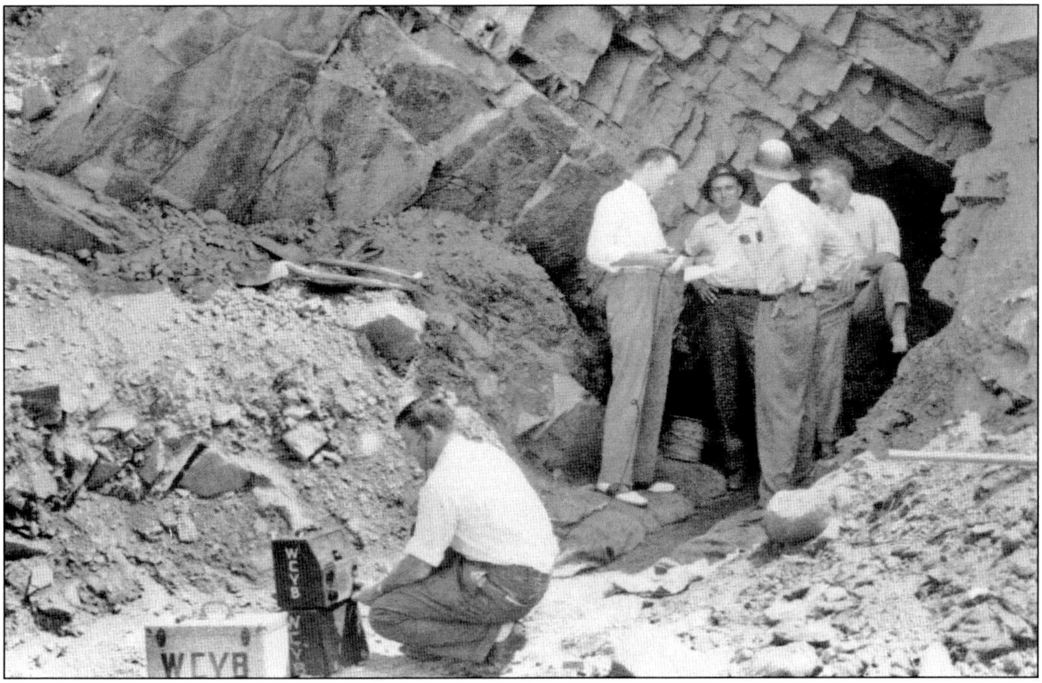

BIG NEWS. Bomb shelters were built for reporters and photographers at the construction site of South Holston Dam. Here a news reporter from WCYB in Bristol discusses the dam-building process with construction officials. (Courtesy of John and Julie Slagle.)

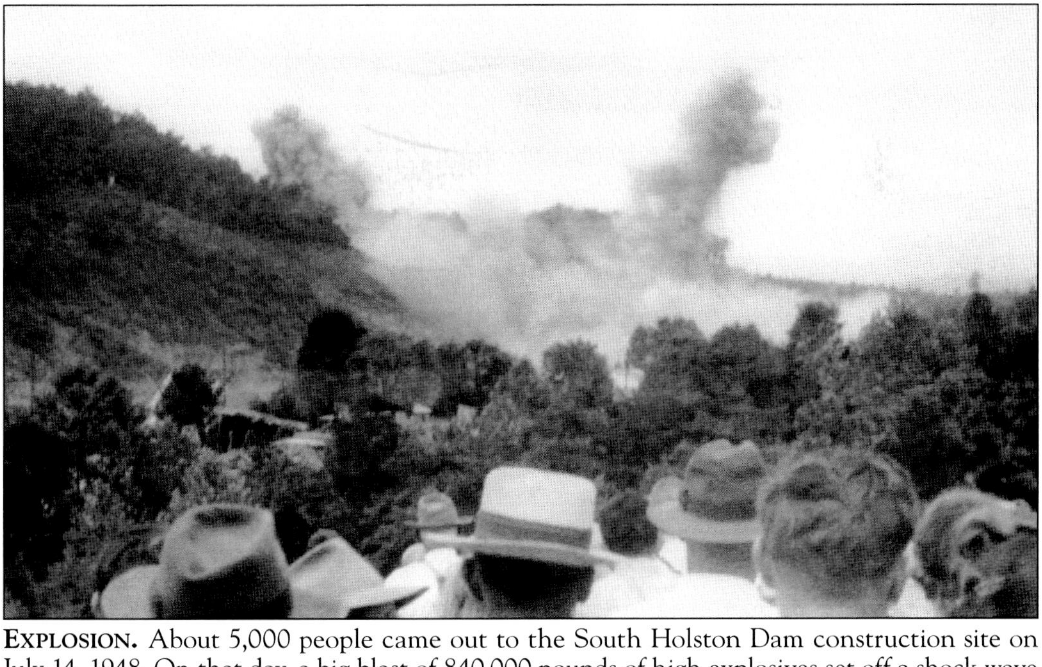

EXPLOSION. About 5,000 people came out to the South Holston Dam construction site on July 14, 1948. On that day, a big blast of 840,000 pounds of high explosives set off a shock wave similar to an earthquake. The explosion, in turn, provided rock fill to build the dam. The following February, another blast shook houses from Abingdon, Virginia, to Johnson City, Tennessee. (Courtesy of John and Julie Slagle.)

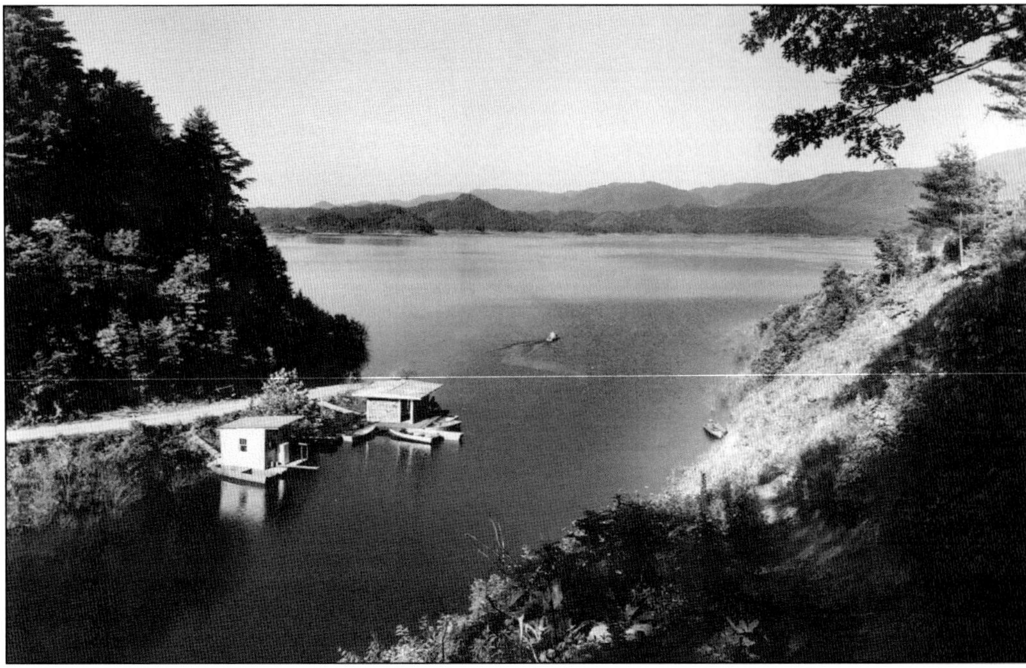

NEW LAKE. Soon after the new South Holston Lake began to reach full pool in 1951, early marina operations began, including Lake View Dock, shown here with rowboats ready to stroke the surface of the placid waters. By 2008, this scene was almost unrecognizable because Lake View had been extensively developed with covered slips and floating piers. (Courtesy of Gary Rose.)

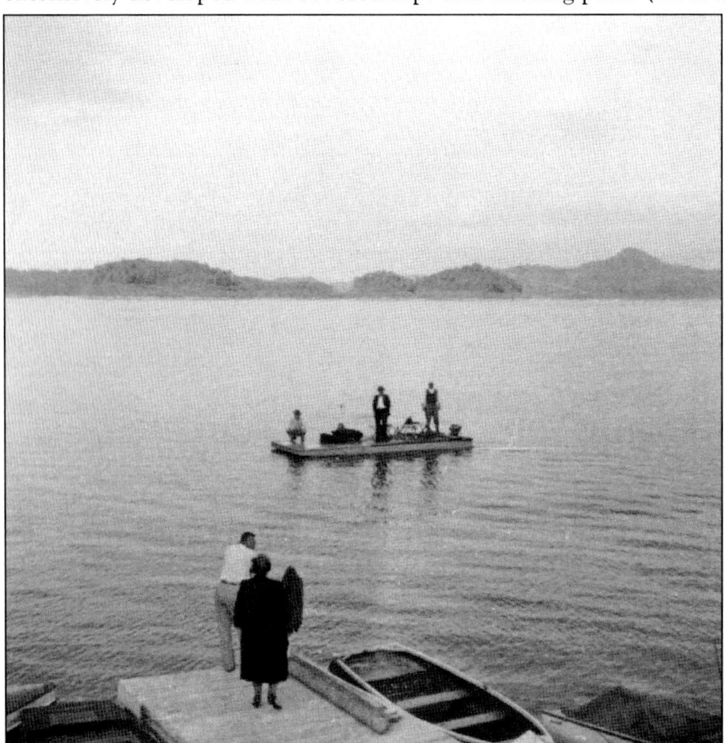

PREHISTORIC PONTOON. Some well-dressed boaters take off on South Holston Lake on a prehistoric pontoon in 1951, a scene that could hardly be duplicated amid today's wakes of personal watercraft on South Holston Lake. Notice the natural landmark of Grandfather Knob, the curvy mountain in the back right corner. (Courtesy of John and Julie Slagle.)

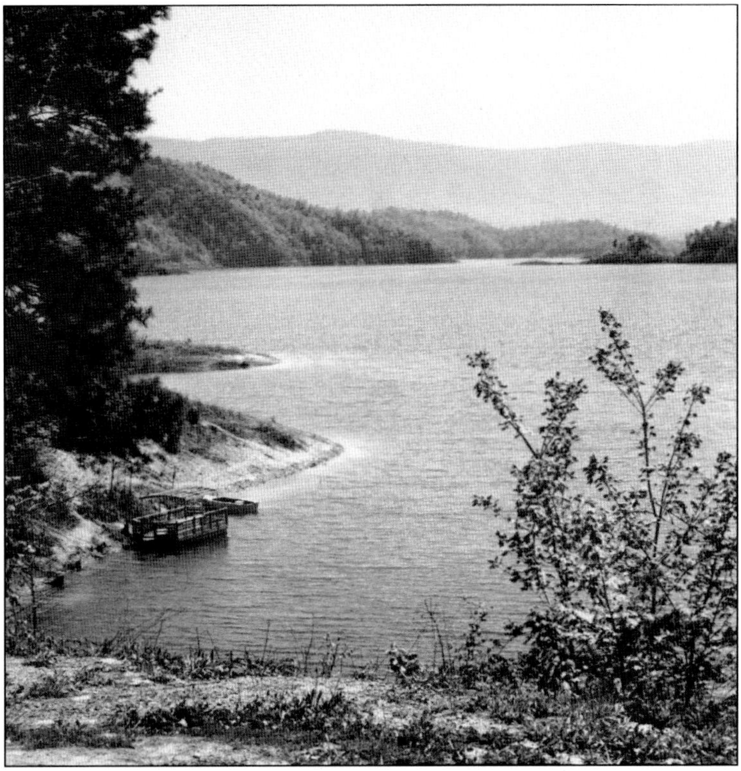

HIGHWAY 421 RAMP AREA. A 1950s-era photograph shows the site of the U.S. Highway 421 launching area before it was paved and became the most popular access for boats with trailers on South Holston Lake. A wooden pontoon lies on the shoreline at lower left. (Courtesy of Bud Phillips.)

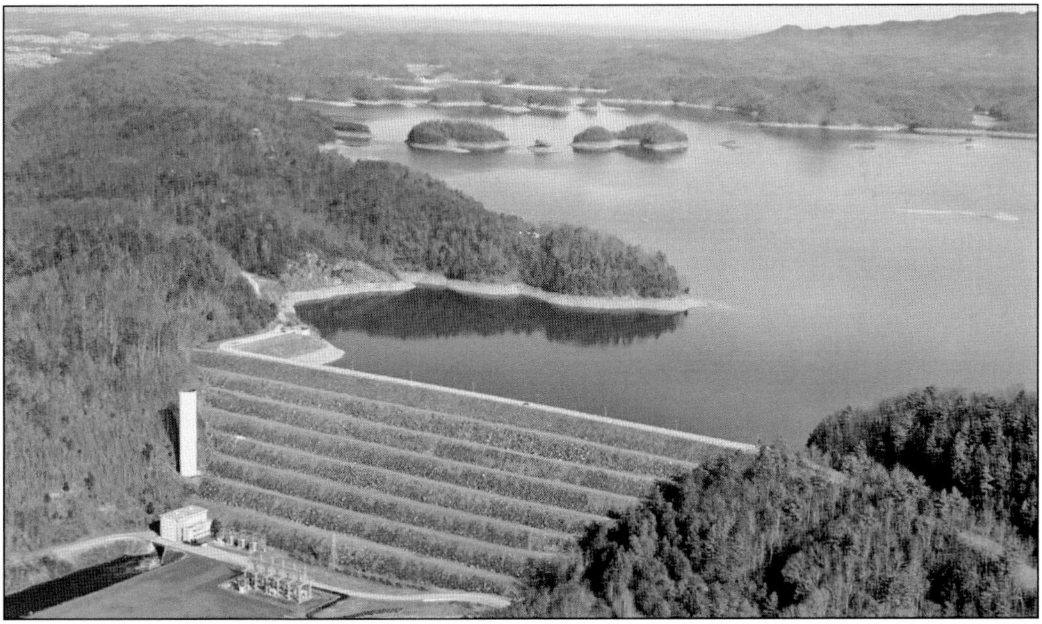

TAKEN FROM THE TOP. Spanning into both Tennessee and Virginia with 7,580 acres at full pool, South Holston Lake forms the largest body of water in Sullivan County. A chain of islands dots this mile-wide reservoir between The Knobs, on the left, and the shoreline of the Cherokee National Forest, right, at the Little Oak Recreation Area. A roadway, center, leads across the top of the dam. (Photograph by Bill McKee.)

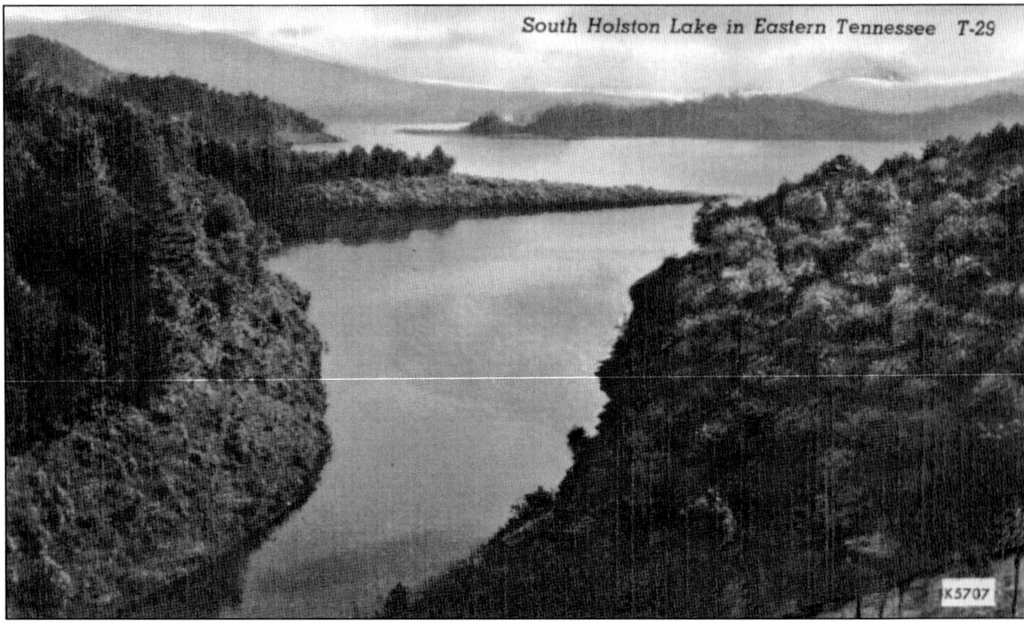

OVERLOOKING THE LAKE. A postcard showcases South Holston Lake as a recreational paradise shouldered by scenic mountains, just off U.S. Highway 421. At the lake's headwaters, the Holston River's Middle and South forks meet at Alvarado, Virginia, near the Virginia Creeper Trail. Streams feeding the lake begin as far north as Wythe County, Virginia. (Courtesy of Shelby Edwards.)

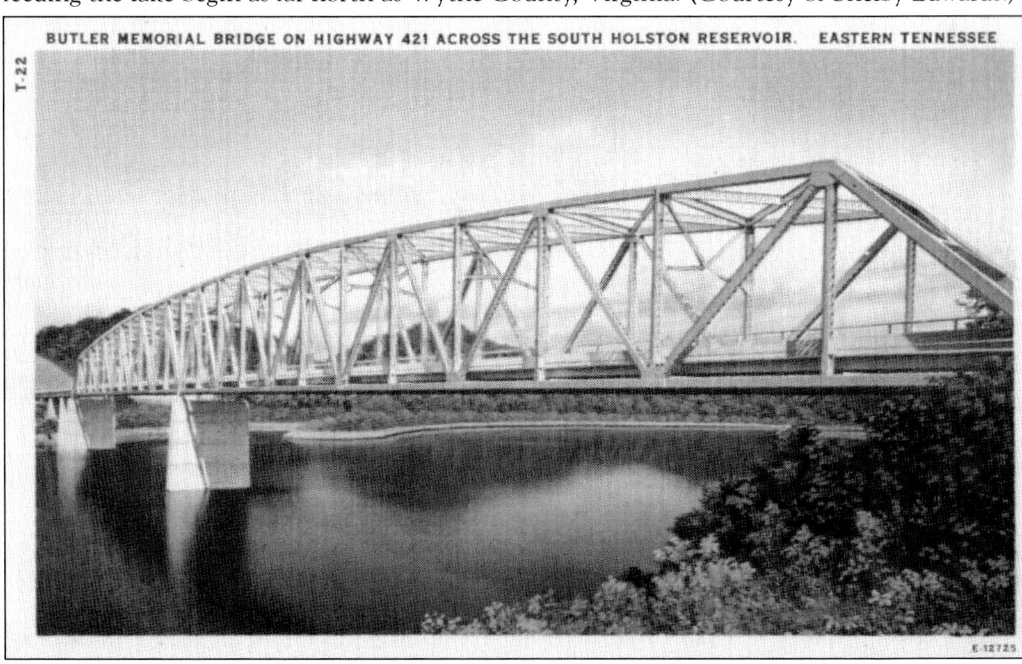

BEAUTIFUL BRIDGE. In 1949, a strike in the steel industry caused work to be delayed while building the steel superstructure of the U.S. Highway 421 bridge across South Holston Lake. The bridge was completed in 1950, replacing an earlier bridge that predated the lake and crossed the river near what is now Observation Knob Park. This postcard shows a shoreline view, looking west. (Courtesy of Shelby Edwards.)

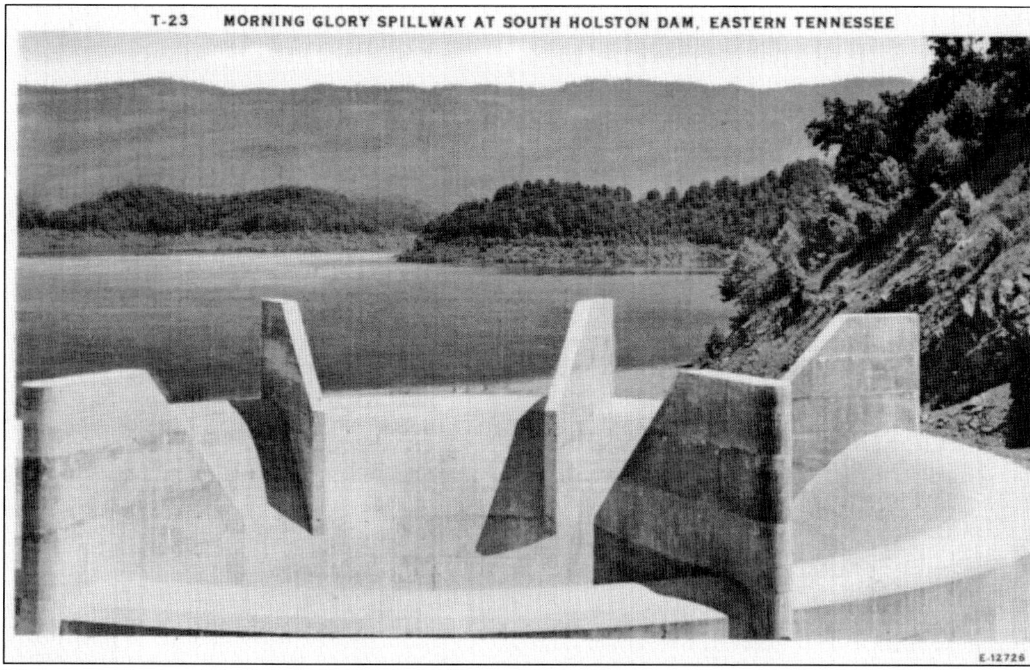

MORNING GLORY. The Morning Glory Spillway, shaped like the bloom of a morning glory, overlooks Holston Mountain and the former site of the Big Creek community. This concrete spillway was installed in 1949 as an emergency device to be used in times of unusual flood conditions so that water would not spill over South Holston Dam. (Courtesy of Tim Buchanan.)

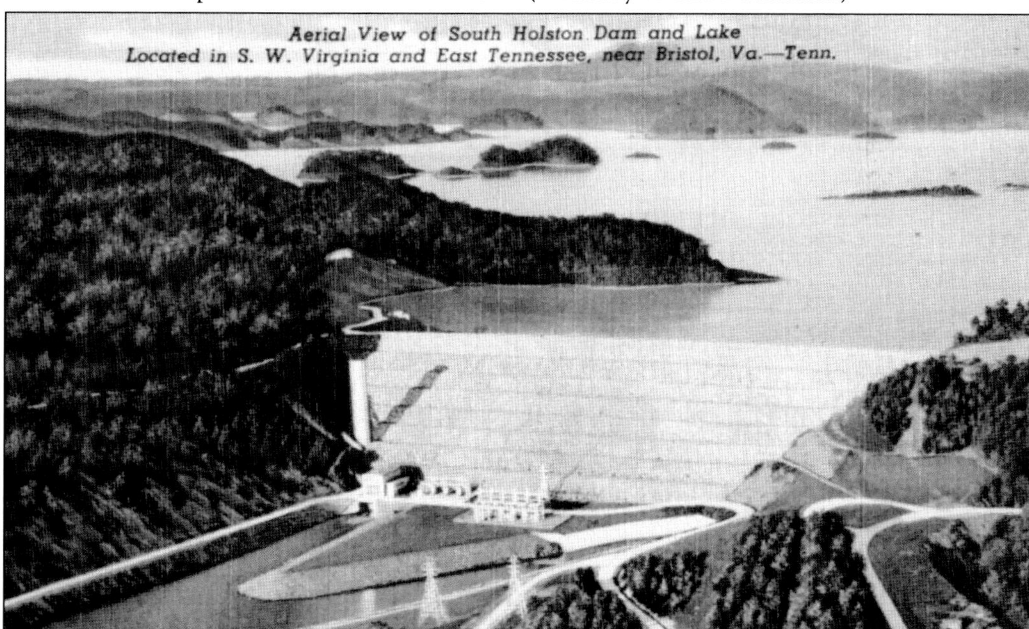

AERIAL VIEW. Bob Greever and Billy Joe James of the Bristol News Agency produced this aerial view of South Holston Dam in the 1950s. The postcard notes the dam "is 285 feet high, 1,600 feet long and creates a 24-mile long lake that stretches up into Southwest Virginia. The mountainous terrain makes this one of the most beautiful of the TVA lakes." (Courtesy of Tim Buchanan.)

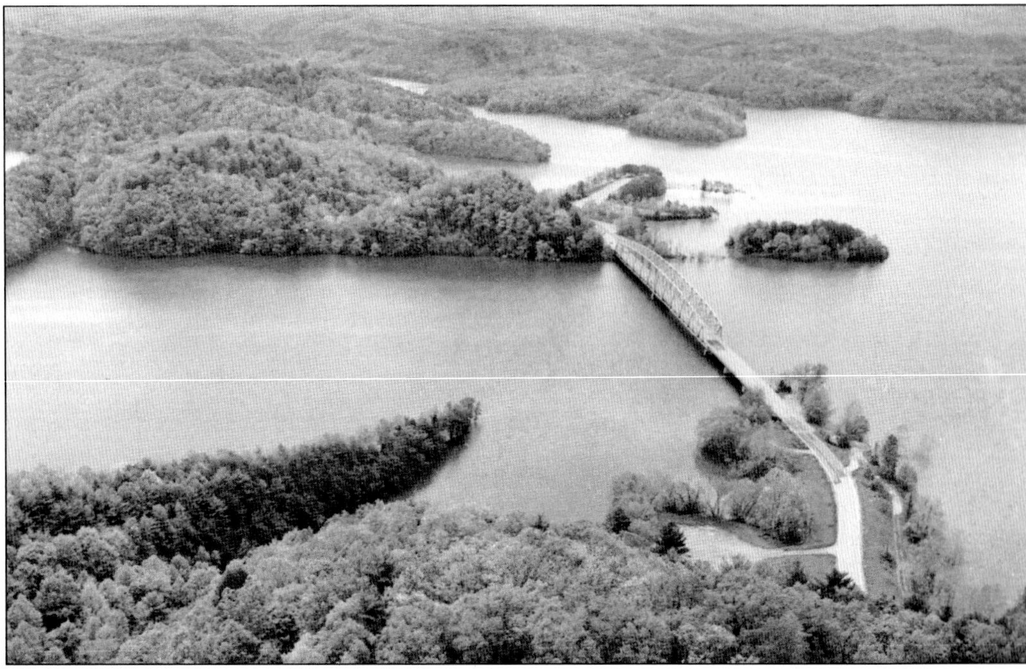

High Waters. A 1984 aerial shot shows flooding on South Holston Lake at the U.S. Highway 421 bridge near Laurel Marina. A popular boat launch area, pictured here in the upper right corner, has been almost completely submerged. During normal seasons, South Holston Lake reaches full pool by June, usually after months of heavy spring rain. (Courtesy of the *Bristol Herald Courier*; photograph by David Grace.)

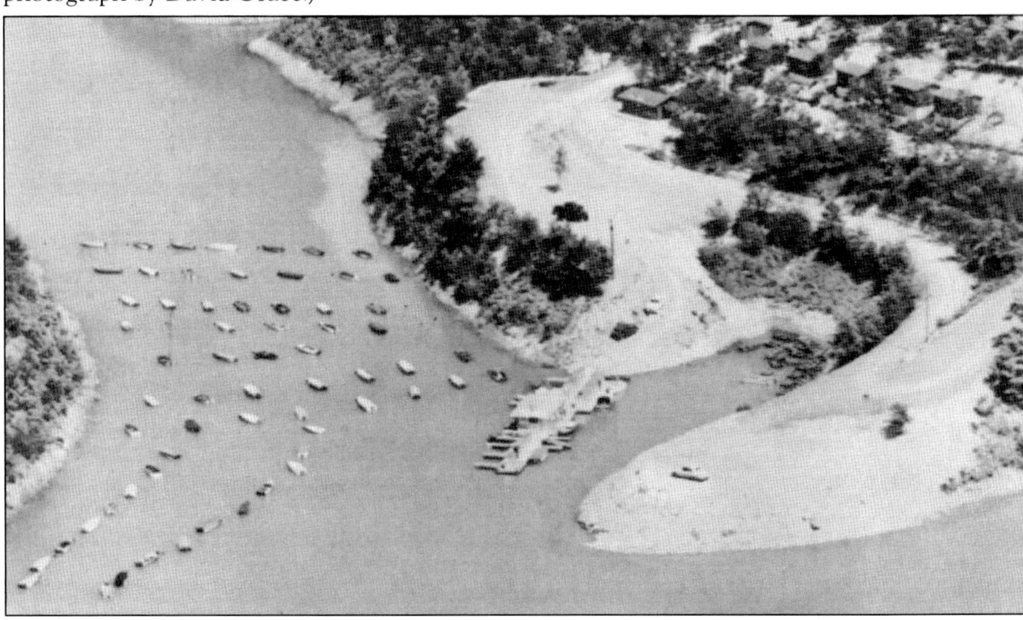

Friendship Marina. No one knows for sure how the lakeside community of Friendship got its name, but locals guess it might stem from the friendliness of residents. This rare postcard from the 1950s shows an early view of the Friendship Marina. Notice how boats are tied to buoy lines before the days of covered slips. (Courtesy of Friendship Marina.)

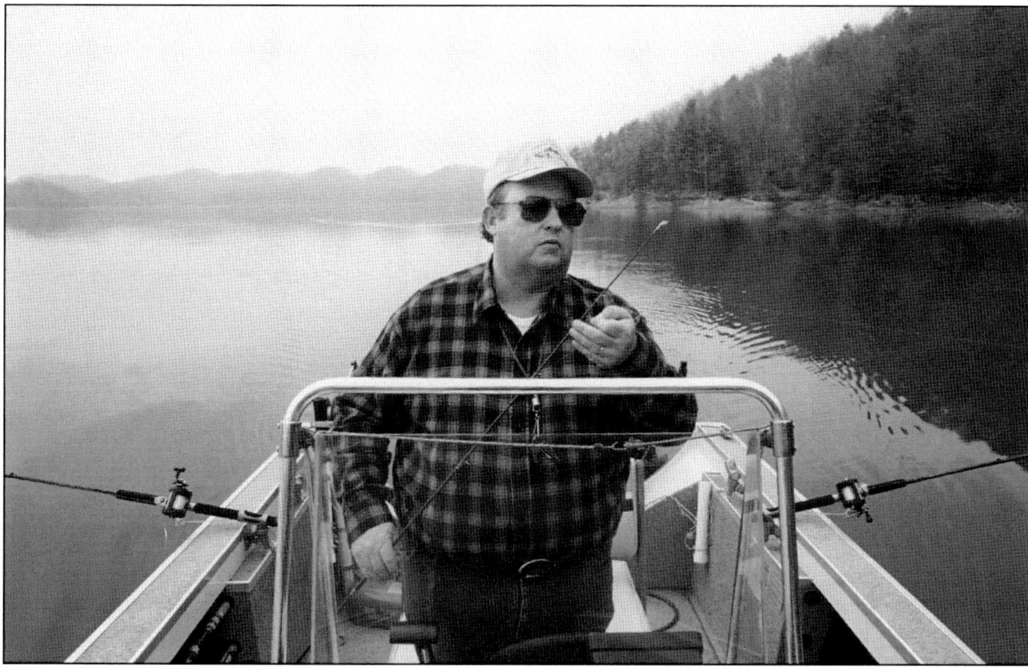

JOHNNY'S FISHING REPORT. Longtime WCYB-TV personality Johnny Wood has become a fishing legend on the waters of both the Holston River and South Holston Lake. Wood is also famous for his folksy fishing reports on morning newscasts. Here Wood shows off his fishing skills during a *Bristol Herald Courier* newspaper interview. (Courtesy of the *Bristol Herald Courier*; photograph by Bill McKee.)

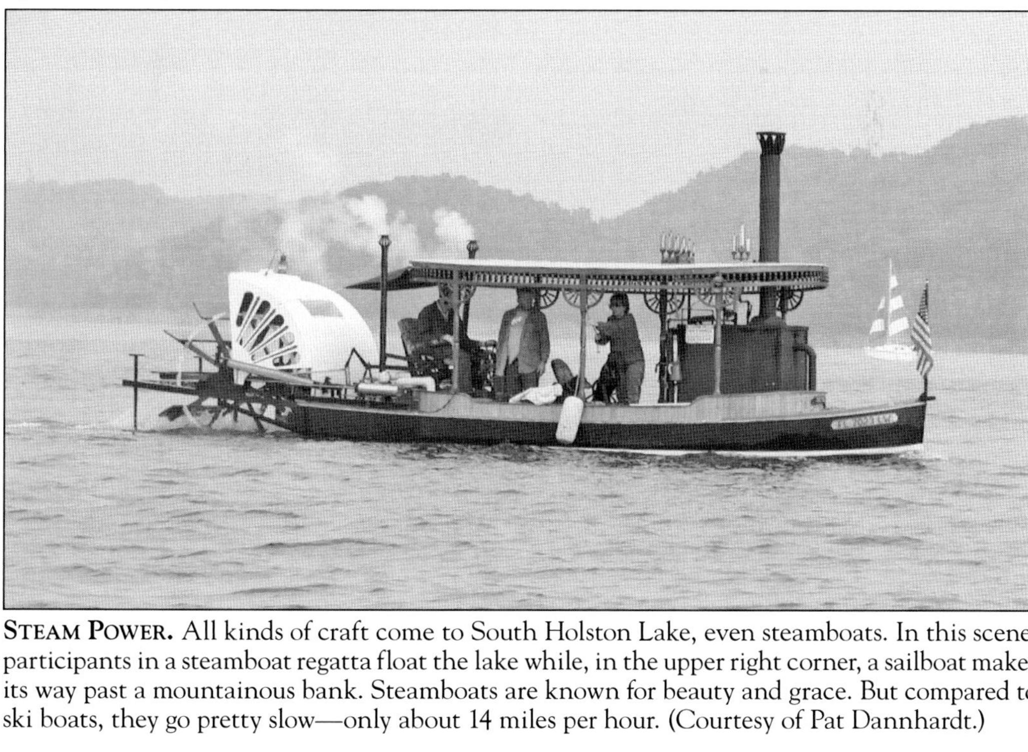

STEAM POWER. All kinds of craft come to South Holston Lake, even steamboats. In this scene, participants in a steamboat regatta float the lake while, in the upper right corner, a sailboat makes its way past a mountainous bank. Steamboats are known for beauty and grace. But compared to ski boats, they go pretty slow—only about 14 miles per hour. (Courtesy of Pat Dannhardt.)

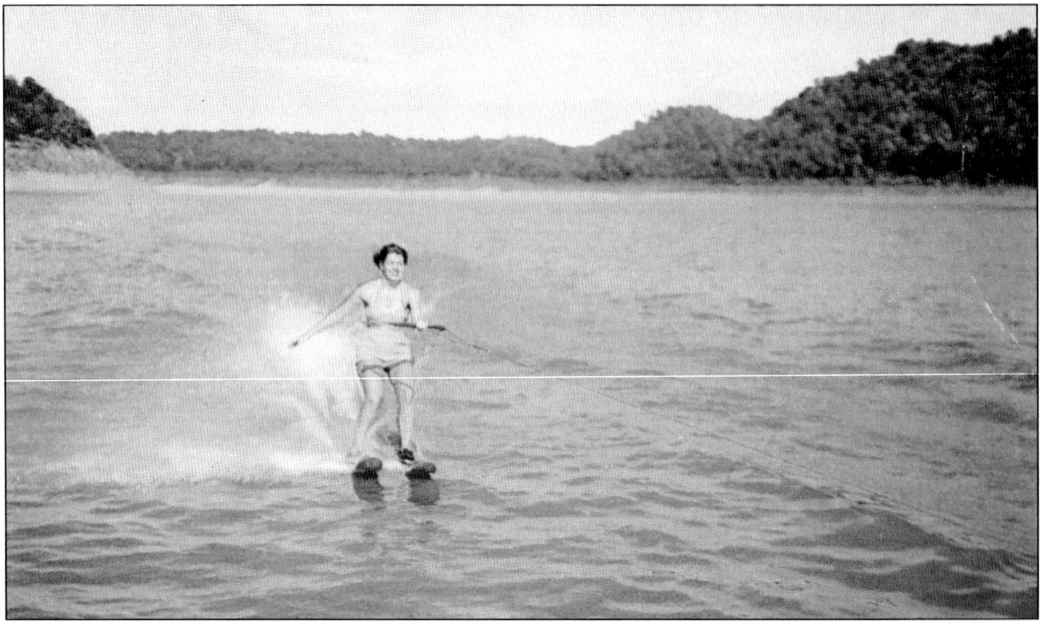

WATER SKIER. A *c.* 1960s postcard shows a skier on South Holston Lake at what appears to be the Tennessee-Virginia line—an area that, incidentally, contains an interesting point of geography. At this spot near Spring Creek, due to the location of the state line, the southernmost tip of Virginia's Washington County Park actually extends a few yards into Sullivan County. (Courtesy of Shelby Edwards.)

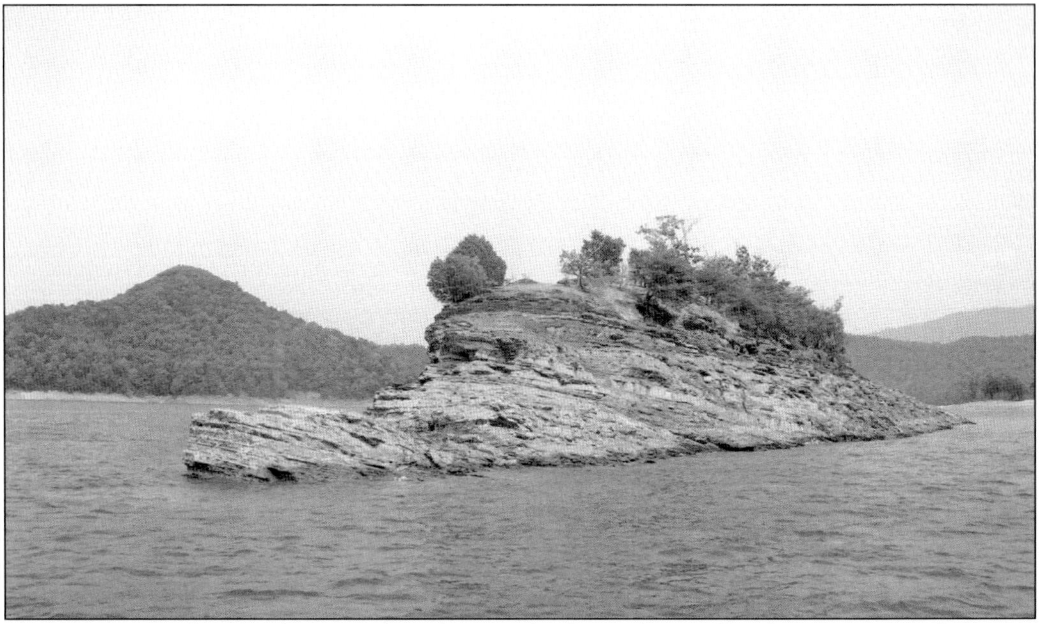

CLIFF ISLAND. The islands of South Holston Lake do not have official names. But reference is often made to "Cliff Island," which rises out of the water like a battleship between South Holston Dam and the U.S. Highway 421 bridge. This rocky isle takes its name from its opposite side, which drops into the water in a sheer cliff and is a popular jump-off point for adventurous swimmers. (Photograph by Joe Tennis.)

Nine

Boone Lake

Water streams down Beaver Creek, running through Bristol, and empties into Boone Lake at a place called Buffalo. Boone Lake also fills up with whatever water comes down the Watauga River, as well as the South fork of the Holston River at Bluff City.

Stretching across 4,300 acres, Boone Lake sits at the apex of the Tri-Cities. The reservoir's rocky shorelines extend from Bluff City and Blountville to the outskirts of greater Kingsport and south to Johnson City. About 85 percent of the lake's 130-mile shoreline is privately owned, and that makes it quite the suburban playground for the Sullivan County neighborhoods named Jamestown, Baywood, and Grande Harbor.

In the 1940s, the Tennessee Valley Authority (TVA) chose a 400-foot-wide section of the South fork of the Holston River to build Boone Dam. It was at the site of a rugged ridge called "Spurgeon Knob," rising about 375 feet above the river's surface.

In 1952, the dam was finished, and Boone Lake began to fill.

The lake's name comes from famed frontiersman Daniel Boone, who roamed the Northeast Tennessee region in the mid-1700s. Boone carved a road from modern-day Kingsport to the Cumberland Gap. Stories say, also, that Boone once hid under a small waterfall on one of the lake's tributaries—a stream now called Boones Creek in Washington County, Tennessee.

Similar to other reservoirs, the TVA provides a man-made tide on Boone Lake. Water rises with heavy spring rains and remains at a summer recreation level, suitable for skiing or floating a pontoon. After autumn, the lake is drawn down during winter, allowing water to rush downstream through the Tennessee River's navigation system at Knoxville and Chattanooga.

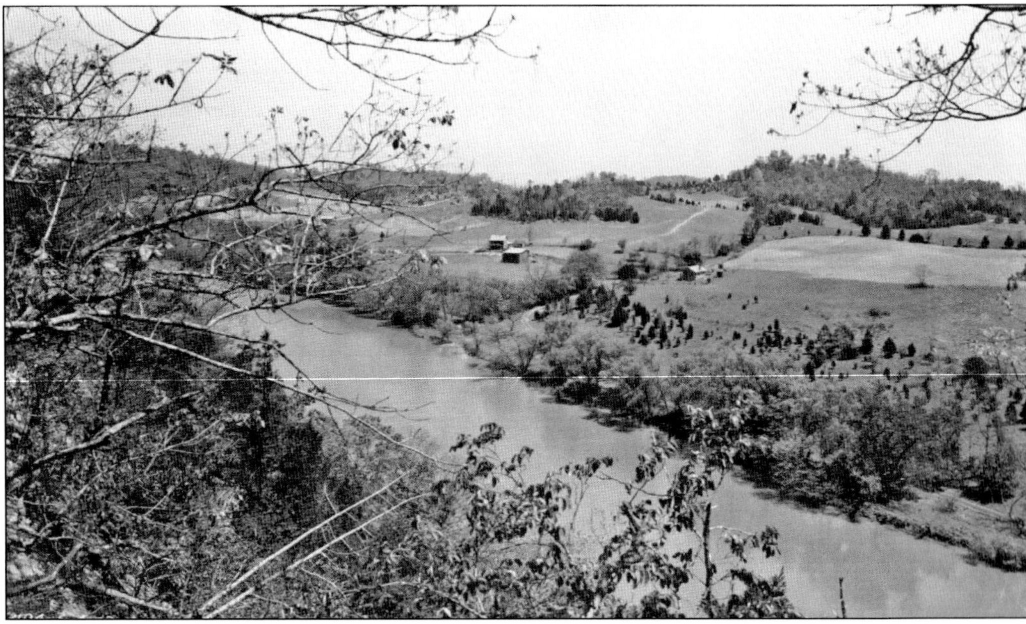

FREE-FLOWING RIVER. This 1949 view shows the Holston River, looking downstream, at the future site of the 4,300-acre Boone Lake. Originally, the proposed name for this reservoir was the "Spurgeon Island Project." The Spurgeon name comes from early settlers. (Courtesy of the National Archives.)

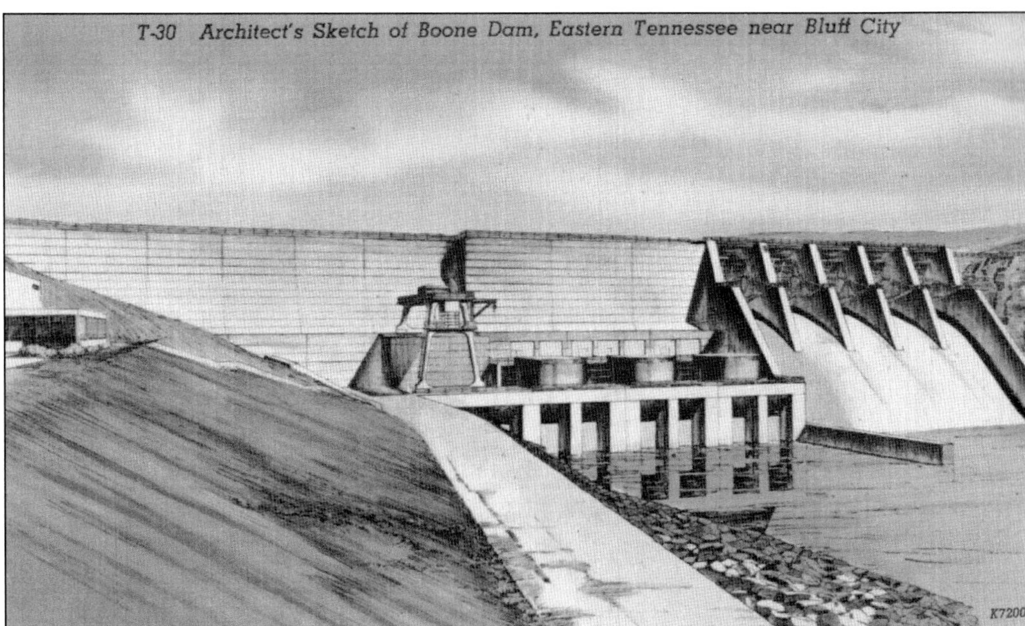

POSTCARD VIEW. An architect's sketch of Boone Dam shows what the structure would look like upon completion. Note that the dam is located "near Bluff City." The headwaters are located at that point on the South fork of the Holston River, but the dam is actually closer to the Tri-Cities Regional Airport near Sullivan County's border with Washington County, Tennessee. (Courtesy of Shelby Edwards.)

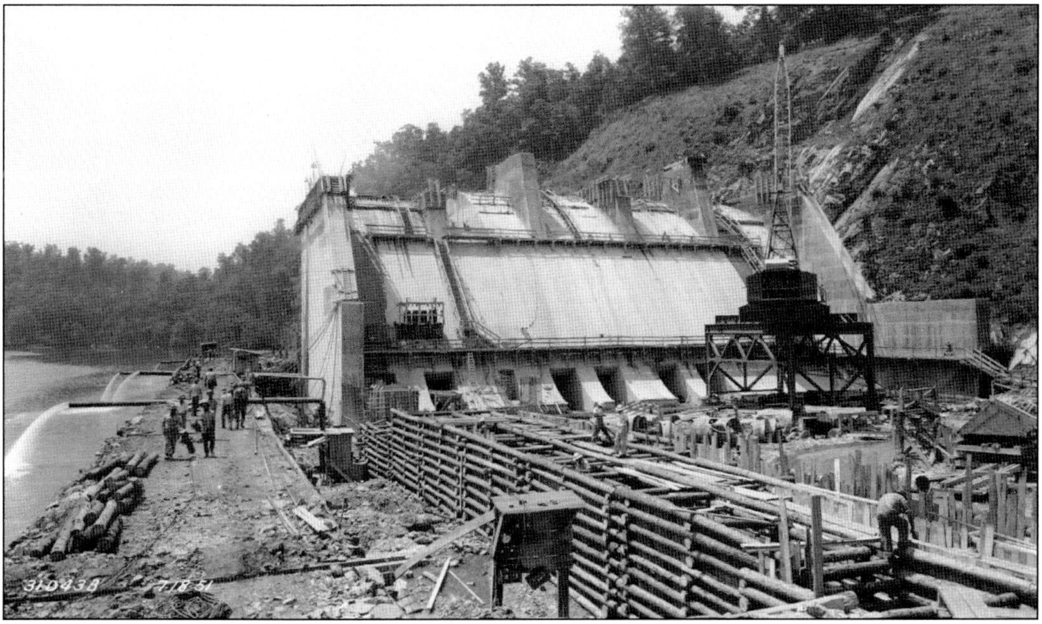

CONSTRUCTION VIEW. Boone Dam was built between 1950 and 1952, with concrete sections standing across the main river channel. This shot shows ongoing construction at the dam site on July 18, 1951. (Courtesy of the National Archives.)

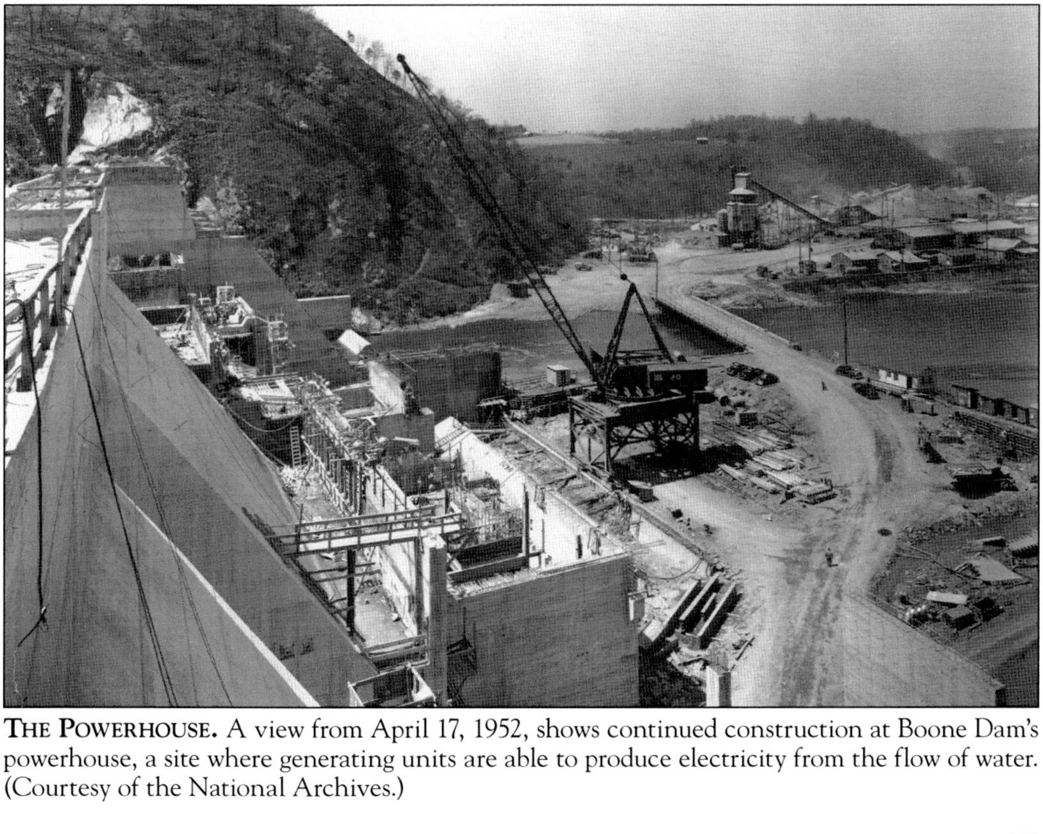

THE POWERHOUSE. A view from April 17, 1952, shows continued construction at Boone Dam's powerhouse, a site where generating units are able to produce electricity from the flow of water. (Courtesy of the National Archives.)

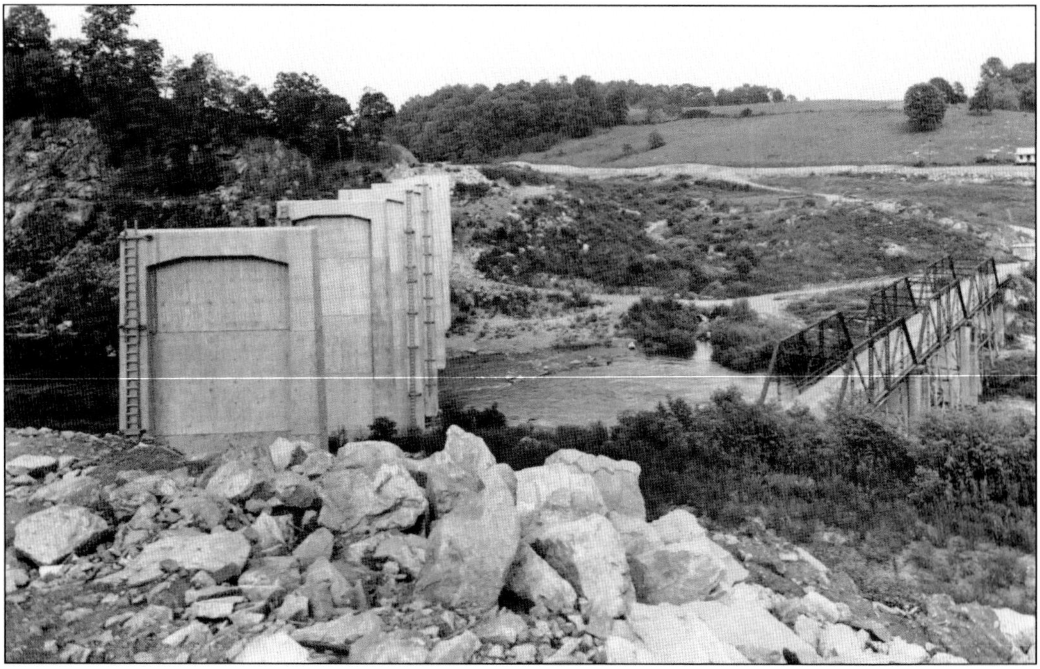

PICKENS BRIDGE. The Pickens Bridge was built over the Watauga River in 1952 as construction continued on Boone Lake. This view comes from the Washington County side of the lake at what is now a boat ramp. Notice the shoreline of Sullivan County and the piers of the Pickens Bridge while under construction. The older bridge, at right, no longer stands. (Courtesy of the National Archives.)

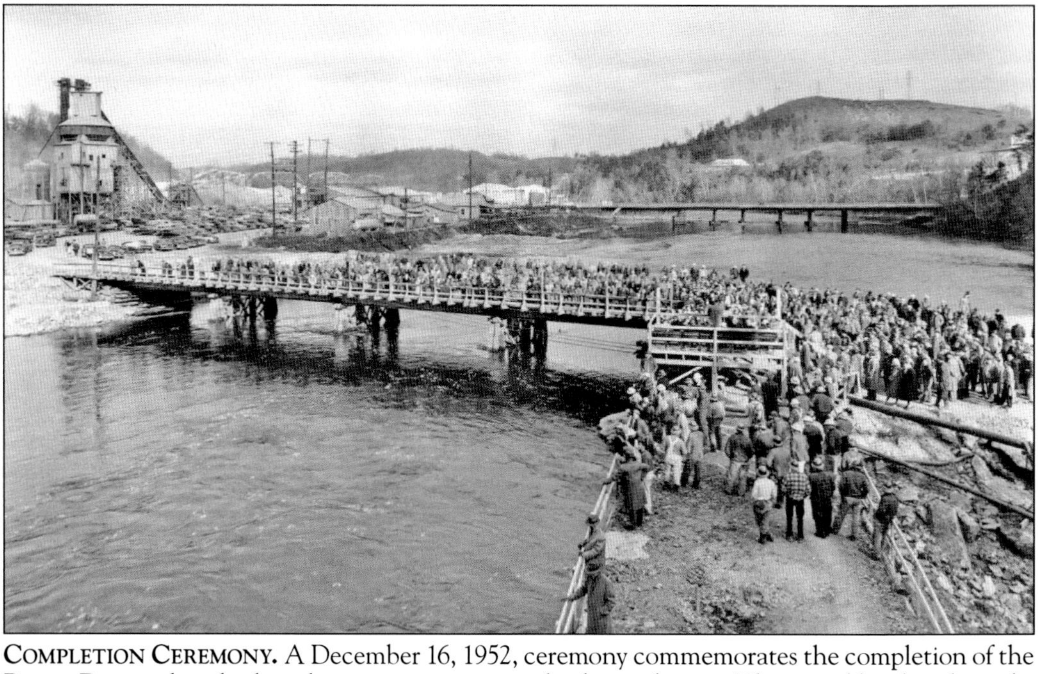

COMPLETION CEREMONY. A December 16, 1952, ceremony commemorates the completion of the Boone Dam, as hundreds gather on a construction bridge at the site. The raised level at the right side of this photograph is a speakers' platform. (Courtesy of the National Archives.)

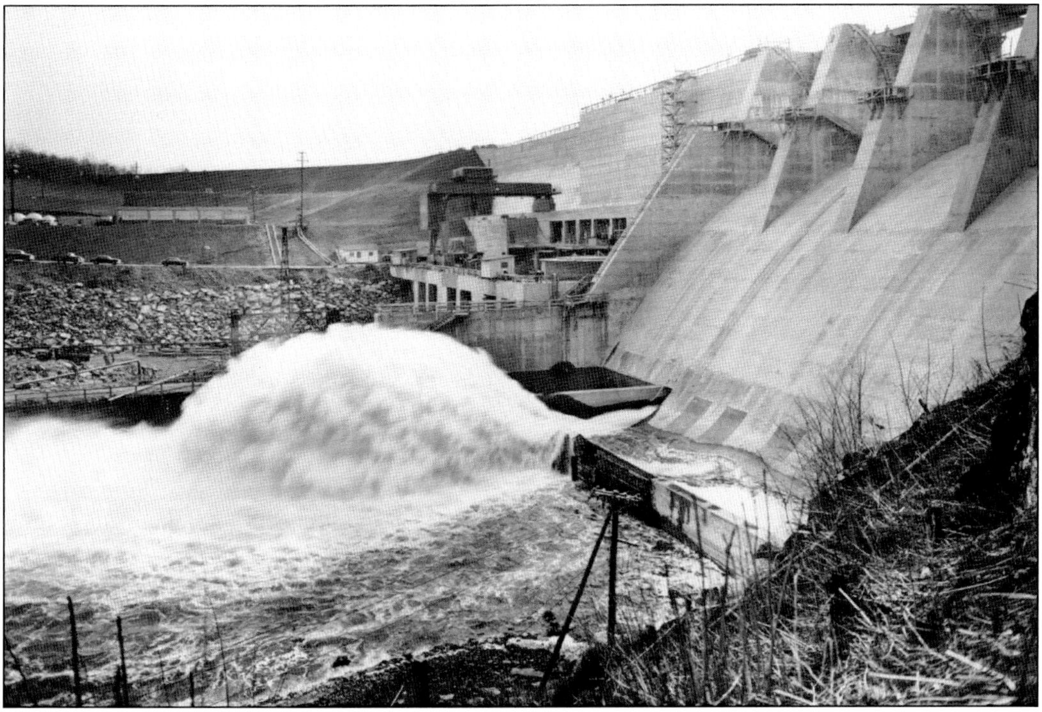

DISCHARGE. This view of the Boone Dam on January 20, 1953, looks upstream from the left bank. The photograph displays the operation of the powerhouse crane as water gushes from the sluice-way gate. The dam spans a length of 1,532 feet and stands 160 feet high. (Courtesy of the National Archives.)

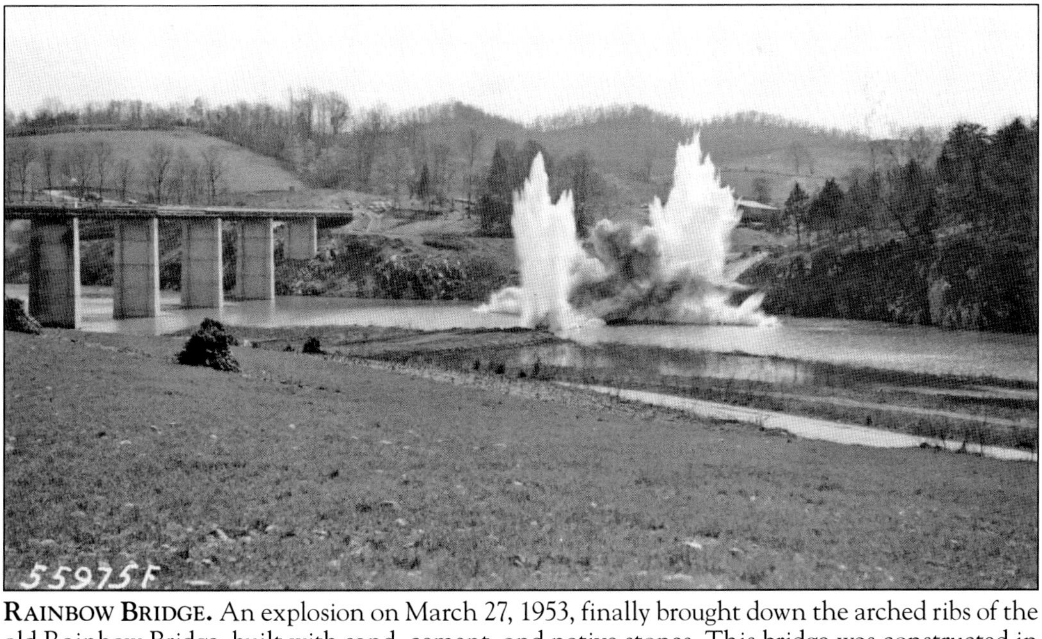

RAINBOW BRIDGE. An explosion on March 27, 1953, finally brought down the arched ribs of the old Rainbow Bridge, built with sand, cement, and native stones. This bridge was constructed in the 1920s over the South fork of the Holston River in the Enterprise community and was called Rainbow for its shape. (Courtesy of the National Archives.)

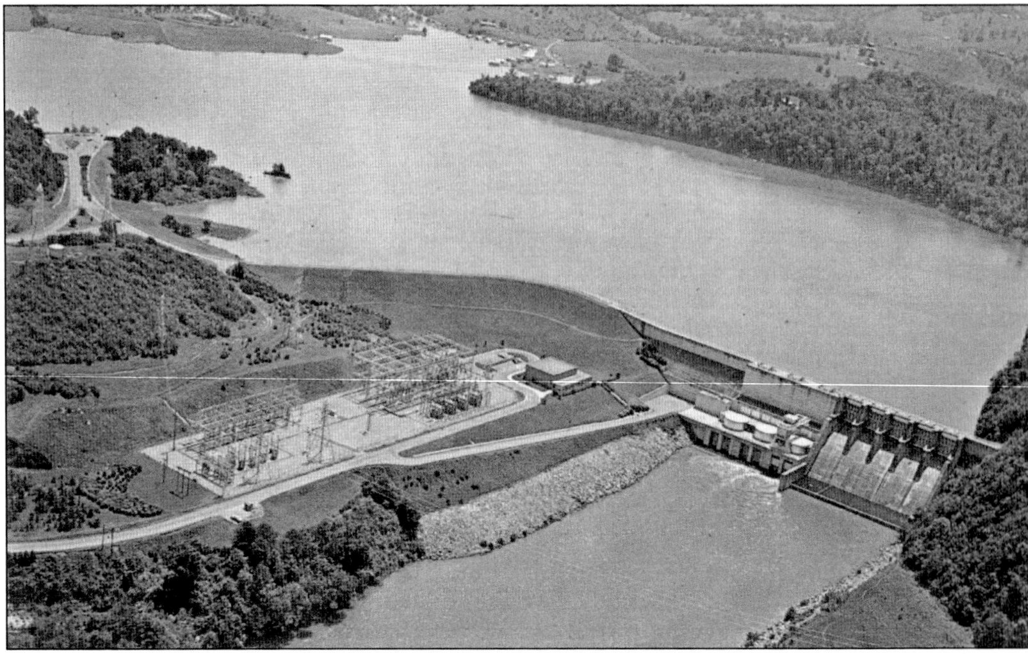

AERIAL OF THE DAM. An aerial postcard by Joyce L. Haynes provides a bird's-eye view of Boone Dam soon after its completion. A sandy beach has since been added in the cove at central left. The road, at the upper left corner, leads to a hilltop overlook of Boone Lake. (Courtesy of Shelby Edwards.)

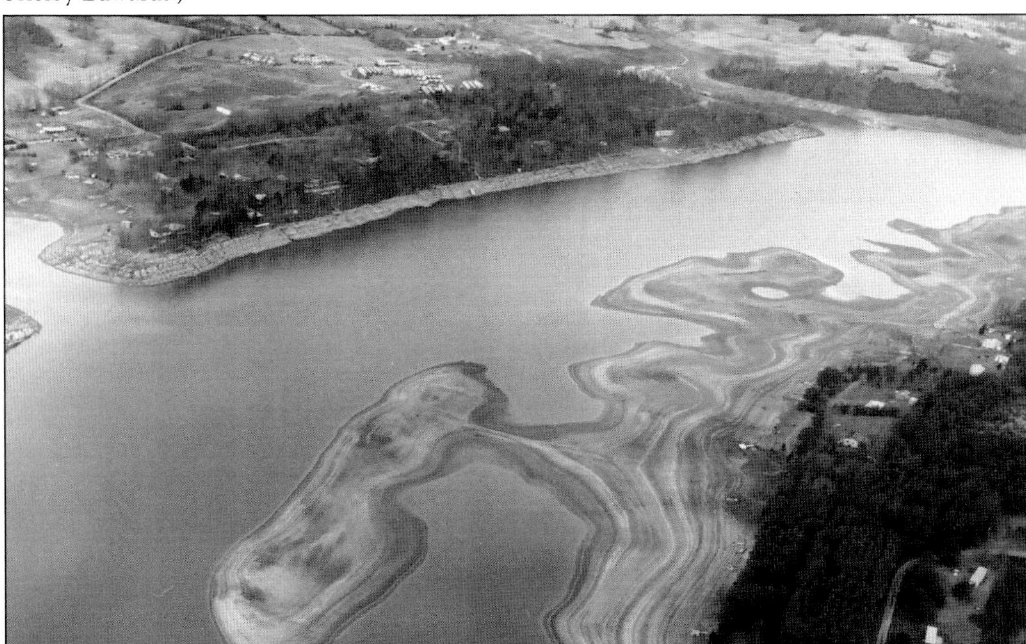

ROCKY SHORELINE IN WINTER. An aerial view of Boone Lake in January 1981 shows an odd pattern in the muddy water at winter's low level. The shoreline on the right side is the Haw Ridge community. The shoreline on the upper left is an area located near the Tri-Cities Regional Airport. (Courtesy of the *Bristol Herald Courier.*)

Ten

Fort Patrick Henry Lake

Early settlers came into the Holston River area and built a fort in 1776 for protection in what is now Kingsport. Naturally, they named that fort for Patrick Henry, who was the governor of Virginia at the time.

Back then, that made a lot of sense. Before the formation of Sullivan County in 1779, no one quite knew where the state line existed. Yet the territory north of the Holston River—including Kingsport—was called the North of Holston Settlement, and it was considered, in the 1770s, a part of Washington County, Virginia.

Centuries later, with the Tennessee-Virginia border firmly established, the industrialized city of Kingsport now prides itself, of course, on being part of Tennessee.

Patrick Henry's name, still, is not forgotten.

For years, "Fort Henry Mall" was the name of a major Kingsport shopping center. Henry's name is also forever emblazoned on a lake, the smallest of the three water holes in Sullivan County built by the Tennessee Valley Authority.

Spanning about 875 acres, Fort Patrick Henry Lake starts just below Boone Dam and stretches about 10 miles. The lake slips beneath a bridge on Interstate 81 at the sides of towering rock bluffs. Then it winds through the woods of Warriors Path State Park, a popular spot to catch rainbow trout, bluegill, bass, and crappie. Finally, the little lake wraps around a recreation area at the Fort Patrick Henry Dam, built in the early 1950s primarily for hydroelectric power but also to regulate a steady supply of water for local industry.

Downstream of the dam, the South fork of the Holston River extends through Kingsport and slips around Long Island. Then the South fork meets the winding North fork at what is now Hawkins County, Tennessee.

At this confluence, when the Holston River was believed to be the state line, Virginia was once thought to end. But now this area simply marks the beginning of a solitary branch of the Holston River slipping south from Sullivan County.

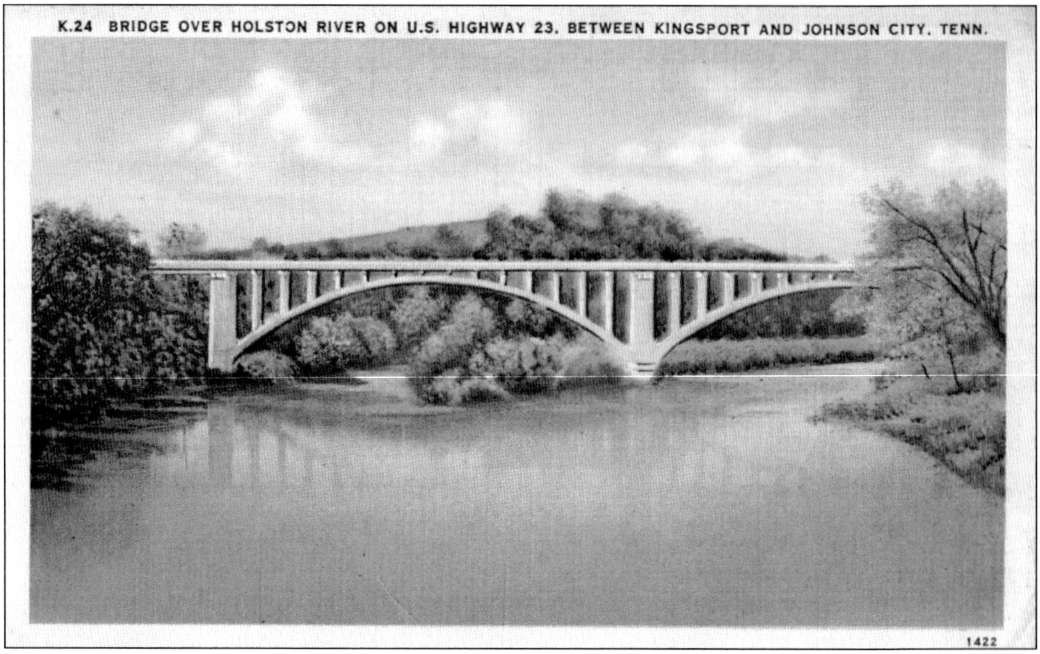

OLD BRIDGE. This postcard shows the elegant arches of the Hammond Bridge, or what was also once called the "Pactolus Bridge," on old U.S. Highway 23. Later re-designated Tennessee Route 36, this bridge, built around 1930, links Kingsport to Johnson City, crossing the South fork of the Holston River immediately downstream of the Fort Patrick Henry Dam. (Courtesy of Shelby Edwards.)

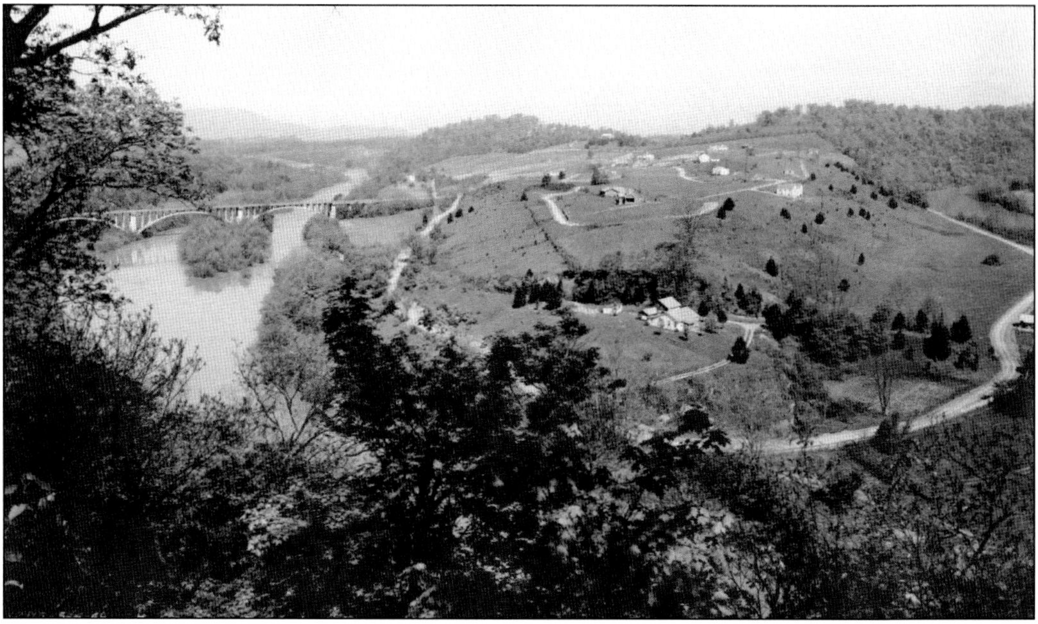

BEFORE CONSTRUCTION. A 1949 view shows the Fort Patrick Henry Dam's construction site on the South fork of the Holston River, slightly upstream of the Pactolus Bridge on old U.S. Highway 23. According to legend, the nearby Pactolus community took its name from the Pactolus River in the ancient country of Lydia in Asia Minor. (Courtesy of the National Archives.)

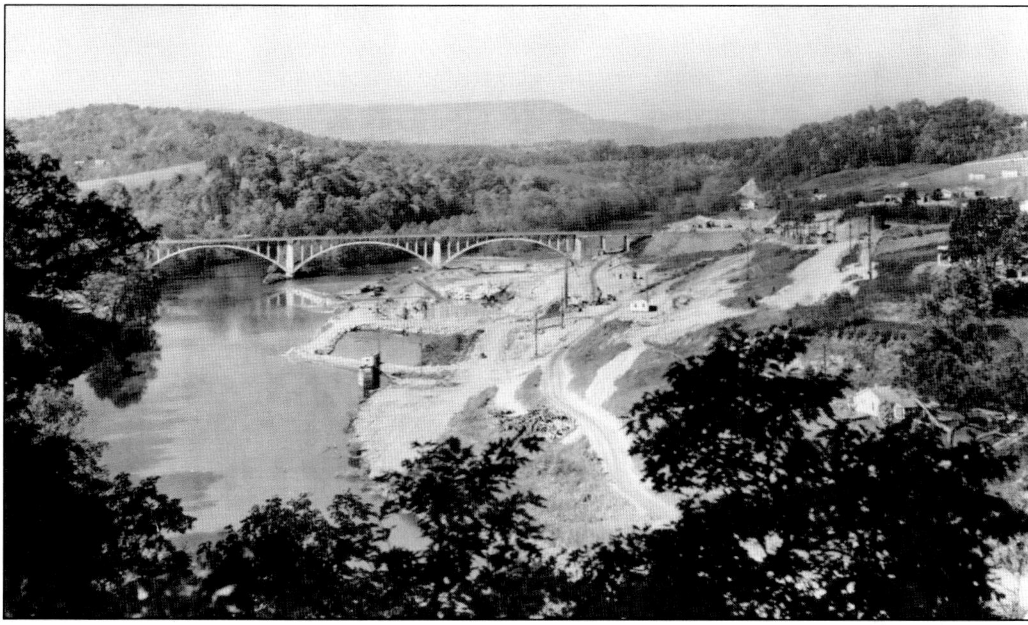

CONSTRUCTION BEGINS. By the time this scene was shot by the Tennessee Valley Authority on October 17, 1951, construction was well under way at what was once called the "Wexler Bend Project," later renamed Fort Patrick Henry Dam. The Wexler name came from early settlers, including Jonathan Wexler, a Philadelphia native who constructed the area's Pactolus Nail Factory about 1811. (Courtesy of the National Archives.)

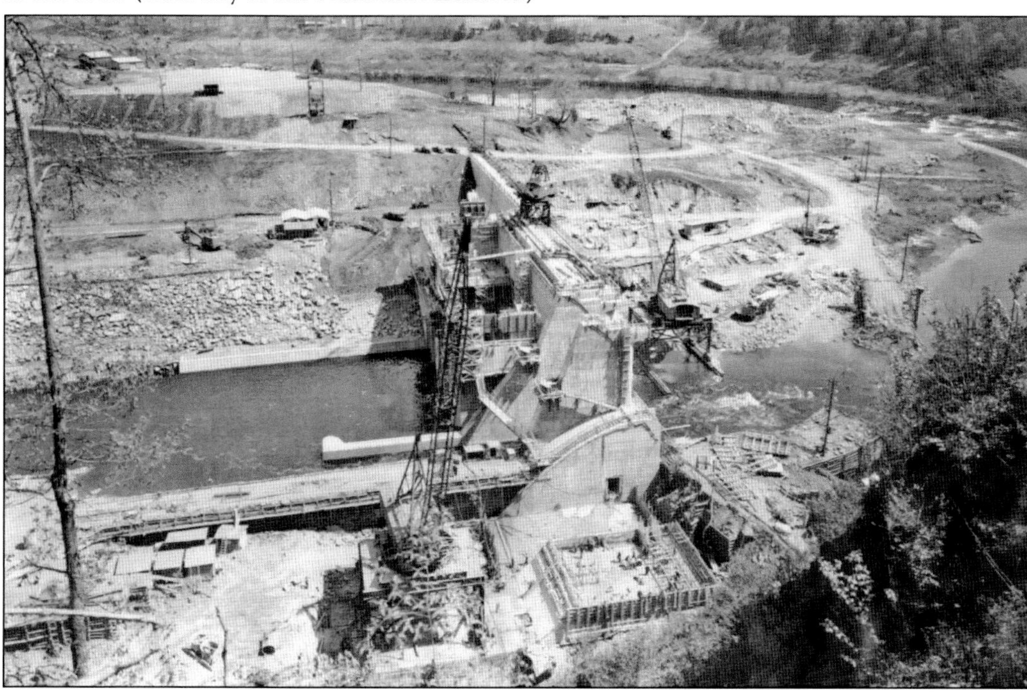

CONSTRUCTION CONTINUES. The construction scene at Fort Patrick Henry Dam just seemed to get muddier as the months went along in 1952–1953. The dam project, in turn, meant the neighborhood bordering the reservoir would be forever altered. (Courtesy of the National Archives.)

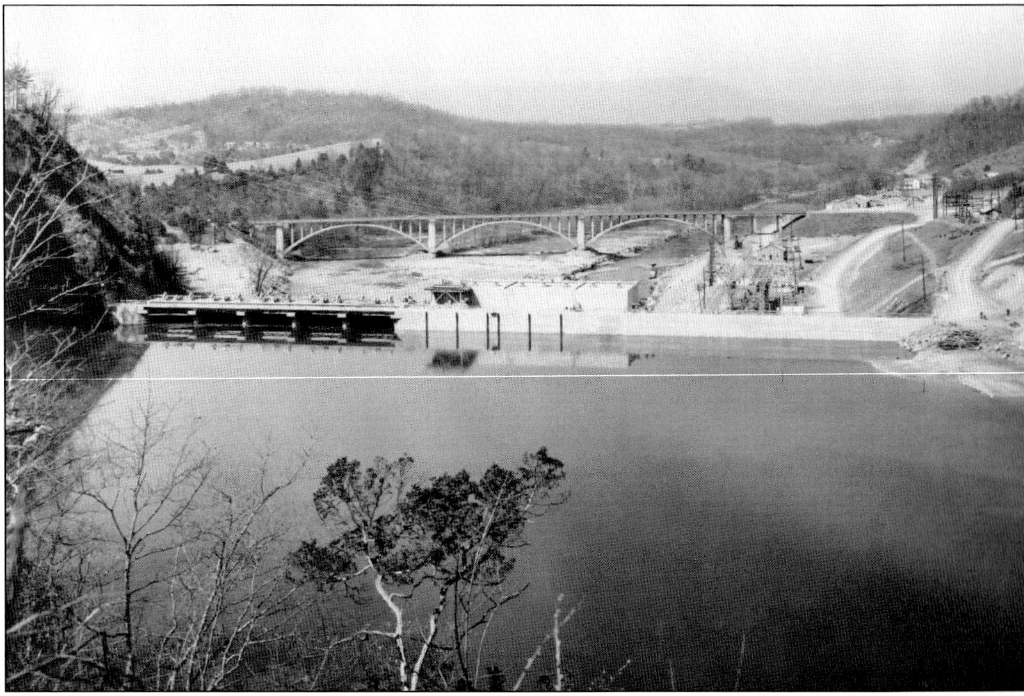

Looking Downstream. Work generally was wrapped up by 1953 on the Fort Patrick Henry Dam project. This photograph, on March 17, 1954, shows the 95-foot-high Fort Patrick Henry Dam stretching 737 feet across the South fork of the Holston River. (Courtesy of the National Archives.)

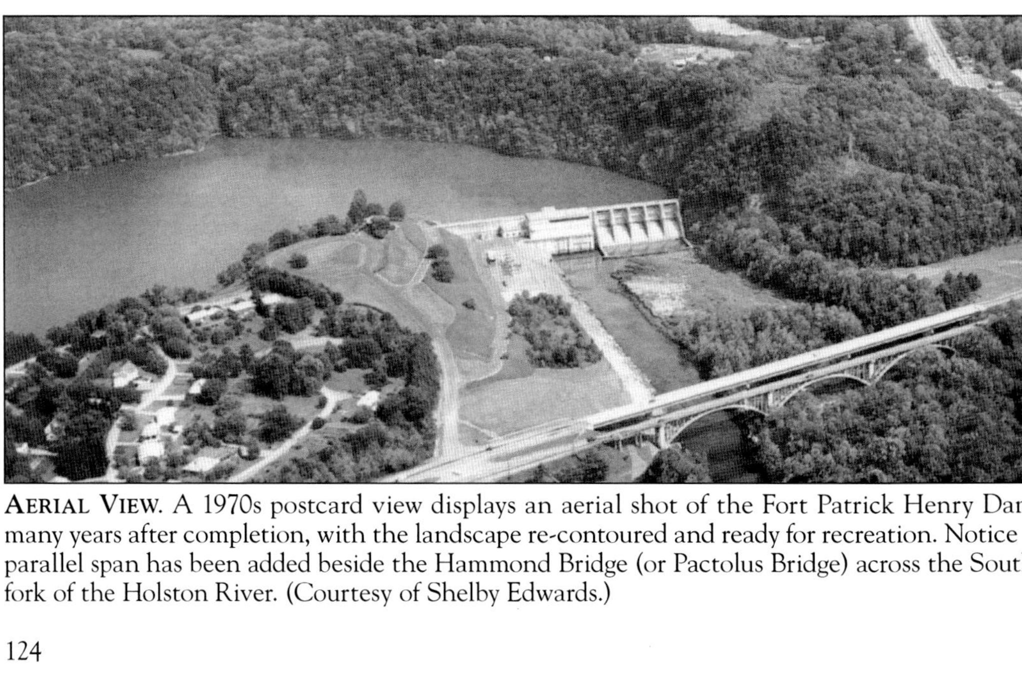

Aerial View. A 1970s postcard view displays an aerial shot of the Fort Patrick Henry Dam many years after completion, with the landscape re-contoured and ready for recreation. Notice a parallel span has been added beside the Hammond Bridge (or Pactolus Bridge) across the South fork of the Holston River. (Courtesy of Shelby Edwards.)

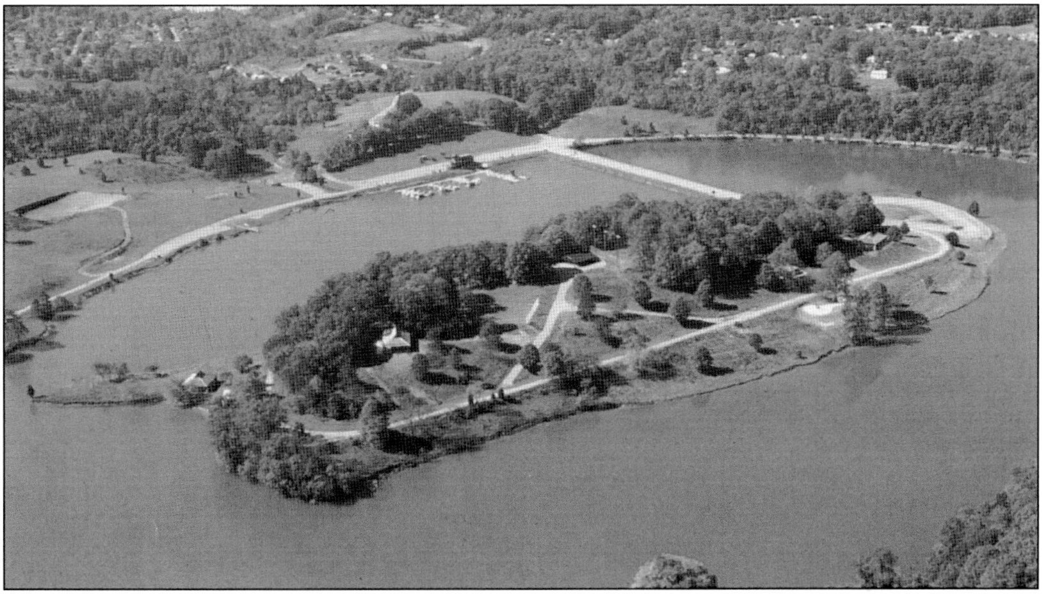

WARRIORS PATH STATE PARK. Fort Patrick Henry Lake wraps around the shoreline of the oval-shaped Duck Island, a centerpiece of Warriors Path State Park. Named for an ancient war and trading path used by the Cherokees, Warriors Path stretches across 950 acres and features a golf course, a campground, a playground, a marina, and a swimming pool. (Courtesy of George Stone.)

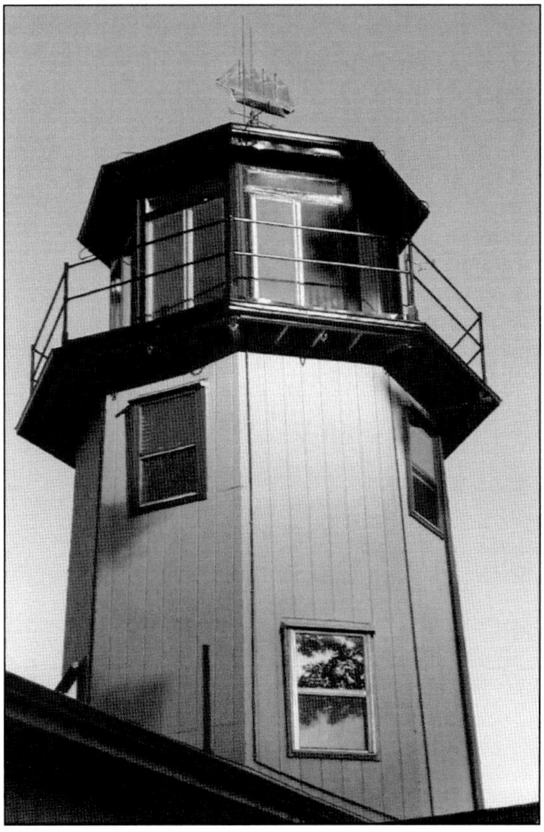

THE LIGHTHOUSE. Kingsport resident Jeff Marek built a six-story lighthouse in 2000 as an addition to his family's home overlooking Fort Patrick Henry Lake. The eight-sided structure stands 68 feet tall and features a working lantern and spiral staircase. (Photograph by Joe Tennis.)

BIBLIOGRAPHY

Barnes, Thelma Gray. *Adventures in Education: Sullivan County, 1773-1983*. Blountville, TN: Sullivan County Retired Teachers' Association, 1983.

Bluff City United Methodist Church. *Scenes from the Bluffs: A Bicentennial Picture History of Bluff City and Piney Flats Tennessee*. Bluff City, TN: self-published, 1976.

Egan, Martha Avaleen, and Nellie McNeil. *Kingsport: Images of America*. Charleston, SC: Arcadia Publishing, 1998.

Holston Territory Genealogical Society. *Families and History of Sullivan County, Tennessee, Volume One: 1779-1992*. Waynesville, NC: Don Mills, Inc., 1992.

McGee, David M., and Sonya A. Haskins. *Bristol Motor Speedway: Images of Sports*. Charleston, SC: Arcadia Publishing, 2006.

Miller, Larry L. *Tennessee Place Names*. Bloomington, IN.: Indiana University Press, 2001.

Porter, Dena Williams. *Sullivan County, Tennessee: Overmountain History Series for Young Readers*. Johnson City, TN.: The Overmountain Press, 2003.

Sakowski, Carolyn. *Touring the East Tennessee Backroads*. Winston-Salem, NC: John F. Blair, Publisher, 1993.

Skelton, William H., ed. *Cherokee National Forest Hiking Guide, 2nd Ed.* Knoxville, TN: University of Tennessee Press, 2005.

Skeirik, Karen. "Deery Inn – This Has Been a Magnificent House." *Bristol Herald Courier.* 26 February 1982.

Spoden, Muriel. *Historic Sites of Sullivan County*. Blountville, TN.: Sullivan County Historic Commission of the Sullivan County Court, 1977.

Stone, George. *Bristol: Postcard History Series*. Charleston, SC: Arcadia Publishing, 2008.

Sullivan County Genealogical Society. *Sullivan County, Tennessee: A Pictorial History*. Paducah, KY: Turner Publishing Co., 1998.

Taylor, Oliver. *Historic Sullivan*. Johnson City, TN: The Overmountain Press, 1988.

Tennessee Valley Authority. *The Upper Holston River Projects: Technical Report, No. 14*. Washington, D.C.: United States Government Printing Office, 1958.

ABOUT THE AUTHOR

A graduate of Radford University and a former Sullivan County resident, Joe Tennis lives near Bristol with his wife and two children. He is also the author of *Beach to Bluegrass*, *Southwest Virginia Crossroads*, and *The Marble and Other Ghost Tales of Tennessee and Virginia*.

INDEX